Leaves from the Fig Tree

Diana Duff

summersdale

Summersdale Publishers Ltd
46 West Street
Chichester
West Sussex
PO19 1RP
UK

www.summersdale.com

Printed and bound in Great Britain

ISBN: 1-84024-363-5
ISBN 13: 978-1-84024-363-5

Cover photograph © Lorne Resnick/Getty Images

Acknowledgements

I want to thank Isobel Dixon, the most wonderful literary agent anyone could have. Without her this book would never have happened.

My thanks to Sheila Palmer for her support and putting the manuscript together. Thanks too to Nick Vujovic for allowing my intrusions into his office and a special thank-you to 'Kitten' (Meriel Latchford) for so many things.

Author's Note

Names, places and dates have been changed slightly in some instances to protect the privacy of individuals.

This book is for Robin and all our marvellous children,
Marnie, Hugh, Jessica and of course Nico

Prologue

It seems such a strange thing to be doing, I thought, however ordinary the surroundings. Waiting in a coffee shop in Oxford Street, with the London traffic roaring outside, for my mother, whom I would not recognise when she finally arrived.

She was already twenty minutes late. Fuller's was crowded. A clutch of London matrons fiddling with cake forks chattered over coffee and walnut cake. The room was thickly carpeted and smelt of freshly roasted coffee and expensive scent. As I waited, two elderly women rose, gathering parcels and vacating a table for two. I took it, peeling off my gloves, butterflies fluttering in my stomach, and wishing that Robin had come with me for support. He had offered that morning before I left the hotel but I refused. This was an emotional hurdle to be handled on my own – or so I had thought.

I had never tried to visualise my mother until now, or given much thought as to what sort of person she was – discussions of her had always been taboo – but when she finally arrived, glancing uncertainly around the room, oddly I knew who she was. She stood in the doorway scanning the tables and I, who had been watching as the glass door swung open from time to time, raised a cautious arm. She moved towards my table, recognising me perhaps, because I was the only girl sitting alone. I saw that she had a man with her, and knew then, feelings of anticipation deflating, that the meeting would be impersonal. With just the two of us we might have reached some rapport – I was better at one-on-one relationships, but with three of us it was unlikely.

Looking back on that strange afternoon – the three of us strangers to each other – my first impression was of the dark-haired man with her, a scar on his lip – you could see the small white marks of old stitches – and then my mother behind him, brown-eyed and blonde in a striped dress. They would have seen me, rigid with tension and nerves, copper-haired and thin in a yellow coat.

Later in the powder room she had been apologetic, searching for the right words. She had plucked at the tortoiseshell handle of her handbag clicking it open and shut mechanically, almost nervously.

'Don't think too badly of me,' she said. 'I knew that night when I was packing that I was doing something unforgivable. Just walking out. The native girl was holding you, I made her promise to stay.'

Her voice trailed off.

'What I did was for the best … Your grandparents. I was terrified of them. They had that huge place, Annes Grove. Were you happy there?'

It was a bit late, I thought, for her to ask that.

'There was always Molly,' I said.

And Kitten, I could have told her. Kitten with her round speedwell-blue eyes mothering me, making things better when my stomach churned on hunting days. I had wept bitterly when Kitten left.

'Molly …?' my mother said vaguely. 'Who was Molly?'

It was hopeless to explain. The gap between this stranger in the striped dress and me was too wide to try to bridge. Decades of living without her in a different sort of world would take too long to describe, and even had we all the time in the world, how could I ever paint a word picture for her to describe brooding druidic Annes Grove, with its cromlech, fabulous river gardens, the Foxy Woman's ghost – and the wonderful eccentricities of old Ned and Molly.

★★★

The past is with me so much these days, but memories of it come in eddies like small summer winds. Before you can savour them they are gone again. One day the past may go for ever, and there won't be anyone alive any more to remember those days in Ireland when the banks of the river below our house were covered with primula and arums, and the catkins were out, and my grandmother rode her blue roan side-saddle, sitting straight in her blue riding habit.

It was on one of those spring days that my father drove away from the home he loved, banned from the house for ever, and on one of those days too, years later, when my grandfather, standing with me in the rhododendron garden in the dusk, tried to explain to me that he loved his son but the entail break had had to come.

All that time the house looked on, brooding over us, as if it had seen so many things, and its thick walls had absorbed so much of the emotion of our family over the last two hundred and fifty years, that it had become an extension of us all.

When I look back on it now in 2003, all those thousands of miles away and decades of years ago, even with Africa just outside my window, I get the same feeling about the place, that kind of odd, inexplicable feeling. I know that it never really belonged to the present and never really will. Just under the surface, hidden from the naked eye, is the past and the people of that time, just as they always were. You can feel them and sense them. Perhaps, simply, time does not move forward as we ordinarily think of it doing, but past, present and future coexist.

I have got to write about it, grasp it somehow before it slips away into its own quiet retreat, the people become faceless, and all those emotions that shaped us as a family into what we all became belong only to the house again.

The story for us as a family begins in 1776 when the Earl of Annesley left Castlewellan, the huge crenellated castle in County Down where the family lived, and came to Cork to buy horses. There he met and married the farming heiress Mary Grove – he took her name as part of ours – and they called her house no longer Ballyhimmock (the place of the mound) but Annes Grove, an amalgamation of their names. He is not a direct ancestor. He died without children and left the estate to his little brother Arthur, my great-great-grandfather – but he was the catalyst, for, because of him, the place became the property of the Annesleys. The Grove Annesleys of Annes Grove: the place that exerts such power on us all and is part of us.

Arthur, inheriting it, was to have seventeen children and, happily ensconced at Annes Grove, set about buying more land. From time to time he took carriage and coach to Dublin to escape from his brood, and then on to visit his other older brother, the new earl, enjoying his lands and title at Castlewellan.

Not that being a belted earl was without hazard, as an earlier Annesley ancestor had found to his cost. James, an orphan – Baron Annesley and seventh Earl of Anglesey – was kidnapped at fifteen and sold into slavery in America in 1735 by his uncle, who wanted him out of the way so that he could snatch the titles for himself. After thirteen abused years of slavery, poor James managed to escape and make his way home, somewhat the worse for wear.

The story has been romanticised in the telling of it in an

ancient book that I own, printed in Dublin in 1798. It is titled *The Kidnapped Earl: A Story Founded on Truth*. But the true facts are well documented as, when James escaped and landed in England, a jury upheld his claims and restored his estates. Not surprisingly, however, the heart was gone out of him from all this, and he never used his titles again although his uncle continued to flaunt them across Ireland.

Various Annesley kinsmen and -women come and go in the family annals. One married Catherine Darnley, a love child of King James II. Another, Susannah Annesley, married Samuel Wesley and so became known as the Mother of Methodism through her son John. Pepys mentions yet another Annesley in his diaries.

As it is in most families, the good and the bad march across their pages of family history, but it was great-great-grandfather Arthur, the General, who settled at Annes Grove and who – marrying at forty – was the one who interested me most.

He had a penchant for gambling and for collecting uplifting books, still scattered all over the house one hundred and fifty years later and perused by me – besides an invitation sent to him to attend Napoleon's funeral, which I believe he did.

I have one of Arthur's books with his name and crest on the flyleaf titled *The Duties of the Female Sex*. Predictably, it mentions the benefits of having numerous children, and that 'wives should at all times remember their domestic duties' and are advised to 'be not snatched into the wild vortex of Amusements', which meant presumably that Arthur's wife Elizabeth (barely eighteen when they married) was encouraged to stay at Annes Grove and rear her brood while Arthur, returning from the fleshpots of Dublin, read her uplifting books in the evenings. Arthur, one feels, had things well sussed out!

But it was not just my illustrious ancestors and the upstairs inhabitants of Annes Grove who gave it life and colour. For me, the Servants' Hall was the hub of the house, and Molly its pulse.

– 1 –

Molly Reilly it was, authoritative, eighteen stone and black-aproned, who after forty-eight years with the family was the pivot, gossip and energy source of the house. She knew about everything, everyone. No nuance escaped her. Family moods upstairs could be checked with her in the Servants' Hall next to the kitchen, where she rocked her chair beside the iron stove. It was no wonder that cars of visiting families were often parked first at the kitchen door instead of the great gravel carriage sweep above, thus incensing my grandfather who deplored her easy familiarity with us all. But she in her basement had her finger on the pulsebeat and from her the whole scenario of the house for the day, on enquiry, could easily be revealed and described, from countdown when the early morning tea trays had gone upstairs at eight, to dusk. Moods of ageing relatives in the rooms above could be gauged before sticking one's neck out, so to speak.

'Grandfather. How's his humour?'

'Raging mad he is today, raging. The young horse is lame. The seeds from Dublin never came. The tractor broke. No spare parts in Mallow. Roaring he was, roaring. And speaking to the steward at the home farm, he didn't need the phone, you'd hear him up there, roaring.'

Acting on this sort of tip-off, one's plans perhaps to ask some favour of the head of the house would, in wisdom, be shelved until the hour was more propitious. The confession of a broken cucumber frame or a branch snapped in error off some rare tree would be postponed until Molly advised contact. Nor was my grandmother always approachable.

'The bill for your hat came from Dublin.' She wasn't pleased. 'And your school report – the only word for that is *desperate*.' Picking at soda bread cooling on top of the Aga, I questioned further so that I might handle this situation with caution.

'Will she be hunting all day?'

'She will. Better to keep away now or she'll ate the face off you.'

'If the hounds find, her temper'll change,' I said.

'And the wind will change and leave your face like that for ever if you screw it up. Leave the soda bread alone!'

Heaving herself out of her basket chair she would pad off to some culinary delight or launch an offensive on a lazy kitchen maid, shouting over her shoulder, 'And another thing. A letter from your father came from Africa. Himself was fit to be tied when he got it. Roaring he was.'

Anything to do with my father seemed to increase the temperature upstairs.

Wisest to spend the day riding, with a packet of sandwiches to eat on horseback, when the airmail posts came from Africa.

My father, because of the feuds that had never abated, had not returned from Africa for many years, but one day, having ridden home in the teeth of an east wind, I went as usual into the house by the kitchen. Moll's stove would be welcoming after the knife cut of the wind.

As soon as I opened the huge oak door I felt the vibrations of tension. Molly was rocking in her chair, her rosary between her fingers, her face wet.

'Sure God help us all!' she said. 'Your father's here from Africa. He has some illness but your granny won't see him. He's going and he's never to come back.' Breaking news gently was not her strongest point. She was always factual.

'Where is he?'

'Upstairs in the smoking room with your grandfather. Don't go in!'

'And Granny?'

'The Mistress? In her bedroom.'

I could hear the shouting as I passed the study. My father's voice: 'Rockvale lands should be mine at least!'

And Grandfather's roar: 'There's nothing for you here!'

Taking the stairs two at a time to the third floor, I went and stood, shaking, in the door of my grandmother's room.

'Couldn't you at least *see* him? He's ill!' I said.

She was lying down on the sofa and, turning her head, looked at me with her fierce black eyes. Her white hair was loosely piled in a knot. She was still handsome, even in her late seventies. '*No!*' It came out strongly, but there was emotion there although she tried to hide it.

'You are turning him into a remittance man,' I said, 'and he's *your* son.' How I dared speak to her like that I don't know.

'He has turned himself into a remittance man,' she said, 'and you, I think, have overstepped the mark. Please leave the room.'

As I went downstairs Molly was coming up with a tray of tea for her, with a plate of thinly sliced soda bread and butter.

'He's gone,' she said flatly. 'To Africa. Doyle took him to the station in the trap. He couldn't say goodbye to you. He was in a state. He left you a letter on the dresser in the kitchen.' And with her stout back to me, mounting the staircase to my grandmother's room, I heard her say, 'Your father. He has Parkinson's disease and there's no cure. He told me that's why he used to drop things. Clumsy she said he was. She didn't know. God help us all. That poor man. And now he's to get nothing from here.'

And the door to my grandmother's room closed behind her.

I stood looking out into the rainy greyness of the stable yard. Something traumatic had happened. The chain of eldest sons was broken, after so many years, and the house knew it, felt it. The whole atmosphere had subtly changed since this morning in 1949 when I'd ridden out. It had been raining the first time he had gone and it was raining again; and now, as then, I was to stay behind.

How did he feel, I wondered, to leave this place which was in all our blood? I hated it – the house, the whole estate – yet loved it passionately too. It was an extension of self, of family. It held and controlled us. Not we it.

As I stood there, Doyle the groom turned into the stable yard and drove the empty trap into the coach house below. I looked down at the coach-house door, a seventeen-year-old remembering the coldness I had felt years before in 1934 when I first came with my father at the age of two, home from the warmth of Africa, from Kenya, South Africa and the Copper Belt, to the chilly formality of this old Irish house.

The whole thing had frozen in my mind in a single snapshot: Molly in the background, her arms outstretched to welcome me, blue with cold from the east wind, and in the foreground my grandmother, the 'Mistress', 'Herself', called by whatever name, facing us. She had no idea of distance. England and, once, Geneva were her furthest points of reference. Africa might, as far as she was concerned, be just around the corner. And then, as now, she was implacable.

It seemed to me it was a day for flashbacks, for replaying the past. Things which had now reached a climax had begun sixteen years before when my father had sent a cable, as he chewed his pencil in an iron-roofed mine post office on the Copper Belt in 1933. He had sent it in French to thwart the curiosity of the postmistress of a Cork village in Ireland, with no projected dates and no address.

'*Femme est partie*,' it said. '*Je reviens*.'

What it hadn't said, Molly told me later, was that he would

return with me, standing beside him that dusty day in an enormous grey felt hat. In all photographs at this time I wore the hat, which made me look like a walking mushroom. My early memories were limited. Possibly the hat impeded vision!

My father had taken me, soon after my mother left him, to the Copper Belt with an ayah from Kenya and his Zulu cook from Natal. We went in an old jalopy. The Copper Belt calls to mind a great gleaming place, a vast smithy with coppery lights, anvils and swinging hammers. In fact it was dry and dusty and full of men who smelt of the dust and the beer. I spent most of my time with the ayah and after a while I could speak only Swahili and Fanagalo from being with the Africans all the time, sitting in a sun-scorched garden of a mine bungalow near clumps of dusty canna lilies.

My father didn't make his fortune there and after a few months, encumbered by me, he had to cable his parents in Ireland and swallow what pride he had left. Swallowing pride was the difficult part, because his parents had tried three years before to stop his marriage to my mother.

As my father was heir to a 200-year-old Irish estate, they felt that choosing his future wife was their prerogative, within reason. Total control was their maxim and that meant that he should marry someone of the right background, who knew about sacrifice and duty and looking after things like houses and the land handed on to you.

Presumably you passed it on at your death to what Grandfather was fond of calling 'the next man in'. Having the right background meant that you understood about responsibilities and you spent your money fighting dry rot and mending the roof instead of having fun.

My father had married, with only his younger brother present at the ceremony, and even he had come reluctantly. There were no cables from well-wishers in Ireland and later, after a series of ferocious and numerous family quarrels –

the Anglo-Irish are talented quarrellers – he left for South Africa on the crest of a rage and took my mother with him. She was eighteen.

The telegram he had sent from the Copper Belt was without an address, nor was it followed by a letter. And so we arrived, he and I, in an aura of disapproval which ever since his Eton days had hung like a fog around his dealings with his parents. The trouble was that my father was constantly expected to live up to the images he had no wish to meet. Fifty years later his wildness would have been accepted, but not then and never by them.

From a mining camp in Northern Rhodesia to a large Georgian house in the south of Ireland was a fairly traumatic transition, and to come to this household, encapsulated in a Victorian regime for over a hundred years, was no small contrast. But I, being young, scarcely noticed and, apart from asking repeatedly where the street was, accepted everything with reasonable equanimity.

'I want Ayah!' I had sobbed at the beginning, but Ayah would never have fitted in.

The house in Ireland was large and beautiful in its own way. A cream Georgian block with sweeping terraced lawns, peacocks and flowering shrubs and a vast velvet green croquet lawn where my grandmother, probably in one of her ancient Edwardian hats, was playing croquet when we returned from Africa.

We were quite unexpected. Weeks of journeying had elapsed since the cable had been sent. No other communication had been exchanged and my grandmother, putting down her croquet mallet, was scarcely welcoming. It was not her way to be so. Once, years later, when I flung my arms in an affectionate gesture round someone or other, she reproved me by saying, 'Do *not* behave like a housemaid on her day off. Emotion is for the lower classes.' Visions spring to mind, Thurwell-like, of a plethora of housemaids launching themselves into the arms of their acquaintances. With her, a light dry kiss was too effusive.

My one memory of that autumn day was sharp cold. The house was set in a bracelet of thick copper beech and oak trees, with a sweep of lawns in front. At the back a river hooped by bridges ran through water gardens of gunnera, spiraea and bamboos, where Edmund Spenser once wrote his *Faerie Queene*. Above the river towered a rock, crested with trees, where one could climb and watch people like ants going about their business. There was a cave there, an IRA hideout during the Bad Times.

In the house lived my grandparents. My grandmother, an autocratic and aristocratic lady, very conscious of her connections, granddaughter of Sir William Howard Russell, the Crimean War correspondent; and my grandfather, who at that time was Master of Hounds, with a scarlet face and a great jutting nose. He seemed to be permanently clad, when not hunting, in bright green tweed plus-fours. He could also roar amazingly loudly for a small man, but practice in the hunting field was no doubt the reason for this.

This was a new world, a muted world of mists and quiet country lanes and boreens and a patchwork of green chequered fields loosely bound together with stone walls. The atmosphere of the old part of the estate was often eerie and the house itself had this feeling of great isolation. Approached by three avenues, two of them long and twisted and bordered with thick dark woods, it stood alone in a clearing and the walls which surrounded the demesne were high and old. They had been built by country people during the Great Hunger of 1848. The landlords couldn't feed all the starving Irish, so piece-work like the walls went out to a few and they were fed. It was they who had built these great towering walls of huge pieces of limestone all around the estate, which shut in the house and old thick trees.

But people had died under these walls when the potatoes

failed, coming too late to search for work, and so the walls were eerie too and there were awful legends of famine walls and famine grass. Near the walls rooks and crows nested in the elms and on the house the ivy grew, tapping on windows at night when the wind blew down the valley.

The atmosphere was predominantly one of rain and mist, one felt. The blazing sunlit spaces of Africa were far from here – but even in later years when a great deal of time had passed, if I shut my eyes I could see a mind-picture of yellow fruits piled in a native market, black smiling faces and African people grouped, talking in a foreign language, under a blazing blue sky.

'When you first came here you were always talking foreign,' Molly said once. 'Like a savage. For shame!'

They weren't savages, I could have told her. She thought that just because no one in Ireland could understand Zulu or Swahili. But I never did tell her, because Africa and the divorce were things never mentioned by anyone at that time.

In my passport it said under 'Place of Birth' Johannesburg, but to all intents and purposes so taboo was the subject of my father's marriage that I might never have been in Africa but left by the fairies under a convenient Anglo-Irish gooseberry bush.

– 2 –

A year or two after I had come back from Africa with my father, he had quarrelled again with his parents and left to prospect for gold in Sierra Leone. Why couldn't he have taken me? I longed to ask. But I didn't dare.

The day he left Ireland it was pouring with rain. The trees dripped, I remember, and the lawns were shrouded with a downpour that blotted out the sky. When it rained in Africa the tropical showers had drummed on the corrugated iron roofs and in the little *dorps* the streets ran noisily with muddy torrents. The rain often stopped in Africa just as suddenly as it had begun and there was a smell of dust, and blue jacaranda blossoms, newly washed, lay on the ground.

No one mentioned my father's departure then or ever again. The entail on the estate would soon be broken, severing his inheritance as the eldest son. After that, he would never again return home to live there.

When my father went off to Sierra Leone, my grandmother decided to undertake my education herself, which she did with her usual verve. Mathematically it was a disaster as neither she nor I understood multiplication or division at all. Both of us counted on our fingers, so sums were something of a mystery. I had a feeling, instilled from those early lessons, that there really was no rhyme or reason to mathematics – at any moment a welcome element of surprise might enter into them. For instance, five and five might unexpectedly make eleven, or nine subtracted from eighteen could perhaps on occasion leave more than one expected. This has brought a great air of optimism into my dealings with figures, which has proved financially fatal.

Reading lessons were a success, and as I grew older I found a feast of books in the house, ranging from some as curious as De Quincey's *Confessions of an Opium Eater* to eighteenth-century books bound in brown leather, flung carelessly into cupboards in the night nursery. The pages of these were badly foxed and the spines of most of them broken from neglect, which was a pity as they were fascinating if one had the patience to convert the old *f*'s into *s*'s. It was years before I was old enough to appreciate them, but I terrified myself quite early by reading Scott's *Letters on Demonology and Witchcraft* under the blankets with a torch.

The top of the house where I slept was, I think, almost certainly haunted. It had a curiously forbidding atmosphere in some of the rooms which was not in any other part of the house. There was one room in particular where I felt I was being watched by invisible eyes and I never stayed in it a minute longer than was necessary.

The room where I slept had a skylight. Fastened to one wall were show certificates won by some relative for her bulldogs and on the other wall a series of lithographs of ferocious-looking Red Indians whose faces, like Medusa, were calculated to turn one to stone. These had been brought back by Grandfather from British Columbia in the late 1880s, and when the moon shone through the skylight and highlighted their sinister faces and jutting noses, I kept my eyes closed, especially if I was up there alone on a windy night.

Besides this, some of the cupboards on the landing had a disconcerting habit of blowing softly open and then creaking shut. They were set into thick walls, and as the backs of several had crumbled with age, the wind would blow through and funnel down inside thick hollow walls to blow open cupboards in other empty rooms or on the landing. Lying in bed, riveted by the book on demonology, I would, cold with fright, suddenly become aware of the creaks and moaning of the wind on winter nights and the eerie opening and shutting of cupboards.

Eventually, with not the slightest idea of basic mathematics but the ability to recite my tables like a parrot and a wide and catholic taste in unsuitable books, I went to Ballygliff House where the Perrotts lived to share a governess with their daughter Maria. In some ways this was a well-thought-out idea. Maria and I would have each other for company, be grounded by an English governess, who was presumably trained, and have some sort of routine.

The only disadvantage was that Miss Maiden, the governess, was a sadist.

No one knew this. She had come with good references and it was to be some time before it was discovered. It was unfortunate for us that the nursery and the schoolroom wing were isolated from the rest of the house by a heavy door, as we were incarcerated with her, and inside the schoolroom she was monarch of all she surveyed. I had to bear with her only from Monday to Friday, as mercifully I went home for weekends, but Maria was continually with her, even to sharing a bedroom.

The schoolroom area was self-contained, with a hall, a huge bedroom and the schoolroom itself where we studied and ate our meals, served by a dignified butler, James, and cooked by his wife Julia. We literally learnt, read, ate and lived in that room. A picture of a bowl of anemones hung over the mantelpiece, the flooring was thick cork-backed linoleum, and there was a wicker chair by the fireplace where Miss Maiden read us suitable books in the evenings.

She must, I imagine, have occasionally been kind to us. But Maria and I were terrified of her. She used to hit us with enormous sticks. On walks she would pretend to be Hitler while Maria and I were Poland and Czechoslovakia and she would lash our calves with an ash plant as we bumbled along in our little red sou'westers and Wellington boots. We seemed to spend hours walking for miles in our mackintoshes in the pouring rain being taught the names of wild flowers by Miss Maiden, who strode along in her lace-up oxfords and shingled hair, hitting us from time to time.

I was wildly imaginative and invented stories with which I regaled Maria, who was stolid and gullible. I spun her such stories about the river people who lived underwater in caves of mother-of-pearl that she very nearly jumped into the river, and as far as I can remember I was all for it! Miss Maiden soon put a stop to my story-telling, saying that little girls who told stories were liars.

One of my peccadilloes was to try to make a concoction from the juice of the scarlet poppies that grew near the gates. De Quincey seemed to have entered a fairyland world after sampling poppy juice and perhaps I felt it might brighten up life at Ballygliff a bit for Maria. All that happened was that I got a headache and Maria was ill all day. I had to learn four psalms from the Bible by heart and got hit by Miss Maiden.

Miss Maiden had a fixation about eating quickly and eating everything on one's plate. Consequently I learnt to eat like a puppy, gulping my food, hardly tasting it, scraping my plate and putting my knife and fork together within minutes of being served. Maria, on the other hand, ate extremely slowly and gagged on anything she disliked, spinach or gristle or fat. She would sit under Miss Maiden's eye with a piece of gristle in her mouth, her jaws moving slowly up and down and tears pouring down her face. Everything would be removed from the table except Maria's plate, on which the food grew colder and greasier every moment. Eventually Miss Maiden would fetch the castor oil bottle and with a large metal spoon ram castor oil into Maria's mouth. Maria would sit sobbing, with tears, castor oil and spinach all over her face, trying to swallow.

And so life progressed, bounded for us by Miss Maiden. If we got out of bed at night and she caught us, we were made to stand on the schoolroom table in the freezing cold in our nightgowns for an hour at a time. We dared it once or twice when she went downstairs to dine with the Perrotts but on each occasion by some sixth sense she heard us and we were caught. Why we never complained at home I don't know. Neither Maria nor I would have dared. We were too terrified of her.

When asked at home if I liked her, or liked being at Ballygliff House, I always answered 'Yes,' or 'Yes, thank you,' or 'Very much, thank you.' She always said that if we spoke about her she would overhear us no matter where we were, and I felt that she might, like a witch, have supernatural powers so I took no risks. When, at last, I was taken away I felt like someone released from prison who has left a companion in enemy hands.

There was, however, a sequel to the saga at Ballygliff. Maria, abandoned to the terrible ritual of being rammed full of castor oil, made to stand on an icy table, being hit on the legs, beaten with an ash plant and generally demoralised, grew desperate. Eventually, at lunch one day, the worm turned and she, confronted with the metal spoon and the castor oil bottle, picked up a heavy Georgian silver mustard pot and hurled it at Miss Maiden's head. A spot of blood appeared on the Gorgon's forehead and Maria, appalled at what she had done, fled sobbing along the landing, through the baize door and down the blue-carpeted stairs to collide with her father at the bottom.

Henry Perrott was a spare, shy man who had been a banker in Shanghai for many years. He had a habit of clicking his teeth together and turning the change in his pocket at the same time. He seemed to spend most of his days in his study, which was full of books and carvings, and paid little attention to what went on about him.

On this occasion he was startled somewhat to be confronted by his small daughter of eight, hysterical, terrified and screaming. She was shaking like a leaf. On being asked what the matter was, Maria cried the more 'Nothing! Nothing!' until the whole story was elicited and Miss Maiden was given twenty-four hours to pack and leave for England. We were repeatedly asked why we hadn't said anything, but she had literally terrified us into silence. We had had Dickens read to us and *Jane Eyre*, so perhaps we thought Miss Maiden's behaviour quite normal in England.

It is too long ago to remember now, but for me some good came of it. She taught me the name of almost every local wild flower – vetch, scarlet pimpernel, star of Bethlehem, mallow, birdsfoot trefoil, celandine, wild scabious and twenty more besides – and this made a bond with Grandfather, who was passionate about plants, so we grew closer. After that I was taught by governesses at home until I went to school.

There was Miss Dolphin who rode my pony bareback and was considered too flighty, and Miss Cowdry well into her late seventies with highly rouged orange cheeks like a cockatiel, and teeth like old ivory piano keys which she picked delicately with a silver toothpick. She had two false sausage curls fastened, one over each ear, with hairpins, and an unpleasant habit of rotating my elbow bones if I vexed her, which was painful to say the least.

When she left, creaking with age, for a retirement home in Dublin, and I saw the dogcart go down the avenue, I danced a jig in the kitchen much to Molly's amusement.

'Wait,' Moll said a few days later. 'Wait till you see who is coming now.'

I was sitting on the Aga top watching her putting a hot lamp into a box near the stove to warm some day-old chicks.

'Good or bad news, Moll? Who?'

But she didn't reply.

'She is only here for three weeks, mind you,' she said mysteriously. 'From Connemara.' And would say no more.

A week later Miss Manning arrived from Tourmakeady in the west, and told me that she was my new governess. She was utterly unlike anyone I had ever seen. For one thing she laughed all the time, had blue eyes, fluffy fair hair, and had never been a governess in her life.

'You don't *look* like a governess,' I said, appraising her.

'What *do* I look like then?'

'You look like a rather nice kitten,' I said, and Kitten she became.

She told me stories of Connemara, of Ballinahinch Castle and Indian princesses who had lived there for a while, of sailing on loughs in her skiff, and fishing for salmon. She talked plants to Grandfather and went riding with Granny. She could play the organ, sing in the choir, and remove a swarm of bees from one place to another. She and the bees had a rapport which mesmerised me. They swarmed all over her with only a veiled hat and gloves to protect her. They crawled up her arms and chest and never stung her, and as I watched goggle-eyed from a safe distance she moved clumps of bees in a seething mass from one gloved hand to another. She told me about drones and bee queens and the different kinds of honey, and that if you had hives on your property you should always tell the bees of any happenings in the family.

Mornings in the schoolroom passed in a flash. Molly too was captivated by her and brewed her up what she called 'coffee-oh-lay' which she sent up with the parlour maid to the schoolroom promptly at eleven each morning. What with the bees, the stories of Connemara, and the confidences I shared with her which I had never revealed to anyone before,

I wanted her to stay forever. She had come for three weeks and she stayed for three years.

Granny, who wanted her conveniently at hand, had now decided that the only sensible way to keep her nearby was to marry her off in the parish. The only bachelor within striking distance – who drank like a fish and was completely unsuitable – was known, according to his brother, to be, 'combing Ireland for a wife'.

He had been away combing for a fortnight after the harvest was in, returning spouseless. So Granny, who had been receiving progress reports, unveiled her plans to Kitten.

'A pity,' she told the startled Kitten, 'that he is not ideal, but he will have to do. I have made enquiries and he seems quite well off.'

Kitten, not knowing whether to laugh or to cry, thanked Granny tactfully for her role as marriage broker, gently pointing out that she was already unofficially engaged to someone she loved. So the Comber – as I had christened him – would have to seek pastures new.

When she left to marry I was her bridesmaid at the cathedral in Cork in a long turquoise crêpe dress, feeling happy and proud and sad all in a jumble together, and she went off to live happily in her house called Rookstown near Dublin.

'Under the Penal Laws enforced by the British in Ireland in 1695,' intoned Miss Nolan in a strong Cork accent, 'no Irish Catholic was permitted to vote or read Law. He was barred from commerce, the army and the navy, could not purchase land nor attend any school either abroad or in Ireland.'

She turned to write Irish on the blackboard, saw it, paused, and started to go red in the face. Maeve behind me giggled.

'Stand the girl who drew the Union Jack on the board!' You could have heard a pin drop. I leapt to my feet.

'I drew it, Miss Nolan.'

'And for why?'

'I'm Anglo-Irish.'

'God save Ireland,' she said, glowering. She was the only Roman Catholic teacher in this Protestant school in Eire – a landowners' enclave of black Protestants where, like Trinity College in those days, you had to be a Protestant to get in and the schooling you got there, particularly in history, was slanted to the Crown.

Any past Irish uprising in those history books used at school, we were taught, was quelled firmly but kindly by the long-suffering, good and gallant British, who were constantly irritated and embarrassed by the truculent, undisciplined and wayward Irish.

'Poor Lord Castlereagh was *forced* by the Troubles in Ireland to sail for Dublin. Yet *another* insurrection had erupted in turbulent Ireland,' said *Little Arthur's England*, the current history book for children.

'Ireland had first been invaded by England in 1169, yet was never subdued. It was a constant source of anxiety to the English,' I wrote on my examination pad, sure of ten out of ten for perception.

A different song was sung by the Irish history books, glorying in martyrdom and with most if not all of their heroes 'trodden under the iron heel of the British'. They had plenty to say on the subject.

'I met murder on the way. He had a face like Lord Castlereagh [England's choice of Chief Secretary for Ireland],' said the Irish history primer.

'Think of all the great men who lived and died for Ireland, killed in cold blood by the cruel brutal British,' Miss Nolan hissed at us whenever she had the class to herself. It wasn't often. She was there simply to teach the Irish language and was on dormitory duty once a week. When she turned off the lights she said '*Slain Lath*' instead of 'Goodnight'. '*Slain Lath!*' we chorused sycophantically in a language never used in our world except by Miss Nolan.

'Think of all the great men who have lived and died for Ireland, killed in cold blood by the brutal British,' I related tongue in cheek at home and then waited for the explosion with a certain amount of glee. It came. Grandfather was eating kedgeree at the breakfast table and threw down his knife and fork at this sedition.

'Christ Almighty! Who is teaching this child this Sinn Fein cant?'

'We learnt it in Irish class,' I said piously. 'All about England and how the North of Ireland belongs to Eire really and one day Eire will take back the six counties.'

But I had gone too far. Giving me a look of sheer fury, he threw down his napkin and stamped into the smoking room to write a letter to the school. I was to be taught no more

Irish, nor be exposed to IRA sympathies of any kind, however diluted.

Back came a letter. The Irish Education Board demanded the Gaelic, even at private schools. Everyone had to learn the Irish. There was a penalty, a fine on any child whose family baulked.

Seizing his pen he wrote back, this accompanied by much roaring and door-banging. He would pay the fine, I was *not* to learn it. Whatever the fine was, it would be paid. He was incensed.

And so, back to *Little Arthur's England* and the Good Good English and no more Miss Nolan telling us severely that we Protestants weren't true Irish at all but only the descendants of English planters put into Ireland from London and bribed with lands and titles to stay and subdue the Catholics.

'Bribed with *our* land,' she hissed, while we wiggled under her beady eye. '*Our* land, confiscated by the British from the Catholic Irish people and given to the likes of you.' This had all happened centuries previously but Miss Nolan, like an elephant, had a long memory.

'What's she on about anyway?' said Maeve that morning. 'Eire's a republic now, has been since 1921. It's only the north that still belongs to England and who wants that place anyway!' But apparently some people did. There were rumblings already near the border and the IRA had begun to paint their slogans on village walls.

The irony of the Irish issue was that Granny, now eighty, was teaching herself Irish in the long summer evenings.

'There is beautiful poetry in Gaelic,' she said, glaring from under her huge hat with her spectacles on the end of her nose. 'And there are wonderful words in Gaelic and descriptions that lose their colour when translated. You close a door in your mind if you turn your back on it.'

But Granny was a Macnaghten and they loved learning, Grandfather said, 'for the sake of it'.

– 4 –

There was much that I learnt and remember of Annes Grove that had nothing to do with the schoolroom. My good friend at that time was Ned Ginevan. He was the estate carpenter, and when the slates blew off in a high wind he would climb out onto the roof and put them back. He fixed the farm machinery, mended the gates and once a year swept the drawing-room chimney. Everything was shrouded in dust sheets for the sweep, and Ned and the parlour maids would move the furniture, knocking heads merrily off Rockingham figurines and Meissen birds during the operation, crossing themselves and muttering 'Jasus, Mary and Joseph!' as another priceless china ornament crashed to the floor. After a while, covered in clouds of soot, Ned would emerge from the drawing room as black as a Moor.

Although in no way like Ayah, with her tight plaits and kinky hair and shiny oiled face – Ned had no teeth and had little growths like grapes all over his neck – he took her place. I thought him marvellous. He was a historian and belonged to what he called a historical society. To add to his charisma, he had written for the local paper. He had a huge room in the yard called the carpenter's shop. There were shavings all over the floor and pots of turpentine and paint, ladders and tools everywhere. He used to stand at the bench planing planks while yellow shavings of wood rained ankle-deep onto the ground. Sitting on the floor, I uncurled them with my fingers until they snapped, while he told me stories about old times.

There was a huge rock, about a hundred feet high, which ran behind the river for about a quarter of a mile. It was covered with thick bushes and ivy and trees. There was a cave there, Ned said, where a hermit had lived a hundred years ago. He told me that during the Troubled Times the IRA had used it for a hideout.

In the workshop, hanging on the beams above, was an old oak cradle belonging to my great-grandfather. There was a cupboard in there as well, where Ned kept his lunch. It had been made by George III, according to him.

'Do you mean George III made it?'

'Well, he didn't make it himself like,' said Ned, 'he was too busy, I suppose, ruling and that, but it was made when he was on the throne over England.'

When I asked in the house if it was true, Grandfather said it was an early Georgian cupboard and disgraceful that it should be left outside. But no one brought it in because it was too heavy to move.

It was Ned who told me about the ghost on the Castle Avenue, the Foxy Woman. She had long red hair and a grave-stained shroud, and he said she walked at midsummer.

'What does she walk for?' I wanted to know.

'She is guarding gold belonging to your family,' Ned told me, 'and now and again she takes the air. An ancestor of yours buried treasure in the hopyard when he was going to the wars. She was alive then and she followed him and watched him digging. He caught her and made her swear on the Bible to guard the gold until he came home, and then he killed her. She was a woman and he didn't trust her,' explained Ned matter-of-factly.

'Maybe she'd dig it up like, when he was gone, so he cut off her head. He did some sort of injustice by murdering her no doubt, for she's been haunting the avenue since. She'll guard it for ever now, for your ancestor was killed in the same wars. There used to be people digging for it at one time, but after she marked poor Mickey Mac they didn't dig after that.'

'But how did anyone know he'd buried it, if he was dead and the Foxy Woman was dead?'

'He left papers for his son. They got them after he died. He said it was buried under the eleventh tree in the hopyard, but sure, whichever way you count the eleventh tree it's always different.'

'How did she mark Mickey Mac?' I wanted to know, but Ned was sick of the subject.

'Away off to your tea and don't be bothering me.'

I went to the hopyard. It was as still as the grave and there were trees everywhere. I tried to count them to eleven but they were growing in lines like the spokes of a wheel. It was eerie there and sure enough there were pits, as if people had been digging and got tired of it, or worse still, I thought, had to make a run for it, pursued by the Foxy Woman in her shroud.

Ned was cross at that time. Rheumatism was bothering him, so I wandered down to the river gardens, to find old Bill Donlan scuffling weeds with his scuffler. Bill had an equable temper and he didn't believe in working too hard, so he was always glad to stop for a while and lean on the handle of his hoe. Bill had heard the Banshee crying on the village hill many years before. When he mentioned it, he used to make the sign of the cross because she had frightened the wits out of him. When she keened behind him and he turned to look, he said, she'd keen to the side of him in the butt of the ditch.

'Was it dark when you heard her?' I enquired, a glutton for punishment. I wouldn't sleep a wink that night.

''Twas. Only a small piece of moon shining.'

'Why was she keening, Bill? Was there anyone dying in your family?'

'Ah sure, it wasn't our people at all. The Banshee only follows some families.'

'I wouldn't like to hear her at all,' I said. 'Is she an old woman?'

'She is. With grey hair streeling down her back and she all hunched up and bent.'

'I wouldn't like to hear her at all,' I said again, sitting down and hunching my knees up to my chin.

'You won't hear her either,' said old Bill, 'because she doesn't follow your family. She only cries in the wind for the Fitzes and the O'Gradys when they are going to die.'

'Would she be walking the woods by day?' The woods were frightening enough without meeting a banshee down in them.

'In the day,' said Bill, 'she takes the form of a hoodie crow, or of a big black dog.'

'Isn't *shee* the Gaelic word meaning fairywoman? And *badthe*? It's a crow or a raven in the Irish, isn't it?'

'Ah, you've great learning,' Bill said, taking off his cap with the peak and scratching his head. Sometimes he would put the peak to the front and sometimes to the back. If he was feeling frivolous he would put it over his ear.

I used to think a great deal about what Bill said to me about the Banshee. Once when I went down below the killeen, the family graveyard, it was going to rain, so I took a short cut through the woods to where the famine walls were broken and you could climb over. The gypsies and tinkers had broken in, looking for firewood, when they parked their caravans outside the demesne wall. I was walking when I came on a wizened old woman, her hair streeling, talking to herself as she picked sticks. She was bent in two and must have been about eighty-five years of age.

It turned out that she was an aunt of Ned's, but I didn't

know that. I got such a fright that I ran like a hare, for I thought it was the *shee*. When I ran I went past the graveyard and a hoodie crow rose and perched on the wall by the tombstones. My heart was pounding as I flew up the avenue. I burst into the kitchen and told the cook.

'The Banshee is below in the killeen! She's below! I saw her!'

'Jesus, Mary and Joseph!' she said, and crossed herself.

It was from old Bill that I eventually got the story of Mickey Mac being marked.

'Bill,' I said, choosing my words carefully, 'did you know about the foxy-haired woman on the avenue?'

'Yerra I did,' he said, slicing a chunk of tobacco off his plug and putting it into his mouth to chew it. 'Yerra I did. Didn't she mark old Mickey Mac?'

'How did she do that?'

'He wanted the treasure.'

'In spite of the Foxy Woman?'

'Well, he had porter took like, below in the public house in Glanworthy and a bottle of holy water in his pocket. Sure with that combination an Irishman will do any bleddy thing.'

'And ...?'

'And he went up from Reagan's pub to the hopyard here at about twelve o'clock at night with a spade. He put the holy water around himself in a circle and he commenced digging. Nothing can touch you if you've the holy water sprinkled. Well, he was digging away for himself like and he hit a big stone. "Jasus!" he roars, "I'm into it!" and at that moment the Foxy Woman came on, her red hair streeling and she in a cold white shroud.'

I shivered. 'But he was in the circle with the holy water.'

'He was, but he came out of it. She must have tricked him some way. She got him by the throat and the two of them went down the avenue. He was walking backwards and she in front of him, forcing him. He was saying his Hail Marys so she couldn't mark him, but in the heel of the hunt he had too much drink taken. He hiccoughed,' said Bill reflectively, 'and it broke the chain of prayer.'

'She hit him?'

'She did. Then she went away and he was in dread so he could not even make it home like, only lying in the butt of the ditch, but there was the mark of her hand burnt into him and he died about a month after. The five fingers of her burnt into his back.'

Bill and Ned were always telling me about long ago. When I told Molly some of their stories she burst out laughing, but going at dusk into the woods was like going back in time. The whole countryside was in the grip of the enchanted past. Down on the avenue by the yew trees was the old pagan burial ground with the cromlech in it, with queer slanty lines all along the top. I asked in the house about the treasure in the killeen and the Foxy Woman.

'The treasure is in the cromlech,' said Grandfather. 'The cromlech must go back nearly a thousand years. There must be an old Irish king buried there or a druid priest. I expect that is where the stories come from. Gold and bronze might be buried with him. It very probably is.'

'Couldn't we dig?'

'In a tomb? Of course we couldn't, and anyway that old burial ground is consecrated ground now. Your great-grandfather is buried there and Great-Uncle Fitz.'

'They're buried a good piece from the cromlech, though,' I said. 'Couldn't we ask people about it? People who know about cromlechs?'

'And have hordes of terrible people coming here? Newspaper people, sightseers? In our own graveyard? Don't talk about it and don't ever discuss it again.'

I talked about it though, to Ned. Ned knew it was there. He could hardly miss it as he bicycled past there every day with his lunch pail dangling over his handlebars.

'It's a tomb,' Ned told me. He was painting the spokes of the threshing mill when I found him. 'This is a very old place. Not just the killeen; there were some class of druids here at one time. I think it was before Saint Patrick.'

The thing about Ireland was the sense of timelessness. A thousand years ago or a hundred were very much the same. Cromwell, Mickey Mac, the druids and the Irish king in his tomb almost seemed like old friends. The countryside remained sleeping in the enchanted past.

Up at the farm, in the forty-acre field, the ploughman found some coins with heads on them crowned with plaited wreaths. They were put into a glass case in the drawing room. While he ploughed he had to navigate a tricky passage because he couldn't plough by the hawthorn bushes and he couldn't plough up the fairy raths. The raths were deep hollows or depressions in the ground, sometimes nearly a quarter of an acre across and usually rimmed with hawthorns. They were reputedly the home of the little people, and the hawthorn bushes and may were sacred.

'Do you believe in the fairies?' I asked my grandfather. He was sitting in his pea-green tweed plus-fours with the waistcoat with leather buttons on it, reading the *Irish Times*. It was a bad time to ask him. He had just finished his tax returns.

'What rubbish are you asking me now?'

'The fairies ... do you believe in them?'

'Of course I don't. Do you think I'm a child?'

'Why doesn't Donlan plough everywhere in the forty-acre field then?' I asked. 'Why doesn't he plough near the may bushes?'

'Because of the raths, that's why.'

'And the hawthorns?'

'He'll plough near no damned hawthorn trees. We've enough problems as it is without bringing bad luck here to us.'

★★★

The Foxy Woman in the avenue continued to fascinate me. Ned said she was never seen in the daylight, but there was a postbox at the lodge gate and often I would be sent down on my bicycle in the dark to catch the seven o'clock post on a winter's evening. The bicycle lamp sent only a small circle of yellow light and the avenue was half a mile long and very bumpy and windy, bordered with dark lonely trees. Down in the valley the river flowed, the noise of it very loud in the silence. I bicycled at full tilt when I was passing the graveyard and faster still by the hopyard. Then there was the really black dark piece where I met the old woman I had thought was the Banshee. If I had had a puncture here, I think I would have gone on pedalling on a flat tyre, so terrifying was the avenue – lonely, remote and so dark and long.

At one end of it I could see the lodge lamp shining through the trees and the vast studded outline of the lodge gate. Inside the lodge house people would be having their supper – boiled potatoes in their skins and a slab of salty butter and sometimes a piece of bacon, like pig's trotters.

I would hurl the letters into the box which still said VR although the old queen was long since dead and George VI on the throne and not monarch of Ireland either, and cycle back as if the Devil himself was after me. The road curved in a steep hill past the killeen on the way back, but I took it at breakneck speed, my heart pounding. Once an owl got up, flying low and clumsily in front of me and I crossed myself as a Catholic would. Ned was half amused, half sympathetic when I told him about my bicycle rides.

'One time,' he said, 'people were always in dread of that avenue at night on account of Herself, the same Foxy Woman. There was a fella, Bill Joe by name, living at the lodge and he married. He was a good-looking fella and he had a wife who was that jealous of him you've never heard the like of it. At him day and night she was, with a shrill nagging voice like a paycock. Sure the poor fella never had an hour's peace, only when he was away from her, God help him.'

'What was she at him over?' I asked Ned, who at this time was tarring boats in the barn for the fishing season.

'Jealous so she was. There was a woman named Norah Casey over in Ballyhooly and Bill Joe's wife was that jealous of her she was eaten with it. "'Tis her you love," says she, "an' her you're after," says she, "an' don't be telling me lies," says she, "for I'm your match."'

We both fell silent, thinking of Bill Joe and the peacock-like voice of his wife, drilling him day and night and filling the lodge with her nagging.

'So what did he do?' I asked. Obviously he must have done something or there would be no story, and Ned was in an expansive humour.

'What did he do, is it?' asked Ned, filling his pipe. 'He did what many a good man did before him. He took slightly to lifting his elbow, and wholeheartedly to fishing.'

'Lifting his elbow?'

'Taking a drop of the crayture.'

'Oh.'

'But of an evening, he'd wait till she'd be inside in the bed and he'd lift his old trout rod down from the nail and go down to the river below the killeen for a bit of peace and to throw a fly.'

'Did that please her?'

'Please her, is it?' said Ned in disgust. 'Nothing would please the likes of that one, only trouble. "Fishing," says she. "Casting your line," says she. "Fishing for Norah Casey," says she, "more likely." She was a sour apple of a woman, that one. Red hair she had, streeling red hair, and green eyes, and a voice as I am after telling you, like some class of a peacock! One night, 'twas in April, poor old Bill Joe takes down his rod and closes his ears to her. 'Twas a fine spring night and the trout were rising below in the river like the dead after the Resurrection. He went down the avenue and then he turned down the steps below the killeen making for the river. Well, Herself was inside the bed and she lying there in her long white nightgown …'

'How do you know?'

'Whisht, will you,' said Ned, 'aren't I telling you the story? Well, she heard him going and she heard the door closing and she lying there in the bed. Up she gets, and throwing an old shawl round her, she starts following poor old Bill Joe down the avenue. Hiding behind the trees she was and stopping behind the may bushes like a bloody gun dog after a hare. When he took the steps down to the river, she stood up on the stile by the killeen, to see could she see him.

'Well, your grandfather was ill that time and he'd a nurse above from Clonmel who was looking after him. She was walking out with the chauffeur. They were coming down the avenue the same night and he telling her the story of the Foxy Woman, hoping she'd hold on to him like, for a bit of comfort. They came on for the killeen and, God save us, there standing in the dusk he sees a red-haired woman in a long white night shift. None other of course than Bill Joe's wife.

'"Jasus!" says the chauffeur, "Jasus God! The Foxy Woman in her shroud!" He let out one unmerciful yell and went over the cliff by the killeen like a Derby winner on the home stretch. Yerra, you need wings to go jumping like that and the poor divil didn't have them, so that was the end of him.'

'And the nurse?'

'She handed in her notice the same night,' said Ned.

'What happened to Bill Joe?'

'His wife died a couple of years after that, of some class of a weakness and he married the girl from Ballyhooly.'

'So he *did* love Norah Casey!' I said 'Maybe his wife was right to fault him.'

'She might have been,' said Ned, putting his pipe away in his pocket, 'and on the other hand she might not.'

– 5 –

Doyle and I waged war. Doyle was a hunchback only about four and a half feet tall, who lived in the stable yard, looked after the horses and drove the trap. He was supposed to look after the harness as well. In the mornings when we sat eating our breakfast, Doyle would pass under the window perched on top of a big Irish hunter, with his bowler hat on his head, taking the animal out to exercise it. He came from Castlecomer in County Kilkenny and he was always saying, 'An' I wish I was back there.'

The maids in the Servants' Hall used to tease him. When a new girl came to work in the kitchen, the cook used to send her out with a message for Doyle's wife. He had never married and for some reason this joke used to madden him. He could be heard roaring in the yard at the luckless girl.

'Your mother should chastise you, begob!'

Some of the jokes they played on him were cruel. But he brought a lot of it on himself as he was as bad-tempered as a weasel.

In the summer time when the horses were out on grass I could see him in the evenings, going down through the green dusk to the inch to fish for trout, and late, at about eleven, he returned, a small bent figure with his rod over his shoulder, and a few trout in his creel.

When I came back from school Doyle was sent in the dogcart to meet the train. He was the first person I saw when the Ballybrack train rounded the curve, perched up high with his old pipe stuck in his mouth and his collar turned up against the rain. We were friends then for a while but we were fighting before a week was out when I stole oats from the bin in the harness room to feed the horses. However well he hid the key, I used to find it. He would shout at me, standing in his buttoned gaiters in the musty hay smell of the stables. He was responsible for the oats and was blamed if he used them too quickly. Looking back on it, I think the truth was that he was getting old and could not hold the horses if they became too fresh from the oats.

The time he was angriest with me was when I decided, one day when he was down at the farrier's, to clean the dingy little room he occupied near the stables. The smell in there was terrible and I slopped soapy water all over the floor and tried to scrub it. Water lay in puddles in the dents in the concrete and I could not get it out. When he came back he was raging and we shouted at each other for an hour. I kept telling him I was a Brownie doing him a good turn but he just kept on roaring.

My grandmother used to knit Doyle the most terrible woollen scarves on big wooden needles for Christmas. The colours were frightful; sometimes they would be mauve and yellow and sometimes purple and chocolate brown. She was getting blind in those days and dropped half the stitches. Doyle used to be sent for, round to the big porticoed front door on Christmas Day and given his scarf, wrapped in tissue paper. He used to do a sort of bob, almost a curtsy, and wrap the scarf around his stringy little neck with a few words of thanks.

When I came back from Africa many years later, Doyle was not there. He had become too old to work and had gone home to Castlecomer. The horses had been sold and there were young calves in the stables and seed potatoes in the harness room. The smell of the horses still hung in the air and neglected pieces of harness, dried, cracked and dirty, hardened in the lofts. No one spoke of Doyle any more. One night, standing near the old loose-boxes under the sycamore tree, with the bats diving and planing in the dusk, I kept thinking about him. I couldn't get him out of my head. I looked at the blackened squares of the deserted stables, and in the quiet it was as if I could hear him whistling through his teeth as he rubbed the horses down.

I wrote to him eventually, care of his sister in County Kilkenny, and sent him money for tobacco and an old photograph I had of him, standing dwarfed by an enormous Irish hunter under the sycamore tree. It had been taken some time after the war. I did not hear anything until I was back in Africa and then one day a letter came for me in a badly formed hand. It was from the matron of an old-age home in County Kilkenny where Doyle had been taken by his sister. The matron wrote that he had received my letter a few months before he died and had shown the photograph to all the old men in the ward. When he was very ill, his eyes used to wander to the photo propped up on his locker, of himself in his bowler hat and gaiters, standing beside the huge horse. He never seemed to have anybody to visit him, she wrote, he had apparently quarrelled with all his relations, but the photograph had pleased him very much.

I was sad when I read it and thought down the years to the first time I remember seeing Doyle. He had been very badly thrown by a new horse from Puck Fair and was being treated for shock in the kitchen.

'That horse is a devil!' he kept repeating. At that moment the animal was galloping loose in the sand ring with a posse of people trying to catch her. She had been bought at Puck Fair from gypsies and was absolutely pure wild. After she was caught it was discovered next morning that she had kicked the loose-box door to pieces. I went to see what was happening and could hear her plunging and striking at the door. You could hear the dull thud of her kicking; everyone was afraid to go into the stall.

'She have a temper on her like a blood stallion,' said Doyle sourly. He had had enough of her already and had an angry black bruise over one eye. I stood up on the windowsill and looked into the loose-box and there she was inside, throwing herself about. In the afternoon the vet came in his horse and trap to see if he could do anything with her. There was a frightful lot of scuffling going on in the loose-box; Doyle was trying to hold her head and old Bill came down from the farm to assist.

The vet didn't look too happy about the situation. I was clinging to the windowsill like a limpet to a rock, but there were so many cobwebs on the glass it was hard to see inside. I could hear shouting and see people milling about, Doyle's language was getting more and more lucid, and all the time the mare was lunging like a fiend in hell. After a quarter of an hour the vet came out, his face was purple, his tie round his ear, and he was flecked with foam. Doyle was still in there, shouting and swearing, and then he suddenly shot out into the yard like a cork out of a champagne bottle. Old Bill was left alone with her, doing his best. He never lost his temper or his nerve, he kept talking to the mare very softly whenever he could get near enough, putting his hand out to show her, letting her sniff it and running his hands gently over her withers. This would quieten her for a moment and then she would start rearing and kicking again.

'There is nothing physically wrong with her,' said the vet, panting. He was obviously fed up with the whole business. Bill and Doyle stood with my grandfather, talking. From inside the loosebox came noises of splintering wood and hammering hooves, and at one time it sounded as if she had fallen.

At four o'clock in the afternoon it was decided to send for the Whisperer. I had been ordered away at least a dozen times by the men, who were in no good humour. Each time I went round the corner just out of sight, and when attention was off me I came back to my position of standing on the windowsill outside the stall. At this new development I couldn't contain myself.

'Who is the Whisperer?' I asked Doyle.

'Go way out that!' said Doyle angrily. 'And don't be bothering me!'

'But who *is* he?'

'He's a Whisperer, that's what he is.'

'But what will he do?'

'He'll go into the bloody loose-box, that's what he'll do. If he can't quieten the mare she'll have to go to the kennels.'

'For what?'

'For to be fed to the hounds, bad cess to her.'

The Whisperer arrived later on in the afternoon. He looked to me like one of the tinkers; he had the same sort of yellowish skin a lot of them have. His eyes were small, black and foreign and his clothes ragged. He came in one of the long gypsy drays drawn by a mule. The bargaining went on in the yard as to how much he was to be paid. Eventually he asked where the mare was stabled and without another word walked towards the loose-box, opened the door and disappeared inside. Doyle ordered me away from the window.

'Do you want the man killed? If you frighten the horse and the fella's inside the loose-box she'll trample him. Come down out that now.'

I sat on an upturned bucket to wait. There was dead and perfect silence from inside the mare's stable – no hammering, no kicking, no splintering of wood.

'What's he doing?' I wanted to know. The suspense was killing me.

'He's whispering to her,' said old Bill. 'He have the gift.'

'What gift?'

'Yerra,' said Bill, slicing himself a plug off his tobacco. 'You know the fella with the peeled willow wand that was here last year? Well, he had some class of a gift in him for finding water like. He found a spring of water for the cows in the forty-acre field with only the wand bent. Now this fella here is another of them queer characters. You couldn't understand at all how it works for them, but the one inside there can talk to a horse like one human crayture can talk to another. He's whispering right into the mare's ear now, God help him, to see can he talk sense to her.'

I'd heard of Doctor Doolittle but this was news to me.

'Bill, why doesn't he always come for breaking in the young horses so?'

'Ah yerra, you wouldn't like to encourage the likes of that fella too much. Bleddy horse thieves the lot of them. They'll whisper a horse out of a field when the notion takes them and steal it.'

'Like dog thieves with chopped liver?'

'They don't give them anything,' said Bill, annoyed. 'Aren't I telling you? They *talks* to the horse.'

At six o'clock the Whisperer came out of the loose-box leading the mare by her halter. She was as meek and docile as a lamb, not showing the whites of her eyes at all, but nuzzling his shoulder.

'She'll be all right now so,' said the tinker.

He took a handful of half-crowns, touched his cap and drove away. I went to find Ned, full of the Whisperer and the mare from Cahirmee. Ned was at this time engaged in putting glass into cucumber frames which were partially rotten and was glad of a little diversion. It was cold outside the carpenter's shop and his nose was blue.

'Did you ever hear the like of that?' I asked him, unfolding the story of Doyle and Bill Donlan and the tinker.

Ned didn't seem at all filled with wonder, but then little surprised him. To me he appeared like the oracle of Delphi.

In fact, the way I prefaced sentences with 'Ned said' had been banned in the house.

'That fellow, the tinker, is a man by the name of Paddy Lynch,' he told me, puttying around the neat squares of new glass. 'He's known well. And I'll tell you no lie either, he knows the dam and sire of every horse in Ireland, I declare to God he does, although his father have him beat. Old Seamus Lynch is the greatest judge of horseflesh going. If he'd ever had the price of a suit for his back and a hat for his head, they'd have had him in the ring at the Dublin Show judging horses with the best of them. But sure,' said Ned gloomily, 'when you are poor who listens to you? It's not knowledge but money calls the tune in this weary world.'

'Go away out that!' This last was directed at a hound puppy who was taking an interest in Ned's lunch pail.

'Tell me about Paddy's father, Ned. Do you know him?'

'I knew *of* him more like,' said Ned. 'I met him a few times convivially in Tom O'Donnell's public house in Doneraile. You would not want to be cheek by jowl with those fellas. Real rogues and hangmen every one of them, I'm telling you.'

'Horse thieves, Bill told me,' I said, stroking the hound puppy.

'And that's no lie. Did Bill tell you the story of Seamus Lynch and the Riordan mare?' asked Ned. Even thinking of it made him laugh. 'Will I tell you so?' But every time he started to tell me he began laughing, till in the end he put down the glass squares, cut a plug of Clarke's and sat on the wall beside me.

'The way it all started,' he said, 'was one time when Seamus Lynch was going to Cahirmee Fair. They used to call it Puck Fair long ago and have a goat there, that's going back to the old days, mind. Anyway, to return to Seamus. He was nearly at Cahirmee one particular night and it got dark and he stopped his caravan outside Major Riordan, the JP's place, over by Ballybeg. He'd a string of horses with him to sell at Cahirmee for a fortune and they weren't worth two damns either,' said Ned, delighted. 'They had broken wind, stringhalt and God knows what, but Seamus had all the tricks of the trade at his finger ends, and by the time he got to Cahirmee no one would know there was anything wrong with them. They'd find out a few weeks later, but by then there'd be a long road between them and Seamus Lynch!

'Anyway, Himself was outside Major Riordan's place this night, caravan and all. He'd turned his horses into a field of red clover belonging to the Dean of Killaloe to furnish them like, to put a bit of weight on them for Cahirmee, and he went over Riordan's wall for firewood. "Heaven helps those who help themselves," he told himself, fastening his eye on a tree with a nice spare branch on it for kindling. He wasn't long cutting that, and the next thing he sees is a young pheasant. The way Seamus was telling it, above in Tomo's pub, you'd think the pheasant was down on its knees and praying to be put in the pot for a stew. Anyway, there's Seamus creeping up on the pheasant and behind him, if he'd known it, was Major Riordan who owned the tree and the bird. And he creeping up on Seamus.

'"You dirty blackguard!" was the first thing he heard. "Do you think it's not knowing you I am when you're up before the magistrate for some theft and roguery every three months? Well, it's three months you'll get inside this time for poaching, thieving and trespass. I'll nail you for the lot!" Frothing he was, the Major. Raging and roaring. He hated tinkers. "Gypsies," he used to say, "I'll pass the time of day with, but tinkers! Not a damn!" So he was into Seamus like a long dog.

'"Jasus God, I'm finished!" says Seamus to himself, his heart sinking the way a stone would sink in the River Liffey. "Three months inside with a string of horses to doctor for Cahirmee. Lord God! Inside in the jail and missing a horse fair, it would ruin anyone." He'd all the plamois, though, that fellow. Great ones for plamois, all the Lynches. All blarney and no reliability.

'Well, like all of them he had the plamois like a professional, so in a voice like honey he says, "Sure God love you, Major. A fine sporting gentleman like yourself." Never mind that Riordan's two eyes were bulging mad with rage.

'"Sure God love you, Major." A soft answer turneth away wrath and the Lynches needed to be good at that if nothing else. "'Twould break your heart to put me inside and Cahirmee beckoning me like a flag in the distance of a week. It's ruined completely I'll be and broke entirely. Let you do me a good turn, Major, like the gentleman you are. Close your eyes to me trespassing just the once an' if it's ever a good turn I can do for you or a tip with a horse you're after, Seamus Lynch is your man, for I never forgets me friends."

'When the Major heard this plamois,' said Ned, warming to his tale, 'the sauce of it nearly took his breath away, but he was a bit of a fly man himself, for all he was a JP. Though he didn't burst out laughing, his face moved a fraction in the direction of a smile.

'"God forgive you for a blackguard," he said, "but you have the blarney of the Devil. Damned if I won't take you at your word and give you a chance." But he swore that if Seamus didn't succeed in doing what he asked him, he'd put him inside for a twelve-month if he caught him stealing or poaching or anything else on his land again.

'You see,' said Ned, 'there was something the Major wanted connected with a horse and it was like this. There was a farmer living over Bottle Hill way at that time and he owning the finest stallion in all Ireland. It was a stallion, beautiful, beautiful, it would warm your heart to see it. This farmer had fallen out with Major Riordan because the Major used to hunt hounds sometimes across the farmer's land.

And so maybe the horses would break the fences a small bit or bruise a bit of young oats in passing now and then.

'So that same farmer, who was a sour whelp of a Mayo cattle dealer, put barbed wire across his ditches, you'll understand, the way when the hounds ran to covert, the legs of the horses would be cut to blazes if they followed up. The Major correspondingly told the farmer without sparing his breath what he thought of him. The hounds ran into Bottle Hill after a big fox shortly after, right across the farmer's land, and the Major by some coincidental chance had a pair of wire cutters in his pocket, which he used,' said Ned, puttying in a pane of glass to the least rotten of the cucumber frames, 'wherever his fancy took him to let the hunt through, and the result was that there was never love lost between Riordan and the farmer, this fella O'Meara, after that.

'The unfortunate string to it was,' continued Ned, 'that the Major had a lovely mare, a little queen she was and a mate for the finest stallion in Ireland, and he had a great and obsessive fancy to mate her to the Bottle Hill stallion, but after the trouble with the wire cutters and that, the farmer told the Major that he'd see him in hell first. You can see so,' said Ned, 'that the Major was in the most dreadful quandary.'

Ned loved long words. He never said 'hit' if he could say 'chastise', or 'problem' if he could say 'quandary'. He always said 'ye' instead of 'you', which gave his conversation a biblical flavour. I admired his vocabulary immensely and, crouching down on my hunkers by the cucumber frames, I was entranced.

'Go on so, Ned ...'

'Well, to return to Seamus. He listened to the Major's talk and he savoured the taste of the story with his tongue in his cheek.

'"Sure I know that farmer well," says he, "and a meaner, dirtier scoundrel never put foot in Ireland since the Black and Tans. I wouldn't be above saying that his father left his mark in the West and he a Black and Tan."

"'Don't talk like that now," says the Major, delighted to hear it, "but the curse of Cromwell be on him, the dirty blackguard – in passing, mind, in passing – but the crux of the matter is, do you know the stallion?"

"'I do," says Seamus.

'All of a sudden there was a pause in the conversation, what you might call a pregnant pause.

"'Wouldn't it be an extraordinary thing now," said Seamus with a sweet thoughtful note in his voice, "if O'Meara's stallion class of appeared like, in the inch below, alongside your mare!"

"'Twould indeed," says the Major, nodding, a light gleaming in his eyes like hope at the end of a black, black tunnel, "especially as she'll be ready to mate shortly."

"'Sure there's not a man living would say how it got there, but then there's not a man living would know what he saw, even if he saw it with his own two eyes. Do you get me?"

"'I wouldn't say that I was with you entirely," says the Major, "but I'm picking up the scent."

'It must have been about two weeks after that,' said Ned, putting his pipe in his pocket and rolling putty for the panes, 'that Seamus passed through Mallow on his way from Cahirmee Fair whistling "The Walls of Limerick" as he rode along. His pockets were full of money and he had the uplifted feeling of a man who has completed good business. He had sold his horses for more than he hoped to get, let alone what they were worth, which was damn all. His caravan was gone from him and he was riding a stallion which had a faint look of O'Meara's Bottle Hill stallion about it, bar the fact that its dam came out of a creamery cart in Ballyadare and it was a chronic whistler into the bargain. Three pounds fifteen Seamus had paid for it in Glanworth and he counted it money well spent.

'He went on through Mallow and turned towards Bottle Hill over the mountainy road. When he got alongside Bottle Hill he got off the stallion and turned it loose, spancelled, into a deserted hayfield belonging to the Dean of Clogher. Then, walking on his two legs, Seamus travelled on towards O'Meara's farm. Clean and tidy he looked, not at all the class of spalpeen you'd associate with a tinker's camp. Up walks he to the hayfield where the floats were drawing in the hay, with O'Meara standing there in the field recruiting labour. Taking off his cap and as meek as water, with a voice like cream, your man says, "It's looking for work I am, sir, and after hearing below in the village that you wouldn't be refusing a hand to draw in the hay."

"'I would not," says O'Meara. An unpleasant looking divil he was, nor no credit to his mother either. "I would not. Have you a reference?"

"'I haven't," says Seamus. "The likes of myself don't be carrying around an advertisement, but I'm a man by the name of Davy Ginevan and working for the Duke of Munster five years past and I'm telling you no lie either."

"'Duke of Munster be damned," says O'Meara, which would do the same duke no harm, seeing he never existed.

"'Let you get up so on that hayfloat and start carting haycocks to the barn. If you're worth your money, I'll hire you."

'All that afternoon Seamus was drawing in hay and the sweat pouring off him in rivers. "Be Jasus," he thought to himself as the Angelus pealed. "Be Jasus, it's better off I'd be in prison at this rate, with a twelve months' relaxation ahead of me." His two arms were dropping off him from the pitching and the piking and he was half inclined to get off the hayfloat and walk back to where he came from and the stallion be damned, when O'Meara walks up to him.

"'You're not too bad at all," he says grudgingly, his two cold eyes raking the length and breadth of Seamus. "Not too bad at all. I'll hire you till the hay's in." Then he took another look at Seamus.

"'You've a way with horses, I see. Not a tinker are you?"

"'Divil a one," says Seamus.

"'Well, when you've untackled the float, let you go down to the paddock below and rub down a fine stallion I have there. Look at him long," says O'Meara, "for you'll never see another horse to touch him, if you work for the Aga Khan himself."

'Seamus went down to the paddock, and when he had unhitched the float and, though he heard talk of the stallion and seen him a few times at Clonakilty Stud, the shine of him and the lift of his head were beyond description.

"'Be Jasus!" said Seamus and he fell silent looking at him. "Sure the farmer's heart will break if he has one, which I doubt, when the pair of us, yourself and I, hit the road for Major Riordan's."

'He looked at him again and then he leaned up and spoke in the stallion's ear; the whispering, alanna, that's what you saw today, and when one of the Lynches whispers to a horse in this country, the animal would jump a famine wall to follow him. That stallion was no exception, for all the arrogant lift to his head. His two ears came forward and he let out a whinny like the music of the wind on the hills of Ireland, nuzzling your man like they were brothers. Seamus rubbed him down, gave him a feed of oats and bran, and left him.

'Three days later Seamus was up on the float drawing the hay and three nights he was down in the paddock rubbing down the stallion, but on the fourth night he went down to Paddy's Hardware in Bottle Hill and bought a pot of a black oily class of stain and a quart of white paint from Paddy O'Reilly's shop.

'That evening, when dusk was falling, he went down to the paddock and this time he stayed below with the stallion. Before night fell, the stallion was a changed-looking animal.

I'll tell you no lie, his own mother wouldn't know him. A black body he had, like a Moorish eunuch, and a white blaze on his forehead, two white socks painted on him and three or four white hairs to his tail. You'd think he was a different animal altogether.

'Seamus threw an old saddle over him and left him awhile, and when he came back he was leading the animal he'd bought from a knacker's yard in Glanworth. In the pink of condition it was and why not! It was bursting with the Dean of Clogher's clover. In as long as it would take you to shut one eye, Seamus had the animals changed over, and as the chapel clock was pealing twelve he was riding the Bottle Hill stallion like the hammers of hell for Ballybeg! Sure the strategy of that, wouldn't it charm you?' marvelled Ned admiringly.

'There's no one to beat an Irish tinker for strategy, real rogues and hangmen the lot of them, but the government could do with a few in the Dail.' He fitted in the last of the glass panes and aimed a kick at the hound puppy.

'As daylight came over the Ballyhoura mountains, Seamus turned the stallion into the inch with Major Riordan's mare.'

'And did she throw a foal of his?' I asked, entranced.

'She did. That's a long time ago, my little girleen. There's a powerful lot of water gone under the Liffey Bridge since, but nevertheless if I tell you that the mating started a line which is registered in the stud book as Bottle Hill Theft out of Riordan's Stolen Victory, would you believe me?'

I nodded. Whatever Ned told me was gospel.

'When the Major's mare dropped a foal after O'Meara's stallion covered her, he wouldn't take fifty thousand pounds for it, and I'll tell you no lie, but to this day when Seamus Lynch is passing Ballybeg, he is inclined to throw his leg over the wall of the Major's demesne and help himself to kindling or a pheasant or two. For after all, what's sauce for the goose is sauce for the bloody gander.'

'Did the farmer get the stallion back?' I asked, liking to

have my *i*'s dotted and my *t*'s crossed. 'Did he lay a charge against Seamus for theft?'

'Ah, he got the stallion back all right,' said Ned. 'He found it in the clover field belonging to the Dean of Clogher, but no sign, which was very natural indeed, of the said Seamus Lynch. They had a job though,' Ned said, standing up to cut a plug of tobacco and tucking it into his cheek, 'they'd a job getting the paint off the stallion. Patchy his coat was, I heard, for a long time after.'

– 6 –

You always said 'hunting', never foxhunting, in the same way as you always said 'riding' and not horse riding. To say horse riding was completely beyond the pale. It was a bit like not saying red coats about the whips' jackets, but pink coats, in the etiquette of the hunting field, although anyone could see that they were red. Once I asked someone muddy and battered from the chase if they had fallen off and was reproached by my aunt.

'You must ask if they were thrown,' she said, 'it's much politer.'

The best part of my contact with the hounds was not in the hunting season – the hunting season was my Achilles' heel, but more of that later. In the summer, when the season was over, the whips Paddy Whelan and Patsy Riordan used to bicycle over eleven miles to the Master of the Hounds' house to give the hounds exercise. At that time Grandfather was Master, and so the hounds and the whips came to us twice a week. Early in the morning when the dew was soaking in the ground and the sun casting tall thin shadows, one could hear the whirr of the whips' bicycles and the sound of thirty couples of hounds' feet on the damp Irish earth. Occasionally the crack of a hunting whip and 'Ho up there, Dairymaid! Hi up there, Parson! Yoo up there, Havelock, yoo up!'

The hounds carried their sterns well up and the whole pack generated an indeterminate current of excitement. They jostled. They trotted. They were enormously happy. You could feel it pulsing through the pack as they grouped and divided and regrouped, Patsy riding his bicycle in front, Whelan at the back. The two men looked odd when they were not mounted on their great Irish hunters, but they rode their bicycles in their velvet hunting caps and white linen kennel coats.

When they arrived at the stable yard the horses, not yet out for the summer, were excited. Their heads poked out of the stable half-doors, and Castlecomer, who was Doyle's favourite hunter, would get news of their coming on the wind and snuffle the air while the hounds were still a few miles away. His eyes would go liquid and warm and his ears curve like little sickles when the pack came into the stable yard. In the next stall Joe, the old strawberry roan with stringhalt, would throw up his head and whinny. My grandmother was still hacking with him when she was eighty-four.

Hunting was his whole life, and his eyes, too, beamed with pleasure when the pack came down the stable hill past the mounting block. They were put into the huge barn while the huntsmen went into the kitchen for a big breakfast of rashers of bacon and eggs and strong sweet tea with soda bread made with a cross on top of it.

Later on Grandfather would come downstairs, shrugging into his kennel coat, his pockets full of stale bread. The hounds went nearly mad when they saw him. They literally sang for joy. By this time they would be milling around in the sand ring where the young horses were ringed for hours to break them in. I used to run out in my old green tweed coat with the big bone buttons, having begged bread from the kitchen. You gave them the bread in a special way, pressing it into their mouths with the flat of your hand. The hounds smelt oily and rank and their sterns waved as they milled about. They exuded happiness and so did the whole summer morning.

After this we would walk across country with Whelan and the hounds, Riordan going by road on his bicycle, balancing Whelan's bicycle with the other hand. He met us later on in the morning, at about half past nine, near the top of the ditch in the forty-acre field. The walk was glorious, past the fairy raths, across the clover fields where the big bumble bees were trundling about their business, pollen already ankle-deep on their legs. Underfoot in the wet dew were celandine, scarlet pimpernel and star of Bethlehem. All over was the intense vibrant green of Irish grass. There has never been grass so green that I have seen as the grass that grows in Ireland.

Hunting itself, when winter came, was not nearly such fun, mainly because I hunted on ponies with mouths like iron, fiendish vindictive temperaments and a tendency to kick, bolt, lie down in the middle of rivers like camels, hoping to roll while I was still in the saddle, or take off for the thickest wood in the vicinity. This often happened and I emerged from the wood looking as if I had been in the hands of the Spanish Inquisition, bleeding profusely, scratched by brambles, eyes watering from the lashing branches of passing trees, and clothes shredded.

'Please don't let the hounds find in Ballygliff,' I would pray to God when I was on Charlie, the worst cob in the stables. But they always did.

'If you don't let them run to Annakissha covert I'll say my prayers twice for a week,' I would bargain. It was a three-mile point and though I was sworn at for riding across new wheat and for bad riding manners generally – my hands raw and bleeding from trying to hold Charlie who, like the wind, went 'where he listeth' – I went the three miles, like it or leave it.

'Why don't you cut your own line across country?' shouted my grandmother, cantering by side-saddle and taking a ditch the size of herself and Joe combined. At that point I was thrown. Cantering on, she shouted back, 'Get on, get on! The next ditch is far worse!'

'You should let your animal know who is the master,' Doyle said, when I returned battered and bleeding from the chase.

'But how?'

'The animal always knows who's the boss,' said old Bill in his quiet way. Charlie did know, and he knew it wasn't me.

'That child is a funk on a horse,' said my grandmother. 'She has no feeling for riding at all. Takes after her mother's family I would imagine. Very bad blood there.'

The day my horse really bolted was, ironically, my hour of glory. I had been lent a highly strung, highly bred light chestnut. It was useless to say I did not want to be lent it, because our family was a riding family, so obviously I was a riding child.

'She is called Comet,' said old Judge Rudd, who lent her to me. 'I think she has Arab blood. She belonged to my daughter.' I did not care much if she had Greek or French blood. She had a wild look in her eye and a way of dancing lightly on her dainty feet that did not augur well for me.

Molly helped me to get ready for the meet. She wound a stock, yellow with age, round my throat. It went round several times and was secured with safety pins and eventually with a gold stock pin belonging at one time, a hundred years previously, to my great-great-grandmother. It was difficult to swallow when the stock was tied, and afterwards in Africa when I saw those African women with bracelets stretching their throats I knew exactly how they must feel.

'Next your bowler,' said Molly through a mouthful of safety pins. The bowler hats from Lock's Hatters of London were kept in cardboard boxes in the airing cupboard. There were over seventeen of them and they were all too large.

'We'll stuff one with greaseproof paper,' said Molly, doing so, 'and make it grip your head a bit.' She had plaited my hair back so tightly that my forehead ached. She put the bowler on like a lid, wrenching it over my forehead and thumping it over a double-door-knockered plait of hair at the back. Hunting boots gripped my calves and I clutched a silver-handled crop which said, engraved on the handle, that it had been presented to me by the children of Ballygliff National School. Why, I had no idea. The children of Ballygliff School were extremely poor, scarcely any of them had shoes in the winter, and they had probably been browbeaten into giving money for the presentation by the remorseless red-nosed teacher I had sometimes seen striding about the countryside.

The mare greeted me with no feeling of warmth. She had a propensity to sidle along dancing sideways. A heap of stones waiting to be broken by the road-mender at the side of the road made her start violently. The hounds, of course, found. The Comet was sweating, trembling with excitement outside the covert as the huntsmen cheered the hounds in. Grandfather sounded the 'Gone away … gone away … gone away' and we were swept up in a wild stampeding rush. It was quite clear to me that I was not going to be able to hold the chestnut.

She went where she wanted to go and, as Donlan would have said, 'like the hammers of hell'. I gripped on with my knees. The song of old John Gilpin came to mind: 'Away went Gilpin, neck or nought; Away went hat and wig!' It wasn't a wig that left me but the bowler hat that became a liability. The paper that stuffed it broke loose from its moorings and hung across my face, obscuring vision. The Comet took several banks in her stride. I jolted forwards onto her withers and jerked back again like a puppet as we cleared a bank which loomed out of nowhere in the mist. The hounds streamed in a straight run across a huge green meadow in the distance, with the fox, an auburn handkerchief of colour ahead of them. A fox covert loomed up, and before they could kill, our fox went to ground. The Comet pulled so suddenly that I slid up her ears. I was past thought. Briar had cut my face, not badly, but enough to make me look mauled. Streams of sweat poured down my face. The day had turned warm. The Comet was soaked through, there were marks of sweat all over her beautiful neck, giving her well-groomed coat a look of patchiness. I put up my hand to tear recklessly at the battered sheets of sandwich paper cascading from Lock's bowler hat, and at that second the hounds found again as a vixen broke covert.

'Gone away ... gone away ... gone away!' sang the hunting horn, the music of the wildly excited pack of hounds chorusing with it, and away we went. The Comet was beginning to tire a little. I whipped her over a ploughed field at full throttle, sorry to do this to her as I was, for she was game, but she was right out of control with a mouth like iron and she had jostled several other riders. I could feel her surprise at the brow of the slope, but just as I managed to rein her in there was a thunder of hooves behind us and she was away like a startled fawn again and now running at the front of the field alongside the whips.

Dear God, I thought, will this go on for ever? Like the Flying Dutchman or the Girl in the Red Shoes, I had visions, not of dancing or sailing, but hunting through all eternity on Comet, unless I was thrown. I looked behind me to see what had startled her and saw Old Bill careering along behind me, bareback, on a carthorse commandeered from the plough, which was going hell for leather. He appeared to be trying to communicate some message, but the wind blew it away. Finally as he came alongside, I heard him.

'Come back out of that!' he bellowed. 'They want you at home!'

I dare say they do, I thought, but easier said than done.

'Keep back!' I yelled, but he could not hear me and, vexed by what he considered wanton disobedience, Old Bill whipped up his mount in even hotter pursuit. The harder he galloped, the faster flew the highly strung Comet. The hounds eventually killed at Two Pot House, and he and I reined in simultaneously.

'You rode a grand hunt,' he said with grudging admiration. 'I didn't know you had it in you. Up with the hounds to the kill and every pelt of the way and out there in front too.'

He told everybody at the house about it and they were impressed in spite of themselves. I felt it better not to say I had no option in the matter.

'Look at the cut of you, though,' said Molly, disgusted, as I presented myself for boiled eggs in the kitchen, bleeding and sweaty, 'and where are the greaseproof papers gone from your hat?'

Molly O'Reilly, Poll Ribs, Moll-Doll or Bonne as she was known by various members of the family, was in her element when any of us were ill. She appeared upstairs as if on cue, placing a soothing hand on the patient's feverish brow murmuring 'Sure God help us!' sympathetically as she soothed away pain. She made poultices for swellings or constricted chests, lemon and honey mixtures for coughs, and cut up ice into small pieces to fold in muslin for an aching head. Fetching and refilling hot jars, her very presence heard mounting the stairs intimated comfort and safety.

Once when I was ten or eleven and ill, she sat by me through the night stroking back the hair from my forehead, rocking me, fetching hot milk or stoking the fire in my bedroom, and when I woke in the small hours I saw her, her thick black hair falling to the waist of her calico nightdress, saying a rosary in a chair in the firelight. Hers was real nursing, not with pills but with care, and she knew instinctively how to bring comfort. She had nursed my great-grandmother years before I was born and was to nurse Gran into her nineties and until the day she died.

Moll, being an O'Reilly, was related on her mother's side to the Wexford Kennedys and so through them to the American Kennedys. So whenever John Kennedy spoke in later years on TV we shrieked at her to 'Come and listen to your relation, Moll! Your relation's on telly!' and she would come lumbering slowly up from her room, her hair white by this time and rolled into a bun, an apron over her black flowered-print dress and a little half-smile on her face.

Resemblance to her relation was obvious, or perhaps imagined by us. She always simply said that she was glad a Kennedy had done so well. It was in March every year that she went on her annual holiday to the Wexford Kennedy family, and one of the worst nights of my life was when she was away and I, without her, was ill with an earache so agonising that the impact of it was like a living thing. I can remember it even now.

The pain was stabbing, like a knife piercing my eardrum. It was agony. Something to do battle with and overcome as best one could. Driven from bed right down to the warmth of the kitchen after midnight, I held my head sideways to the Aga, pushing back my hair behind my ear and pressing against the slightly greasy hot enamel of the range so that there was temporary relief. Upstairs I had tried pressing my ear to the cold marble of the Victorian washstand, then gone down to the Aga again, and so walking at three in the morning, to and fro, to and fro, I eventually invaded Grandmother's room. She was awake at once, switching on the light beside the bed, illuminating her French biscuit jar with its climbing life-size china mouse, her *Imitation of Christ*, her glass of whiskey and milk with a saucer over the top of it, and Herself in a pink hairnet with blue rosettes.

'I think,' I said flatly, tears welling in my eyes, 'something quite serious is the matter with me. My ear hurts.'

'Poor child. Be brave,' she said, looking slightly alarmed. 'Put some 4711 on your poor hot face and try to sleep.' She shook some drops of eau-de-Cologne onto linen.

'I *can't!*' I said desperately. 'I absolutely *can't!*'

I had been creeping up and down four floors now, from marble washstand to Aga, in the pitch dark. My feet were like ice and my face swollen, as if with mumps, on one side.

'At least *try* the eau-de-Cologne,' she said crossly. 'Never say die. Perhaps you can see Dr Foley tomorrow. Have a Marie.'

Feebly, to oblige, I chewed on a soggy stale biscuit, the pain now like a red-hot needle through my eardrum.

'Courage, you know, is the most important of all virtues. Think of Edith Cavell and Macnaghten in Kabul: people who have faced great pain and danger with enormous courage.'

'I think,' I said weakly, 'I'm going to be sick,' and fled to the green bathroom.

By six the next morning I was in agony until the abscess on my eardrum eventually burst outwards, and by the time Dr Foley arrived, soothing and kind and smelling of antiseptic, I was better, but was removed on his orders to the Bon Secours Nursing Home in Cork for endless injections.

Dr Foley was appalled by my grandmother's attitude to illness.

'Only the lower classes complain. Too dreadful. On and on about their insides,' she had told him a year before, while he nodded and looked bemused. Called then, as I lay semi-delirious at the top of the house with an about-to-burst appendix, he appeared to listen to her politely while feeling around my stomach with practised fingers, but I had an idea he heard only half of what she said.

'She'll have to have an operation in Cork. Can I have the phone? I'll arrange it. She'll have to go straight to the theatre on arrival.' He had been courteous but firm then, overruling objections. A marvellous man, caring and attentive in spite of the fierce opposition at home to the medical profession.

'Pillboxes' was what Grandfather called doctors. 'Keep away from 'em,' he often said. 'Get into their hands and you'll have every disease under the sun if you listen to them. Got to … stands to reason. They've got a living to earn, same as other people.'

'They have to take an oath or something,' I said vaguely. 'I've read about it.'

'Rubbish! Lot of pillboxes. Nothing but trouble if you get mixed up with them. Kill you off as soon as look at you. They're all in it for the money.'

This rather unusual attitude scarcely endeared him to the medical profession, particularly as the pills they prescribed were hurled more often than not into the nearest wastepaper basket. Although there was a medicine chest in the house, it was full of feeding cups, ipecacuanha wine, Vapex and Thermogene wool.

When I'd returned from Cork, having had my appendix removed in the nick of time, Grandfather stumped into the Blue Room where I lay convalescing in bed, gazed at me as one miraculously returned from some great danger – not of death, which had missed me by a whisker, but from the hands of the pillbox fraternity – and anxious that they should not brainwash me into believing them infallible, glared at me with his pale blue eyes and twiddled his moustache, saying, 'I suppose they told you to stay in bed? Never happy unless they are throwing pills about or keeping you laid up. Damned pillboxes. All in it for the money.'

And having thus reassured the patient, he stumped off to breakfast to eat his kedgeree made with delicious Blackwater salmon, or grilled kidneys and buttered toast.

Illness was scarcely a time for tender loving care should Molly not be about, and a visit to the dentist was a nightmare. Not approving of injections, the Cork dentist gave me what was called a magic stone to hold, tightly gripped in one's hand, which he said took away the pain. Too polite to say it didn't seem to, I would grip it for dear life, squirming round in the dentist's chair in agony.

'Courage!' was Granny's great cry in the hunting field or the sickbed. Her great heroes were Edith Cavell and William Macnaghten, an ancestor who, because of his courage – or foolhardiness, depending on how you saw it – ended up just before the massacre of Khyber Pass decapitated and on a meat hook in the Kabul market.

Courage, it seemed to me, had definite limitations. Gran, however, had a portrait of him on the plains outside Kabul in 1826 before his unfortunate demise. This curious little painting, which hung near her bed, showed Macnaghten, the British envoy, bespectacled and in a top hat, seated on a magnificent white horse to receive the surrender of Dost Mahomed, an Afghan chief loved by the Afghans and deposed by England. Dost Mohamed's surrender was just prior to Macnaghten's wet-nursing, instead, a puppet prince called Shah Soojah-ool-Moolk, installed and favoured by the British government.

Brave Macnaghten undoubtedly was, and tricked viciously by Akbar Khan, but the culmination of his courage was to lose his head, his hand – which was severed and thrown into his wife's bungalow – and his body which, for a time, as I said earlier, was exhibited in Kabul on a meat hook. So the tale of Macnaghten's courage only served to confirm my suspicions that being too brave could kill you off extremely unpleasantly. Bravery was not my greatest attribute. The boy who stood on the 'burning deck' and 'The Charge of the Light Brigade' left my blood totally unstirred and to me their attitude spelt lunacy, although I never dared say so; and in the hunting field I despicably looked for gates while Gran, even in her late seventies, soared over enormous fences and ditches, riding side-saddle.

– 8 –

Driving with either grandparent was really in its own way as much of a hazard as hunting. Risks were taken in both instances, and both operations were conducted with scant regard for personal safety. I was with my grandmother on her last drive, so to speak, and the memory will stay with me for ever.

We were driving to a house called Clifford, where I was to share an imported English governess with a child called Geraldine. I, like Geraldine, had begun to speak broad Cork, and costs were to be halved by sharing the benefits of English diction. So we set off in Gran's car, a black Opel with red seats, which always smelt appallingly of rotten fish. Whether a piece of fish from some long-ago shopping trip to Cork had escaped from its packaging and lodged behind the seat I don't know, but the smell was enough to make one retch, and in hot weather and if the windows were up it was overpowering. I don't think Gran, who knew little about cars, realised that the seat could have been taken out and the fish mystery solved, because although she often remarked on the hideous smell, nothing was ever done.

Gran had taken her driver's licence for the first time in her early seventies. I don't think 'taken' is quite the right word, as no test was necessary in Ireland then. You paid ten shillings at the local police station and that was that. No tiresome training was needed; you were launched at the wheel and onto the roads with the receipt. Having got her licence, Gran then developed her own curious style of driving, a bit like cutting her own line across country. It culminated that day in our rounding a corner and having a head-on crash with a donkey-cart full of the Magner family, of which there appeared to be many, plus a milk churn and various other appendages. Magners flew through the air, the donkey bolted and Gran, dismounting from her car, enquired crossly whether they had not heard her hooter. There appeared to be no reply from the unfortunate Magners, who were lying about in heaps rather bumped and bruised.

The impact had wrought a good deal of damage – milk was lying in rivers all over the road, the shafts of the donkey cart were smashed, and several small Magners, unnerved by Gran's Boadicea approach, were giving tongue from all quarters. It appeared that none of them was seriously hurt, but a court case ensued which the Magners won and Gran never drove again, declaring the roads were far too dangerous.

Grandfather, however, continue to operate in his own style on the roads, which entailed coming in from a small side boreen and increasing speed on approach till he launched himself, hooting wildly, onto the main arterial highway. As he geared himself up for this, he had the air of a rider approaching a water jump. I noticed he sat well back, as if in the saddle, while, with hooter blaring, he hurtled like a bullet onto the major highway. This seemed, by the very nature of his approach, to cause a sensation. People, ashen-faced, swerved or blew their horns, but he, with the air of a rider having taken his fences rather well, slowed down, as it were to give his steed a breather. People often overtook, shaking their fists and shouting, but he genuinely never noticed this and trundled along in his enormous American car, gathering himself together on the outskirts of the city for another burst of speed. Volkswagens he detested, muttering about 'nasty little Hun cars!' as he passed them and giving them scant courtesy.

The Germans were not his favourite nation and the flowers I put on an unknown German's grave in the churchyard in Ballygliff were a continual source of annoyance to him. Try as he might to prevent me, I was not of my grandparents' stock for nothing and refused to be intimidated. Christmas and Easter I sat in the back of the car on the way to church, clutching a bunch of daffodils or snowdrops or Christmas roses for the grave of the young German who had, for a reason never clear, parachuted onto a field at the farm only to be apprehended by a puffing Garda Siochána on a bicycle.

Later the German had had to be buried in the Church of Ireland graveyard. The Catholics would have no truck with suicide. He had been very young when, on interrogation, he had swallowed a cyanide pill in the barracks at Ballygliff. There had been a family snapshot in his breast pocket and nothing else, so there was not even a marker with initials on the green mound which was his grave. Too young to know patriotism and reared in a neutral country as I was, his early death struck me as tragic and to be buried among strangers terrible. So I persisted with the flowers, while Grandfather roared at me disapprovingly all the way through the morning service.

'Damned Hun. Taking flowers to a damned Hun's grave.'

'He belongs to somebody and they aren't here to do it. He's lonesome,' I said, sticking to my guns.

It wasn't only that he was a German that put Grandfather off him. Anyone stupid enough to commit suicide during an interrogation by Guard Mangan was, in his language, a damn fool.

'How could Mangan interrogate him anyway?' said Granny mildly. 'He doesn't speak any German and his brogue … Well, *I* can't understand a word he says.'

'Probably clinched it,' Grandfather said, glowering at me

and the daffodils. 'Probably took one look at Mangan and cyanide was preferable! He must have been a high-up Hun. Knew too much. Didn't know where he'd landed and was afraid it might be tortured out of him.'

But torture seemed improbable, unless it was the torture of Mangan mangling the English language or having a waft of his Guinness-laden breath. Just seeing Mangan bicycling around the village with his guard's hat with the silver sunburst perched on the back of his head made one feel he could hardly pose a threat to anyone, even a German spy. He got a lot of free drinks in Sheehan's pub over it, and a reporter from the *Cork Examiner* came down over the mountainy road to interview him.

But I was sad for the German boy who had no identity on him, only a photograph of his parents, and who had died pointlessly in a neutral country. Dying so young and in Ballygliff barracks seemed a terrible waste. I felt an affinity with him because he was young like me and the war seemed to be not our war at all, but created by faceless strangers.

Doyle enjoyed the war. He was made a commandant in the Local Security Force and got a thick khaki great coat with brass buttons on it. It came right down to his feet and kept him warm when there was a frost.

– 9 –

On summer evenings, when Grandfather went off after tea to the river to fish for salmon, Granny, who was twelve years older than he was, retired earlier for the night than usual, especially when she reached her mid-eighties. She liked to have what she called a 'light supper' on a tray in the drawing room, usually consisting of poached salmon or trout, prefaced perhaps by a bowl of watercress soup and followed by yellow Chinese raspberries and thick cream or a jam omelette. She had either a small half-bottle of champagne or a glass of wine and often, still wearing one of her large hats, she sat in the bow window in the evening sun and, as she got older and more mellow, reminisced about her early life.

She had grown up in the north of Ireland at Dundarave near Bushmills, an enormous house where I had often stayed. It had a beautiful staircase and gallery and a domed roof, and a vast billiard room where Gran and her brothers had prevailed, through table-tapping, to induce an enormously heavy billiard table to rise, unaided, six feet in the air. Another surprising thing about Gran was her interest in planchette, table-tapping and ghosts. All the Victorians had a penchant for table-tapping and mediums; and she, to crown it, had twice seen ghosts at Galgorm Castle, her sister's home near Ballymena.

Sometimes she took me with her on her pilgrimages to the north and we stayed at Dundarave or Galgorm, or at the great Gothic red mass owned by the Macnaghtens called Runkerry at Portrush, on the cliff near the Giant's Causeway, which is now an old-age home.

Gran had had a very unsatisfactory childhood. Her mother, Lady Macnaghten, had run away with an attractive land agent, leaving her father, stern Sir Francis, to bring the children up in a house where every picture of their rebellious and beautiful mother was then turned to the wall and her name never mentioned again in his presence. Her only brothers died abroad, one in India and the other in the Sudan; there were horrific tales of her much-loved dog being shot on Sir Francis's orders – Sir Francis didn't like dogs – and a frightful Spanish governess called Bonarandy, who whipped her; and worse still, a woman who chaperoned the Macnaghten girls in the hunting field and constantly locked her own children in a wardrobe for misdemeanours until, carelessly forgetting to let out a seven-year-old, it died of suffocation. These doleful tales, interspersed with stories from *Struwwelpeter* and *Les Malheurs de Sophie*, not to mention *Carrots: Just a Little Boy*, made me grateful to have been born sixty years later.

One particularly ghastly storybook was called *A Peep Behind the Scenes*, about a circus performer and her child. This tale was particularly well loved by Gran, and as far as I can remember was about a wretched woman dying in a caravan. She became more and more riddled with tuberculosis as the book wore on, coughing blood and falling back ashen on her pillow between acts on the trapeze. Eventually she breathed her last, leaving her weeping child shivering in the caravan with, I think, a drunken father.

As bedtime reading this was bad news and I went off to bed filled with gloom. As I grew older, sometimes Gran had retired to her room before I went up to bed and was helped to undress by Molly by the fire, who then brushed and plaited her long hair. As Molly brushed, so Gran scolded her on a theme which recurred weekly, to which Molly paid no attention whatever, naughtily winking at me from behind Gran if I was perched on the sofa at the foot of the bed listening to the talk and feeding biscuits to the corgi.

'We must cut down,' Gran would say. 'Enough for an army at lunch. Fourteen potatoes between three of us! You must not use Mrs Beeton, Molly. Twenty-eight pounds of butter a week from the dairy! Quite ridiculous.'

Nobody took these homilies very seriously, and the Servants' Hall continued to be crowded with hangers-on tucking into delicious joints because there was no proper supervision, Gran despising people who were keen housekeepers and relegating them to the ranks of the 'kitchen-minded'. She herself did a little foray into housekeeping every morning when she went downstairs to see Molly in the kitchen, her keys jangling, to order meals and give out supplies from the storeroom. As Molly had a duplicate key, which she had procured from somewhere at least twenty years before, it was a pointless exercise, but Gran was fortunately vague about the contents of the storeroom, and if more jam and flour disappeared than she gave out, she didn't notice. The keys gave her the feeling of having her hands on the reins of the house and some sort of control over Molly, and she continued with her lecture on economy from time to time as Molly brushed her hair. Meanwhile, any joint or food that came up in the small hand-cranked lift for upstairs meals and then returned to the kitchen was never seen again.

Among other curiosities in Gran's room, beside her picture of Macnaghten, was a twelve-bore shotgun near her bed, the barrel polished and gleaming. A clip of cartridges rested in her glove cupboard, and once, when I was coming back in the aqua-green dusk on a summer's evening from the farm, the loud crack of a gun going off in the quiet fields startled me out of my wits. Shortly afterwards a bullet whistled past me, making a zinging noise.

'Oi!' I said nervously, as Granny, slightly stooped, emerged from behind a rhododendron bush in a brown felt hat, bare feet and a thick square-necked nightgown embroidered by the nuns in Limerick. In her hands she held the gun.

'Why the hat?' I asked, my voice wobbling. After all, I had narrowly missed being shot.

Ignoring the question, she unloaded, explaining, 'A hare. I saw him from my bedroom window and came down, but you startled him.' She was clearly miffed. Jugged hare in port wine was a favourite dish and hare terrine ranked even more highly.

'Missed him twice,' she said crossly. 'You came along at the worst *possible* moment.' She had crept down in her bare feet straight from bed, hoping to pot him. When I told Molly, she gasped.

'There's no one like the Mistress, never will be. She's a breathing marvel, so she is. Eighty-five years old this December. You'll never be as good as her, or as brave.'

Sadly, I had to agree. Had *she* been in Afghanistan with Macnaghten, Dost Mohamed's followers would not have stood a chance. I could picture her riding side-saddle, straight as a rod in her blue habit, across the plains of Kabul shouting, 'Reload and *fire!*'

– 10 –

The Castle Lodge at the end of Castle Avenue had an ornamental tower with castellations and a flagpole. It looked like a little chess castle stuck on the side of the big wooden gates. The windows were mullioned, and inside there was a twisty spiral stone staircase which went out onto mini-battlements above. Once perhaps the Earl or the Groves had flown a flag to show they were in residence, but there never was anything to see except the bare flagpole when I was small. Outside the gates was the VR letterbox to which I had pelted so often, frozen with fear of the Foxy Woman, to catch the post on a winter's night, and inside the Lodge, where John Joe's jealous wife with the peacock voice had lived, was Mary now. She was a great friend of mine, and her husband worked on the land at the home farm.

The Lodge was as cold as charity, with stone floors. Mary, constantly tinged blue with damp, battled against a good many odds, the main ones being no running water, no loo and no electricity. The Lodge had remained picturesque without and unchanged within, exactly as it was in the eighteenth century, and murderously uncomfortable. Early on most days Mary, buckets in hand, set off to fill them at Saint Bridget's well. Although a certain amount of rain water was available from barrels fed by down gutters, it was not enough and the well was a good half-mile away. I remarked on the inconvenience of this to Grandfather, who did not receive the information at all well and said he was against my bringing 'Bolshevik ideas home', and that if I 'dabbled in Bolshevik ideas, the country would lie in ruins about us'. Obviously nothing was done and eventually Mary, who knew I would be sympathetic, told me that she and Mick had managed to get a house about half a mile from the Lodge gate and that it had nice linoleum floors and running water.

The idea of telling this to Grandfather was discussed and discarded, because the situation was awkward. He had seen the small brick houses going up nearby and, although none were on our land, he had roared that they were an eyesore, ruining the rural look of the countryside. He had even discussed this with Mary herself while exchanging a few words with her one morning at the gate.

'Damned awful houses, Mary!' and she, pop-eyed with guilt, had agreed sycophantically.

'Oh terrible, sir!' earning a smile of approval and a wave as he drove off. He liked people to agree with him.

The position was that Mary and her husband had the dubious privilege of living in the Lodge for nothing. Free milk from the dairy and free firewood were also part of the deal, with a little extra money thrown in for Mary when she did the plucking – the plucking was done in an outhouse full of feathers and down, where she sat and plucked and sneezed for a couple of hours a week. In return for this honour, when Grandfather (or anyone, come to that) hooted outside the Castle Lodge, someone – usually Mary – had to rush out and open the gates, even at midnight. Although this was fairly standard practice in the lodges of the larger houses in the district, it was not particularly restful for the slumbering incumbents, often wrenched from warm beds at night. All our three gate lodges had houses; the Front Lodge, which was reasonably comfortable and decorated with hanging pots and gay flowers; the Middle Lodge, where the laundress lived; and the Castle Lodge.

The Castle Lodge was perhaps used less than most, so Mary was in some ways fairly safe. But the disadvantage was that the gates were difficult to open from the road and you had to stand on tiptoe and hook an arm over the bars as you struggled to push the bolt back, so if Mary was not to be found, a certain amount of hooting and an enormous amount of roaring were bound to ensue, followed possibly by an enquiry as to her whereabouts.

'Just *tell* him!' I said, without much confidence when Mary and I had batted the subject to and fro over a cup of tea without finding a solution. 'Just tell him that you have found another house at fifteen shillings a week.'

'He'd ate me,' said Mary gloomily. 'He'd ate the face off me.' She was fond of him but knew the implications. 'And when he starts roaring, I'd be in a dread. Maybe he'd fire Mick.'

Sitting in the silence, weighing up the pros and cons, we eventually hit upon a piece of strategy which pleased us both. Mary would have two residences, the Castle Lodge and her new house. With them so close together, she would be in commuting distance, and if she ran at speed she could do the stretch of road between them in five minutes.

Grandfather never got up before nine in the morning now that he was getting older, except during the hunting season. He was no longer Master at this time but followed the hounds in his small blue van, hotly pursued by everyone else in cars, on foot or bicycle, who knew that he knew every earth for miles and where a fox was likely to make for at any given time. If *he* reversed, *they* reversed, and when he went up a side lane, twenty cars changed course to follow him. This was gratifying to a degree until once or twice, sneaking up a side lane to obey a call of nature, he found himself ringed by admiring followers imploring him to tell them tidings as to where the fox might run next. Puce with rage, he had roared at them until they finally got the message that he wanted to

'*Pee, Goddam it!*' and twenty cars and bicycles had backed off, crestfallen.

'If he doesn't get up till nine,' I had said to Mary while we discussed Plan One, 'you can cook breakfast for Mick and then rush back to the Lodge and be there for the gate all day.' At night, we decided, two paraffin lamps would be left burning in the Lodge as red herrings, one in each window. Two weeks later, when Grandfather was away in Dublin, Mary moved into her modern abode.

For a long time everything went swimmingly until one night Grandfather returned after dark with me from Cork. We had been delayed by ice on the roads and were late home. He put his hand on the hooter for the gates to be opened and as no one appeared he left it there, making an almighty noise like a foghorn. An owl rose and a couple of agitated rabbits rushed across the road.

'I'll get out and open it,' I said nervously. 'Maybe they're asleep.'

This inane statement received no reply, as the noise from the hooter by now would waken the dead. To use Ned's expression, Grandfather was now 'commencing to roar' and the hooter was taking a terrible hammering.

'I'll do it. I'll get it,' I said, and leapt out, fumbling with the bolt and hurling the gates open. He was in such a rage by this time that he nearly ran me over, drove off without me in fury and had to reverse back.

The next day, passing Mary on her way from the well, he wheeled down his window and bellowed, 'Sleep well last night?'

Mary, unnerved, dropped her buckets of water as he drove off. For weeks after that she slept at the Lodge, but for some reason it was many years before he went that way again after dark.

In many ways he was a very kind man, not arrogant, nor did he in fact see himself as being entitled to make demands.

It was simply that for a hundred years, before he had inherited the place at eighteen, customs like the Lodge gatekeepers had been established and he made no concessions to change whatever. That was how things were always done, so that was that, and to him the fact that life was made particularly convenient for us was quite natural. For instance, several times when interested garden visitors were lunching late on their last day and it was possible that another scoop of Stilton taken or a water biscuit eaten might mean they missed their connection, I was sent to telephone the station to ask Mr Cronin, the stationmaster, to hold the train. Haste was made and the train never held for more than four or five minutes before the car or pony trap rounded the curve, and as the visitors were bundled hastily into their carriages the green flag went down. But it seemed no great privilege. Indeed, so normal did this appear to Grandfather that once, seeing me off to England on the *Innisfallen*, he ignored calls for people who were not sailing to 'Leave the ship' and was very nearly carried out on the Irish Sea to Fishguard in his green plus-fours, with his Jack Russell under his arm.

The problem with these attitudes was that, as a family, when we went out into the world we were very often inclined to take the law into our own hands, with disastrous consequences. What we saw wrong we occasionally felt obliged to put right, not always to the gratification of other people. My only excuse is that our interference was usually connected with any form of cruelty to animals, which none of us could tolerate.

Once Molly showed me an owl which she had found in the daylight in a state of stupefaction, in the woods. It was transfixed by sleep and probably concussed. She had it in mind to have it stuffed by a taxidermist in Cork so that it could stand in a glass dome in her cottage. To my horror she put the still-living owl into a shoebox punctured with holes and posted it to Cork, with instructions to the taxidermist to kill and stuff it.

I ran, appalled, to Grandfather, telling him the horrific tale, and he and I immediately drove to Mallow in the dogcart, thumping on the door to rouse the sleeping postmaster and intercept the mail. Grandfather pointing out to the reluctant official, who grumbled that it was an offence for us to rummage in the mail bags, that it was an even greater offence to accept a parcel containing live animals. We then returned home victorious, after dark, to release the owl in the hopyard. He seemed none the worse for his five-mile excursion and revived in the gloom.

Molly, however, was not informed of this incident and, waiting daily for the return of the owl stuffed and glass-eyed from the taxidermist, was displeased not to receive so much as a word of acknowledgement from him. Various correspondence was entered into and many letters like this were received – 'Dear Miss O'Reilly, Ref your letter with regard to an owl. No such bird has been received in our offices, etc. etc.' – until eventually she gave the whole thing up as a bad job.

11

The wilder parts of the estate had not been visited, sometimes for years. Grandfather was getting old and stiff. He refused to cut down trees, so some fell and blocked entrances to places where only the foxes came, along with the rabbits and occasionally a badger who liked dark, leafier, damp-earthed places.

Down in a thick pine wood only someone child-sized could stand up and walk through, because the trunks of the trees were so close together and the low thick pine branches shut off the light. It was a womb-like, silent wood. Silent as if it had a secret in it or was caught in a spell. Not sinister, but full of promise. At the end of it was a brilliant clearing, dazzling after the dark wood. Here were flags growing, the fat wild irises, yellow and blue. Butterflies drifted over clumps of purple mallow. There were a few waterlilies here too, with exquisite dragonflies in deep greens and blues hovering and darting like arrows of colour. It was utterly quiet here except for blackbirds and thrush who, like opera singers, pushed out their chests and sang.

It was a territory of children and little wild animals, who scarcely bothered (provided I stood perfectly still) to do more than watch me cautiously and then go about their business.

This was a friendly wood, not like the haunted wood beyond the Front Lodge. There I never went alone, but took the dogs. It was as much as I could do to make my feet move into the stillness of it and there was never a single bird there that I ever saw, only an ugly watchful silence.

That wood was full of menace. The dogs never ran in front, coursing ahead of me, but hung nervously around my heels – slunk, if you like. Not a rabbit stirred. You climbed over the stile and penetrated into that ominous silence. Why I ever went there, God knows, because the sound of my own thumping heartbeat drummed in my ears like a water ram. The Awbeg flowed at the bottom of the wood, but here the river was dark, sluggish and appearing to move without a sound. The place seemed always dark, with never any sun. There was a huge old stone there, so perhaps long ago it had been a place of druidic rituals. Three men had been hanged there in 1820, according to old records; the reason for their miserable end was lost in the mists of time, though what residue of fear there was, left there so long ago, remained.

In the days before governesses, when I was as free and wild as a bird and there was no other child about the estate for a companion, there was another place, this one magic and silent, that Ned had described to me and that I had found: the cave of the hermit Darby.

Darby fascinated me. He had moved about these woods and groves a century ago. Sitting on dry leaves in his cave, with my knees under my chin, I thought about him often. He probably knew more than I about this ancient demesne. In my mind's eye, he was a lonely figure slipping quietly through the woods and rocks. I imagined him poaching a rabbit or pheasant or tickling for trout for his supper and returning at night to the cave which Ned called Darby's Bed.

Darby had probably known where one old salmon always lay, a dark shadow near underwater tree roots, in just one place on the top inch under the rock. Sleeping where he did, he would have heard the vixens bark sharply in Ballywalter

Rock on frost-crisp nights and perhaps felt the vibrations, mystic and still stirring, in what Ned called the Druid's Stones.

Sitting in his cave retreat he would have seen the panorama of life at Annes Grove. It was just across the two arms of the River Awbeg, so the cave known as Darby's Bed would have been high enough up on the rock to see straight into the grounds and all the comings and goings of the house, with the cleft of the valley between. The beauty of that valley had so entranced Edmund Spenser, the poet, that he called the Awbeg River the 'gentle Mulla' and wrote his stanzas of the *Faerie Queene* sitting on its banks.

'But who *was* Darby?' I asked Ned.

'He was a hermit. He lived in the cave. It was called Darby's Bed, and that,' said Ned, 'was the sum of it.'

Why had he lived there, shut off from everyone? No one knew. I read about him in an old book, but it said little or nothing. Was he a saint or a drunkard, an unfrocked priest or a soldier on the run from the British Army? I doubted he was a drunk. The way to the cave travelled up so steep an incline that you would need to be stone-cold sober to negotiate it. Even I, clinging like a bat to the ivy lianas, struggled up the rock, with twigs catching at my hair, to the cave mouth.

There always seemed to be a robin watching me and hopping from twig to twig, or a little crowned wren bird. Poor little wren. Doomed to be killed and hung on a broken branch by the Wren Boys on St Stephen's Day. It was an ancient rite, its meaning lost in the mists of time. 'The Wren, the Wren, the King of Birds,' they sang, 'On St Stephen's Day it was caught in the furze.' They blackened their faces and went from house to house begging money.

No one goes to Darby's Bed now. It is impossible to find, so overgrown is it, with the entrance obscured with a tangle of weed and ivy, keeping its own secrets. I know, because fifty-five years later my daughter and granddaughter tried to find it, tore clothes, pierced their trousers and jeans in the thickets, and gave up.

But the birds were still there, or their descendants. A robin and a wren had followed their struggling progress.

There was a hazel bush around there too, on the rock, which carried its own story. Hazel bushes came into many Irish folk and fairy tales. I ate the nuts, green and bitter, before the squirrels got them, and washed the bitterness from my mouth at the Ballywalter spring.

The spring was over to the right of Ballywalter Rock. Clear water bubbled up and filtered through a small patch of snow-white sand. It tasted as cold and sharp as a crystal in your mouth.

Some spring mornings I woke early, crept down the stairs and went out into the three yards, washing my face in the heavy dew before going into Grandfather's smoking room to remove a few Laylor cigarettes out of a lapis lazuli box for John Joe Lynch. I stole a few copies of *The Spectator* for him and a box of matches for the cigarettes. John Joe would rather have had Woodbines than Turkish cigarettes but I had no money to buy Woodbines and he only had a few shillings a week so he would have to put up with what he got.

John Joe was up at the Home Farm in the cold, paid to chase the crows off the young wheat and looking not unlike a living scarecrow himself. He was about sixty, but to me he was older than Noah and full of wisdom. I squatted down beside him, looking at his hands, which were purple, swollen and blue, with lumpy fingers. His wrinkled clothes were in rags, and binder twine around his trouser legs kept them away from the mud.

'I brought you *The Spectator*.'

'May God love you.'

'And matches, but only the Turkish cigarettes, the ones with the winged heads on them.'

'May God be good to you.'

We squatted side by side over a small fire he had made, while I plucked at wisps of sheep's wool picked off the barbed-wire fence behind us, and rubbed the lanolin on my fingers.

'I was a scholar when I was young,' he said, puffing at a cigarette. The rich odour of Grandfather's tobacco scented the air, while crows and jackdaws wheeled about us in a cold grey sky. The Turkish cigarettes were sent over to Annes Grove from a shop in Pall Mall, packed in maroon oblong boxes. Grandfather would have been less than charmed had he known who else was enjoying them besides himself, but I never took more than three or four at a time in case they might be missed.

Close to where we sat was a circular depression like an old lime quarry, a fairy rath. There were four or five on the estate. I asked John Joe why there was no ploughing done near them – as I had asked Grandfather before – and why they weren't filled in.

'The *shee*,' he said. 'They were the homes of the *shee*, the fairy people.'

'Were the little people really here?'

'They were indeed, small, small people like the Picts. The Firbolgs were here one time too,' he said, coughing on the pungent tobacco.

John Joe was a storyteller. He would have been at home in the days of the bards and those tellers of tales who wandered through the courts of Tara and from high place to cottage. They were the ones who held the people spellbound in the long winter nights, passing on stories that were older than time.

I asked him again about the raths and about the history of the little people – if they had ever really existed.

'They were here all right and real,' he said. 'Small, small little people like the Picts and the Firbolgs, free as air, until the men from the sky came, the *Tuatha de Danaan* – the children of Danaan the Woman. Danaan,' he said, as if he knew her personally, 'and all her children were skilled in the arts of magic of all sorts – music, poetry, and all of them with the second sight. The *Tuatha* came from the sky and the first place they put their feet was on a green mountain in Munster.'

John Joe told stories full of power, that held you in the palm of his hand. It was from him I heard about the Nine Hazel Trees of Wisdom. Those who ate the nuts were gifted with the Sight, he said, and could tell the future. They could make poetry so exquisite that none could refuse the writer any of three wishes.

I asked John Joe how he knew about all these people. There were plenty more of them. The Firmoire of the Islands and the Sons of Mil. People whose gifts came from knowing a story with a spell in it, or eating magic salmon, and the story of poor Deidre of the Sorrows who was turned into a swan. I could see that the countryside seen through John Joe's eyes was full of magic, which lingered in the haunted woods and the raths, in a landscape only nudged by the material world.

'I didn't know any of this before,' I said, chewing on a stalk of sorrel and watching wild ducks flying in a V towards the north.

'But you see, little girleen, you're not really Irish. You learn at your lessons all about England.' True that was – a mishmash about Ethelred the Unready, King Alfred burning the cakes, William Rufus and Queen Anne. 'Queen Anne's dead,' I would be told when I made some new discovery, new to me at any rate, but stale news to my grandmother.

But I *was* really Irish – as Irish as any Firbolg. My great-great-great-grandfather Ned Kelly had hunted his hounds near Dublin with a bottle of whiskey in his hand, and a knowledge of Irish ballads second to none. He in his turn would have been very surprised to know that his grandson, little Willy Howard Russell, would end up with an English title and a close friendship with royalty – Edward VII and his beautiful Danish wife. But Ned Kelly was never mentioned or thought of. It took a lot of digging to find him buried among the titles and rank of the Ascendancy, but I found him and, as a bonus, a Tipperary Mahon (no name is more Irish than Mahon) who was a great-great-grandmother.

It was hard to live in two camps, the starched damask of upstairs where the portrait of the old Earl hung and a painting of a man with six fingers, Grandfather calling for a copy of *Debrett's* to check a bloodline; and then the other spent with Ned or John Joe, or lying on my stomach sucking clover heads near the barrow that led into the cromlech. The dogs went into the barrow a couple of times after rabbits. I could hear the echo of them barking deep underground in some hollow chamber far down towards the killeen. If Darby's cave fascinated me, it was nothing to the hold the cromlech had on me.

'No one will ever lift the stone or dig down there,' said Ned, crossing himself. 'There's a curse on anyone lifting it.'

Time flew by in a world of my own, and trailing home, grubby, with most of the morning gone and a dog or two behind me, I would as often as not be accosted by Molly at the back door.

'Look at the cut of you! Filthy dirty! Change your dress! Put on clean sandals! The Duchess of Devonshire is over from Lismore for tea,' (or Elizabeth Bowen, or best of all Sir Fitz Grove-White, a relation who told me he had seen a leprechaun).

When I left Annes Grove for good, I felt as if I had left the psyche of my childhood behind me for ever, but no one growing up and eager for life can live in the past, however gentle and enchanted it might be; a past that John Joe and Ned, like the opening of a door, had unlocked for me into a magic world.

12

Life upstairs always seemed to be involved with visitors, or with doing flowers and the writing of endless letters. If one set foot in the drawing room, criticism was inevitable.

'Your posture is appalling.'

'What have you actually achieved today?'

'Don't keep fiddling with your hair.'

'You are talking with the most frightful brogue!'

'Have you helped Doyle exercise the horses?'

'Your jersey is far too tight.'

Visitors arriving called for furious activity. Trugs full of flowers were laid all over the floor on newspapers and endless cans of water carried to fill the vases. Down in the kitchen eggs were whipped, mayonnaise prepared with thick cream for poached salmon. The lunch table was laid with silver and crystal by the parlour maid. After sherry and lunch, the visitors would be escorted on a tour of the flower gardens, shrubs, rhododendrons and river gardens, which took up the whole afternoon until, muddy and exhausted, the party returned gasping for tea.

My favourite visitor was Elizabeth Bowen, the novelist, on one of her fleeting visits to Bowencourt, her Irish home made immortal by her famous book. Tall and majestic, with a deep throbbing voice and a slight stammer, her long fingers square-tipped, she wore heavy barbaric jewellery and used her hands slowly to emphasise a point. Her poise and humour made me a great admirer of hers and I used to sit, beady-eyed, as near her as possible. She usually came with her husband, Alan Cameron, who was with the BBC. Once I told her that I wanted to write and she showed great interest and kindness, correcting one or two of my immature manuscripts and advising me to read as many books by great writers as I could, to try to develop a good style. She brought Vita Sackville-West to tea with her when I was very young. Of her I remember nothing except her great vitality. Another time she came with Lord David Cecil.

Once, two Siamese princesses from Bangkok arrived to see the gardens. They came in a huge hired Rolls-Royce, driven by an enthusiastic Irish driver who had clearly never had such exotic clients before and who kept rolling 'Your Royal Highnesses' off his tongue with relish and a thick brogue. The princesses were tiny, not young, rather yellow and very regal. They wanted ideas for a rhododendron garden outside Bangkok. They graciously invited us all to stay with them in Siam and afterwards sent us a catalogue affair with pictures of where they lived, with each bedroom appearing to have a curious carved headrest made of wood, with a curved niche for one's neck, instead of a pillow.

The reason for such a cosmopolitan polyglot of visitors was the gardens, at that time world-famous and filled with rare and beautiful shrubs. Some which were as yet unnamed and only numbered were part of an exotic collection brought back from Tibet and bequeathed to my grandfather by an explorer, Captain Kingdon Ward. People came to us clutching introductions from gardeners abroad. They made copious notes and went away with cuttings, photographs and information to put to use in their own gardens.

Two particular visitors stick out in my memory. I have no idea who they were. One, a very aristocratic lady in one of those rose-petal-cluster hats, had an exquisite complexion and white hair. Sitting on a garden bench to rest and exclaiming over the beauty of some of the meconopsis poppies, she took out of her pocket, tamped, lit and enjoyed a large black pipe.

'Excellent for keeping the midges away,' she remarked.

The other, a lady with bright sky-blue hair which she wore casually tucked under her hat, seemed unable to control it. It escaped in brilliant flowing tendrils as she skipped through the gardens, popping off at flowers with an ancient camera. Her resonant trilling voice and bright blue hair mesmerised me. She had had a number of husbands and had concluded her matrimonial career by marrying a chef from Belgium, whom she installed in her castle in County Tipperary to produce such gastronomical delights that the country flocked, half shocked, half titillated, to her door.

'She was married to Lord Somebody or other,' said Grandfather, 'but he couldn't take it, poor devil. He pegged it. Turned his toes up. Do you wonder? Then she got hold of some other fella – General or something. He stuck it for a bit, then he gave up as well. Died last year, I think.'

'Well, she seems happy with the chef.'

'Yes, poor devil. Probably got more stamina. Can get away from it all and make buns or whatever he does.'

Uncle Warden Beresford came to stay, but only very occasionally, as he was rather a trial. He was well into his eighties, becoming senile and looked like a benevolent Father Christmas with a white beard and bright blue eyes. He was extremely eccentric, even for Ireland. He brought his bicycle with him, which seemed to annoy everybody. He was very keen on religion and told me confidentially that the world would come to an end when all the Jews in the world were baptised as Christians. This was a relief to me as I couldn't see that it was going to be very imminent. At least it would give me time to grow up and get out into the world before the Last Trump. He was always praying and consulting the Almighty about everything.

'Don't you think he is a very holy man?' I asked my grandmother.

'No, I don't,' she said shortly.

When he arrived he said how pleased he was to see her, but she had flipped at him with the long white kid gloves she always carried and said that the feeling certainly wasn't reciprocated.

'He asks the Almighty about everything,' I said. 'He talks to Him about every single thing he does.'

'Well, all I can say is that it must be extremely tiresome for the Lord,' she said crossly. 'Imagine having Wardie bothering one all day. I find him quite tiresome enough and I only see him at breakfast.'

My grandmother was going through a rather difficult phase. She was nearly ninety and she often said she was sick of us. All the interesting people she knew had died, she told me, and there weren't any left that could hold a candle to them.

One evening, when we were all busy about things in the green dusk and I was cutting bamboos on the avenue with a long-handled pair of secateurs, Breda came flying down the boreen with a wild look in her eyes and gasped that the Mistress was 'dying'. I sped up the avenue, sending messages to alert the family. When I got to her room she was sitting up in bed with her pink net nightcap on, looking very determined and extremely well. At the foot of her bed stood Molly, tears streaming down her face, holding a pencil. My grandmother was giving her instructions.

'The silver candlesticks are to go to Miss Daphne and the pictures in the anteroom I bequeath to Master Francis. The Marley bronze to Miss Sylvia.'

Molly was sobbing so much that she could hardly hold the pencil. The old corgi was snuffling under the bed and the room smelt of the white-rose scent my grandmother always wore.

'Gran!' I burst out. 'What *is* going on?'

'I've decided to die,' she said briskly. 'All my friends have passed on. There is nothing for me to live for. "And may there be no moaning of the bar when I put out to sea." You may kiss me goodnight,' she said. 'I shall not be here in the morning.'

I did not know whether to believe her or not – she had never been one to underestimate – but in the morning her bell started ringing violently at about ten o'clock. She had overslept with all the excitement of the night before.

'Is the Mistress all right this morning?' I asked Bridie, whom I met coming down with the breakfast tray.

'Ah, she's all right in herself,' said Bridie, clearly ruffled. 'But she's going pure wild above in the bed, for Breda is after burning the toast and her bath water's cold again.'

Uncle Beresford spent hours in the bath in the morning. He and I shared the same bathroom and I used to shiver outside in the freezing morning air waiting for him to finish. I thought he was probably praying, and one morning, on his ninetieth birthday, after being driven to total exasperation, I was sure of it. In a dirge-like chant he intoned amongst the clouds of steam, 'O Lord, shall I get out of the bath?' Thoroughly annoyed and very cold, I intoned back through the keyhole, 'Ye … ee … ees. Get out of the bath.' He was in a very good humour for the rest of the day, but I felt as guilty about it as if I had committed sacrilege.

He went away after about a week, pedalling down to the village station on his bicycle with his battered monogrammed old pigskin case fastened to the carrier.

– 13 –

Breda came to work for us as a kitchen maid in 1950. She was only sixteen. She had straight bobbed hair held with an enormous Kirby grip, a wide smile and freckles. She had to go to bed very late and was supposed to get up early to stoke the boiler so that my grandfather's bath water would be piping hot in the mornings. She usually overslept, and by eight o'clock the master of the house was aware of it.

'Where's that damned wench?' he would yell from the top of the stairs. 'My bath water is stone cold. Can't get up in the mornings, that's her trouble.'

He threatened to tie a fishing line to her toe and run it up the side of the house to his bedpost so that he could tweak it at five a.m. Breda never knew whether to believe him or not. She clapped her hands to her mouth when she heard him roaring and threw her apron over her head. Breda's mother had placed her in the charge of Molly. They were related and it was her first 'place'.

When I went down to fill my hot water jar at night, Moll was in bed but Breda was not. She was usually reading at the kitchen table, mouthing the words to herself and waiting to stoke the boiler for the night.

She used to put her book down and take the bottle from my hand to fill it. We made cocoa on the Aga while the clock ticked away on the twelve-foot dresser, and the huge brass and copper covers, over a hundred years old, winked down on us. Breda used to start telling ghost stories, and at that hour of the night they had a ring of authenticity.

'Are you ever afraid of this house at night?' I asked her once.

She said she wasn't, but she said she wouldn't sleep at the top of the house where I was, for anything.

'Some people died there in the 'flu epidemic in 1918,' she said. 'There was a cook working here for twenty years and she died up there. She was one of the O'Gradys and they heard the Banshee that night out in the yard.' Her voice was soft and low from the brogue and I got shivers up and down my spine.

'Lights follow the Barrys,' she said, talking of her own family. She stirred her cocoa and looked away from me. 'When anyone in our family is going to die like, the rest of us see bright lights shining or moving in the rooms of our place and we hear knocks too. Me mother heard knocking at the door the night me brother was killed in the bombing in Liverpool. The knocking started just before twelve. Whenever she opened the door there was no one there, but the knocking went on all through the night. Sure we got no sleep. In the morning we got a telegram to say me brother was dead. I think me mother knew that night. After a while she would not even let us open the door to knocks but we sat up most of the night. Sure you couldn't sleep with the noise. The old dog was howling and going mad as well, and when we let him in he'd every hair on his back straight up.'

'Was your mother lonely after him? Your brother, I mean.'

'She was lonely all right, but she had the nine of us.'

After this conversation I didn't feel like going to the top of the house alone, so I persuaded her to come with me. We stole up the stairs to my room where there was a wind-up gramophone and I put on a record. She sat on the edge of my bed as nervous as a cat in case Molly should waken and miss her.

'I have a dress in my wardrobe, new, that doesn't fit me,' I said. 'I think it would be all right for you. Would you like to try it on?'

She put it on and I combed her hair back.

'Put some lipstick on, a pink one. There's some of my aunt's in that drawer somewhere.'

She wouldn't. She covered her mouth with her hand and started laughing.

''Twould be a sin,' she said, between giggles.

'Never mind then. The dress looks nice. Keep it if you want it. It came from London.'

'London must be great,' she said wistfully.

I looked at her, the only person remotely near my own age in the large cold house. The wind was howling outside like a banshee and the cupboard doors were opening and creaking.

'Do you ever go out here? I mean, are you going out with anybody?' I asked her. 'Have you got a boyfriend?'

'I'd be afraid of the priest,' Breda said. 'My sister has a lovely fellow, but the priest is out hitting ditches and banks on a Saturday night with a big stick.'

'Why?'

'Sometimes the people do be courting and you know the banks where the wild white violets are in springtime? On the bend of the big hill near Ballyhooly?'

I nodded.

'They do be sitting there at night with the bushes overhead and Father Riordan coming along with a big stick do be threshing the hedges and banks. Me sister said the first time she saw him, there were people running everywhere before him shouting, "The priest is coming!" They were jumping over the dykes and everywhere. I'd be in dread of the priest.'

Suddenly we heard a voice from the bottom of the house. 'Breda! Come down out of that. You've a boiler to stoke in the morning!'

Breda tore the dress off and flew as if the Devil were after her.

I thought about Father Riordan when she was gone. He always walked, mouthing his breviary, in the middle of the road between Ballygliff and Ballyadene, so that everyone had to slow down. His house was the largest in the village, set back from the road, square and yellow with an air of sanctity about it.

Shortly after my conversation with Breda, Father Bourke came to the village for a period while the older priest was away. He was very good-looking. He came up and spoke to me in the post office, where I stood clutching a puppy and waiting for stamps while the postmistress gossiped with one of her cronies. He didn't appear to understand that we couldn't be friends because of our differing religions and that a firm line divided us. I understood it. It had been drilled into me from an early age.

'That's a nice little dog you have there,' he said.

As he seemed to be under a misapprehension, I corrected him.

'I'm a Protestant,' I said politely, by way of putting an end to the conversation.

He looked interested but not particularly bothered one way or another.

'Is that so?' he said, looking amused and trying to keep a straight face. Later on when we became friends he asked me to tea, but I dared not go. There would have been war at that time in the family if I had been known to go to a Catholic priest's house. No one in the Protestant community had ever done such a thing, although we gave the first salmon of the season to the priest. Then you just rang the bell and gave the fish in a basket to his housekeeper and later he wrote a note of thanks.

Father Bourke came up to the house to see one of the maids one day and he came to find me. I was up in the haylofts catching the wild kittens who hid under a broken floorboard, to tame and feed them. He threw off his black hat and sat down on top of a bale of hay to watch me.

'How's the black Protestant today?' he asked me, his very blue eyes laughing.

'Do the Protestants and Catholics really hate each other so much?' I wanted to know, sucking a scratched finger.

'I wouldn't say *hate*,' he said. 'It's a strong, powerful word, but there were things done long ago that caused a lot of trouble, you know. The Catholics at one time were denied education for the reason of their beliefs and then the soupers … during the Great Hunger … sure when people were starving, they'd be given soup if they left the Catholic faith. Another thing was that no Irish Catholic would be allowed to own a horse valued at over five pounds. Any Protestant could make him a force offer for any horse he had and only give the Catholic five pounds and he'd have to take the offer willy-nilly.'

I knew about that. Stories had been handed down about Catholic families who had bred beautiful horses and kept them hidden because of that law. One woman had hidden her fine Irish hunter up the stairs in her bedroom.

'It's their beliefs that are different,' he said. 'People will die for their beliefs.'

'You know,' I said, as he deftly fielded a kitten, 'there was a house near Ballygliff that was haunted. It was so badly haunted that the two old Catholic ladies who lived in it could get no sleep. They sent for the priest in the end, to come and exorcise the ghost. Things were flying around. Pictures and everything leaving the walls and with no one touching them. Could you exorcise a haunting?'

'I could.'

'Well, the priest came and sprinkled the holy water and he brought a bell and a Bible. They did the Stations of the Cross there even.'

'What do you know about the Stations of the Cross?'

'Breda told me.'

'And what happened after that?'

'The hauntings got a lot worse the night after the priest had left. The two old ladies had to leave the house in the end. The priest made the ghost furious and it started lifting heavy furniture into the air and throwing it around after that. There was no stopping it. Afterwards they found it was the ghost of an old Anglo-Irish Protestant who was haunting the house. It was raging mad on account of a priest coming in to interfere with it.'

'I could see that it might be,' said Father Bourke, laughing. 'It was careless of them not to get to the root of it first. I must be on my way. Shall I take one of the kittens? You've got the grey one nearly tame.'

I thought it was odd, thinking over the story after he had bicycled away with the kitten in a box on the carrier, that Catholics should in any case be living in a house that had belonged to a Protestant. There were Protestant houses and Catholic houses in our area, Catholic schools and Protestant schools, even certain shops more used by Protestants than Catholics. Sometimes the Protestant shops had a white horse in the window as a sign, and at the time the whole curious system of taboos between the religions was highlighted by the story of Charlie McCarthy and the chess game. I could see it, though, about the Protestant ghost. If any of my family had been haunting a place they would have been beside themselves at the idea of being exorcised by a Papist.

– 14 –

Religious intolerance had always been rife in Ireland. It was religious intolerance that had caused a rift between the Irish who were Catholic and the Protestant planters settled with grants of land and title in Ireland in the sixteen hundreds. In fact it was that intolerance which negated Whitehall's greatest fear, that Anglo-Irish settlers and the native Irish might at some time join together and, horror of horrors, rise to proclaim the seventeenth century's equivalent of UDI. The religious rift, however, wrecked any possible bonding and meant that the new settlers stayed loyal to the Crown, remaining, from England's point of view, in a most satisfactory state of segregation.

England's maxim 'divide and rule' hadn't worked out as smoothly as planned – nothing in Ireland ever does. Some of the newly settled Anglo-Irish became more Irish than the Irish themselves; but all the same, the wedge had been driven between. Even now religious intolerance has lingered in Ireland for centuries and anachronisms still exist there, which are relics of the early planting.

There was talk as late as the 1950s of people who married out of their religion doing a shocking thing. Mixed marriages were spoken about in hushed voices, particularly if a Protestant spouse should take the religion of another. 'He turned RC!' they said, appalled, or 'He turned!' and ripples of horror ran round the Protestant dinner tables.

Some Protestant neighbours sent their child to a Catholic school and the neighbourhood was aghast. The talk for months was about the frightful danger of it. 'They found rosary beads under the child's pillow!' I remember someone saying, to shock waves in the dining room. 'But what did the mother expect? O God! The risk!' My grandmother, involving herself with a couple who had a mixed marriage, urged the husband whenever she met him to 'stick to your guns and not turn'. He listened with great enjoyment to this while she bent his ear, remarking to me afterwards with glee, 'She has the whole thing wrong. I am the Catholic, not Philippa, but don't tell her. We're having lovely chats about Rome while the hounds are drawing!'

Before Ireland became a republic it was the Protestants who were the landed gentry and the Catholics, suffering from years of being penalised, who were usually the middle classes. After Ireland became Eire, the Anglo-Irish, poorer in power and having had some of their land snatched back by the new government, stayed on in their crumbling Irish mansions because, although they considered themselves Anglo, in their hearts they were totally Irish. Some of them struggled to keep up appearances in huge freezing houses behind demesne walls till they sold to the Germans in the 1960s, chortling with malicious delight at the prices offered by the Ellerholtzers, Schultzes and Brauhausens who poured into Ireland, scattering Deutschmarks in their wake.

Gleefully believing that these mad Germans had bought a pup every time and wildly overpaid for freezing ruins, dripping faucets, leaky gutters and nonexistent heating, they themselves rushed joyfully to the banks to pay in their German cheques, which bought them warm, hideous bungalows to crouch in. It was from these vantage points, pop-eyed with amazement, that they saw central heating installed in their erstwhile houses by Herr This or Fräulein That.

'Damn Huns crawling with money!' they told each other in astonishment, watching trucks full of electric geysers and marble baths turn in between the gates of their old homes and crossly picturing the Huns lying in lovely boiling baths, soaking after hunting. 'Perfectly good baths there already. Been there seventy years and now that Hun is putting in marble, if you don't mind. Must have money to burn. Could have bought a good brood mare with that sort of cash.'

Comforts like central heating and unlimited hot water had never seemed important in Irish country houses. A cousin fresh from a Japanese prisoner-of-war camp who came to us to convalesce after the war was heard to say that the camp was much warmer and more comfortable, except for the food! But at home, so long as there were horses in the stable, flowers in the house, whiskey in the cellaret and good food on the table, a bit of damp and cold was something one lived with. And as for a bit of dust here and there, 'Sure wasn't man made from it and returning to it in any case?' Molly used to say, which made dusting it away seem a little unfriendly. The only time I was conscious of acute discomfort was when Gran decided to use damask tablecloths, leftovers from Edwardian dinner parties thirty years before, as sheets. Getting into bed in winter was like inserting yourself between two shiny slices of ice.

Among the people who didn't sell but remained ensconced long after most of the Germans had decamped disillusioned from the south were Leila and Charlie McCarthy, who lived in a vast freezing cold grey castle on the mountainy road thirty miles from Ballygliff. The drawing room was as big as a ballroom and the wind literally whistled through it and rattled the gilt picture frames on the walls. You could have held a dance there for five hundred people and hardly noticed them. The whole room was warmed, or rather not warmed, by a beautiful minuscule Adam fireplace wrecked by a hideous tiled Victorian surround. The Georgian windows didn't fit properly, so that draughts came in from every area, and the entrance hall was enormous, with a cold flagged floor and stained glass windows with two panes missing. What with the chill rising from the stone floor and the stained glass, you felt as if you were in a badly heated church. Portraits of Charlie's ancestors were dotted about, none looking particularly happy. The heating could have been no better in the castle in the eighteenth century, judging from their pinched, frozen faces.

Just in front of the hall door there was a painting of Mrs McCarthy, who had died in 1919. She had been a beauty in her day and Charlie, painted as a child, stood at her knee in the portrait. He had had a great look of his mother then, and a delicate chiselled face, but when I met him fifty years later there was not a trace of this. He was as small and stooped as a sparrow, with a red-veined face and a beaky nose. He wore grey plus-fours and badly knitted golf socks with moss stitch around the tops. Leila had been lovely as a girl too, judging from the portrait of her in the dining room. She had striking huge dark eyes and a creamy skin crisscrossed with tiny wrinkles when I first knew her, but the Irish climate is kind to complexions and she was easy on the eye even in her sixties.

Charlie and Leila were typical of the impoverished Anglo-Irish feeling the pinch, rattling around in a castle, half frozen to death but carrying on the best way they could. Leila played the organ in church and Charlie took the collection plate round.

We always had to go to church, rain, hail or snow, to 'show the Catholics'. To show them quite what I was never sure – perhaps that although we had never embraced Rome we were not totally heathen. But they, the RCs, as they poured out of chapel full of plans for following harriers or rabbiting with ferrets, didn't seem particularly bothered one way or another about our piety. Our own church was not destined to fill us overmuch with the Holy Spirit. The Canon had a very strong brogue and it was difficult to make out exactly what Moses and Elijah were up to, as most of their prophecies became imbued with a curiously Irish flavour when the Canon read them.

On top of that, the organ wouldn't work unless air was pumped into the bellows at the back of it by a choirboy, who worked hard at it for the hymns but slacked off during the responses. A small weight attached to a piece of string behind the organ moved from a pointed sign which said 'Empty' to 'Full' when he pumped hard enough, but a slight miscalculation meant that the organ ran out of air occasionally, and Leila, who for this reason wore a constant air of apprehension, would find herself hitting mute and silent keys. Everyone rallied at this point, some straggled, some raced, and the Canon, oblivious of all, roared away at his own pace, sounding like a supporter at a hurling match. Grandfather, who was very musical, physically shuddered when this happened and could be heard muttering loudly 'O my God! O my God!' at the discordant yowling.

During the sermon Grandfather read the Bible, which gave him an air of piety and concentration as well as total detachment from the Canon's sermon. The reason he found it so particularly engrossing was that it contained a glossary at the back of every plant and its genus mentioned in the Bible, and he would be heard exclaiming about a particularly fascinating piece of flora which came up in Exodus, 'By Jove! That's damned interesting!' As he never talked below a roar and couldn't possibly be referring to the sermons, which were excruciatingly boring, the congregation craned their necks, hoping for a bit of crack, and even the Canon paused.

We always sat in the front pew, and if the preaching went on too long Grandfather cleared his throat, looked pointedly at his wrist watch and, returning with a sniff to the Bible, gave the pulpit a warning glance. Occasionally this acted as a brake on the Canon, who, unnerved, cut short the sermon and announced the closing hymn.

Services at the church were seldom uplifting but always stimulating because of the by-play, and when part of the gallery once collapsed or the string broke on a Harvest Thanksgiving arrangement, hurtling jam pots and vegetable marrows to the floor, we felt we'd had our money's worth.

Leila came to church one Sunday and asked if someone else could take the collection for Charlie as he wasn't well. His leg had been giving him a lot of trouble for some time. He had been wounded in the war and his leg always ached in cold weather, but now it appeared it was not the cold weather or the war wound but something worse, a disease which would eventually kill him. No one knew how serious it was then, but there was a lot of sympathy about his illness in the neighbourhood.

Gran drove over in the dogcart to see him and took him *Field* and *Country Life* and a book of chess problems. Charlie's two passions in life were Persian rugs and chess, both interests which he had been able to cultivate in Persia during his time with the British Army out there. Persian rugs lay about the floor in the drawing room and the library, and he liked talking about patterns and types of Shiraz or Bokhara to anyone who showed any interest in them. He was a great conversationalist, but as illness sapped his usual cheerful spirits he talked less and less and spent most of his time in bed working out chess problems. Leila said she had never learnt to play and, even if she had, she would not have had the time to sit. She was always running up and down from the kitchen to Charlie's bedroom on the third floor with trays. Someone got him a wheelchair but it was only of use on one floor because of all the flights of curved stairs. Without a lift, and with only Leila and Mary Kate the maid, the chair even if folded up was too heavy to carry up or down eight flights.

In spite of this, Charlie had the odd outing. He ventured

up to Dublin and went to the Kildare Street Club to see all his old cronies. We heard that he and Leila had spent a night at the Shelbourne Hotel and he had seen a specialist in Fitzwilliam Square about his leg. The prognosis was not as bad as first thought, Leila said, but financially things were becoming more difficult. Afterwards we heard that to pay doctors' bills and for an occasional bottle of whiskey to keep the cold out, Leila had had to sell one of Charlie's rugs, a particularly fine Bokhara, to one of the Germans in the district.

Old General Mulgahy, Leila's brother, went over to see Charlie from time to time, and gave us bulletins about him because sometimes weeks went past without anyone else calling. The bad potholes in the mountainy road put people off and it was unfortunately a long way to go to the McCarthys in the winter afternoons when it got dark so early. So we didn't hear very much news of Charlie for a while unless General Mulgahy rang to report on him. Leila told us at church that now winter had come, with the soft rain falling endlessly and a few rooks cawing outside the windows, Charlie was happy enough to doze with a rug over his knees in front of the turf fire.

The trouble was, she said, that on days when he felt better he was listless and bored with no one to talk to and Leila too busy running up and down the stairs all the time. The castle was intended to have five indoor servants, and with only herself and Mary Kate she was killed from work. She used to pray, she told Gran afterwards, that people would call to talk to Charlie and play chess with him, because when he was bored he was very often unreasonable and in a black mood, complaining that she couldn't be bothered to sit and talk to him.

She was always telling him that he was getting better though she knew he wasn't, and wished she could spend more time with him, but her workload was killing. The boiler had to be stoked and the beds made and hot-water bottles filled to keep him warm. Dogs had to be fed, peas podded and potatoes peeled, while downstairs Mary Kate washed miles and miles and miles of tiled floors on her hands and knees and scrubbed the kitchen table till her fingers were purple. It seated twenty comfortably, but although there was only herself below eating a slice of soda bread or a bit of bacon and cabbage all alone most days, it had to be kept clean. So did one hundred and eighty windows. Then there were the dresser shelves to scrub, chickens to pluck, silver to polish and plates to wash up in the butler's pantry. Everything was so far from everything else, Leila often sighed, that the walking and the to and froing would destroy you.

It was in the middle of this daily struggle, with Charlie very down in the mouth upstairs, that a knock came on the door one dreary rainy evening and Leila opened it to come face to face with the parish priest, a man whom she hardly knew. He was standing out in the rain bareheaded and holding a wooden box under his arm, an educated man from Maynooth, with a kind and gentle face.

'Oh hello, Father,' she said, a little taken aback. 'Do you want Mary Kate?'

'No. In fact,' the priest said, 'I heard that your husband wasn't so good and that he was after a game of chess. Someone in the village told me.' He looked shy and apologetic. 'I have a board here and a set of men …' His voice trailed off and he said hesitantly, 'I met him a few times before, over the fishing.'

Leila was in a quandary, she told us later. This was something for which she was unprepared. She scarcely knew this nice middle-aged priest, but suddenly feeling old, tired and lonely she opened the door, flying in the face of every rule she had ever been raised by, and said, 'Come in, Father. He'll be delighted.'

Later, when she had time to go upstairs, she was glad she

had done it. In fact she never regretted it in spite of what happened later. When she went up that night she found the two men engrossed over the chessboard, a glass of whiskey on the arm of each chair and the turf fire throwing a warm glow on Charlie's face.

They only played one game and she heard him say to the priest when he was leaving, 'Come again, I want a return match,' his voice seeming stronger and more cheerful for the chess and a bit of company.

After that night, apparently, it became a regular engagement. Every Tuesday and Thursday evening the priest's small black Renault car was parked outside the castle wall and a friendship appeared to spring up between the two men. Some nights they did not play at all but talked for hours about Charlie's service in Persia, about the Zoroastrian religion out there, about rugs and about the priest's days in the Vatican.

'Don't you find it stifling?' Charlie asked him one night over the chessboard, 'Ballygliff after Rome, with all these country bumpkins gawping at you from the pews on a Sunday?'

'Ah, but I'm needed here,' the priest explained, castling his king. Charlie said that if he did as much good for all the people in the parish as he did for Charlie, he would be a loss if he left. Even Leila found herself wishing that the dear old Canon was as good company, and then caught herself up, horrified. To compare a Roman Catholic priest with the Protestant rector – dear God! Charlie's illness and the worry of the place must be getting to her, she told herself, going downstairs to peel the potatoes.

That was when the thought crossed her mind to write to cousins in Connemara. If Charlie was able to be moved at all, she would take him there for a short visit and let the castle to Americans for the summer. Americans loved castles, especially in the warm weather. 'So romantic!' they told each other, paying well for the privilege.

But it was that week, before she had had time to have a reply from the cousins at Lough Corrib, that Charlie took a very bad turn. He had had a fall from his chair one evening and the doctor came over and told Leila then that the prognosis was very bad. He was a bluff, disagreeable man from Carlow who much preferred his greyhounds to his patients. He was reputed to use veterinary medicines for people but it was never proved.

'Ah, he's a great man after the greyhounds,' his patients sighed, but he had no bedside manner at all.

'Expect the worst,' he told Leila bluntly. 'He's going.'

It was only when the priest came at his usual time with his chess set, Leila said later, that she realised she had forgotten to send a message down to him with Mary Kate, so he didn't know that Charlie was sinking. When she told him, the concern on his face warmed her after the abrasive manner of Dr Murphy and she was glad when he asked if he could go up to Charlie anyway.

He stayed about an hour, and when she came in with Charlie's hot jar it occurred to her that she hadn't even heard the door close. The priest had slipped out quietly so as not to disturb her.

Charlie died the next morning. The news flew around the Protestant community. Wreaths were ordered to be made by gardeners in Ballygliff, and the village people were lonely after him because he had been well liked. We took over some things for Leila, and I was left to answer the door and the telephone as wreaths arrived and cables came through. The front door rang a lot in the two days following: people coming to pay their last respects to Charlie.

On the day of the funeral, flowers poured in from all over the country. White azaleas, pale yellow rhododendrons, wreaths of lilies and moss – there were rivers of flowers wherever you looked. Charlie was to be buried at Ballygliff church and the funeral cortège left from the castle. There was no undertaker's parlour for Charlie. He went straight from his own bed to his coffin, which, gently lifted by men from the farm, was placed in the hearse and driven by a man who stopped earths in the hunting season.

As the procession, followed by over a hundred cars, approached a blind bridge four miles from Ballygliff cemetery, it came to a halt. Cars at the back slowed and stopped on the narrow road, bumper to bumper. It was impossible to see or know why they were being held up. Ten minutes went by and men began to get out of their cars, pulling up their coat collars against the rain and asking each other about the delay.

'Hell on poor Leila,' they told each other. 'Has the hearse broken down or what?'

News came trickling back that two priests with their hands raised were standing bareheaded in the road and had halted the hearse.

'What's happening?' everyone asked at the back. 'Why are they here?'

'These fellows say Charlie died a Catholic,' said General Mulgahy, coming down the line of cars, thunderous with rage. 'He took the last rites before he died, so they say, and embraced the Catholic faith. They want the body.'

The priests asked that the cortège should proceed to the Catholic chapel, and now a lot of people began to get out of their cars and started to crowd up to the front. Altercations broke out. It started to drizzle quite hard in the half-light of the winter's afternoon. The narrow road was choked with cars and it was impossible to go either forward or back. Eventually Leila, frail and white-faced in a shabby black suit with a very beautiful diamond brooch on the lapel, got out of the leading car, supported by her brother. She was very pale and shaking slightly with nerves. She came face to face with the priest who had been Charlie's friend. Distressed though she was and in spite of her anger, she was still aware of the warmth and genuineness of the man.

'Charlie died a Catholic, ma'am,' he said. 'It was his wish. We spoke about it often in the evenings, but he was afraid to grieve you. He needed the warmth of the Catholic faith. I gave him the last rites myself.'

'Why do this now? Damn you! Without warning! It's a damn scandal!' said Mulgahy, spitting the words out.

Very quietly, looking at the ground, Leila asked that the funeral should proceed to the Protestant church and that Charlie should be buried with his own family in the crypt there. The hearse driver looked at the parish priest for guidance. The Father nodded, the procession of cars snaked on to Ballygliff, and Charlie was finally buried a Protestant.

The talk was terrible after that. People were outraged.

'Playing chess,' they said; 'the same story as the rosary beads. A foot in the door and you're gone. Leila must have been quite mad to allow it.'

Nobody appeared to wonder what Charlie would have thought or what Charlie would have wanted. He was, after all, an Anglo-Irish landowner and so the idea of him 'turning' could not have been entertained, but the scandal of the funeral was talked of for months.

– 15 –

Breda and I went to visit her mother one afternoon in early spring. Mrs Barry was walking a hound puppy for the hunt, but that was not the only reason for the visit. I had had warts on my hands since autumn and Breda's mother could cure warts with a gold ring. She could also cure the whooping cough, tell fortunes with cards, charm the birds off trees, and pike hay in the harvest faster than any man.

We went in the pony trap. It took a long time to catch the pony and we were exhausted by the time we had chased it up and down the inch and dragged the trap out of the coach house, where there was still a coach mouldering with its coat of arms on the door. We tied pieces of the pony's harness together with binder twine to hold it. It was pouring with rain – but then it usually was. A mackintosh rug lined with wool kept the worst of the rain off. The pony was inclined to hice, which meant he raised his backside violently in the air and drummed his heels on the bottom of the trap. We were uncomfortably close to his mangy black posterior and the trap lurched about as if pulled by a bucking bronco.

'Give him his head there,' advised Doyle, who was leaning on a pike watching the performance with some amusement but making no effort to help or hold his head. 'Are ye in dread of him? Give him the stick there!'

We whirled out of the stable yard like dervishes, passing the mounting blocks at speed and praying the binder twine would hold.

'Dear God above tonight,' breathed Breda, 'but that animal is pure savage, so he is.'

When we got to a hill we sat forward, or got out and pushed from behind to assist George the pony, who had now settled down. When we went downhill we sat right back. On the tarmac roads we had to keep well into the side or George's metal horseshoes would slip. We met two motorcars on our journey and it felt that the roads were becoming overcrowded.

When we got near the Barry homestead we had to unharness the pony and tie him to a tree by a rein, with a few ferns stuck into his halter to keep off the flies. Leaving him there, we climbed a stone wall to the farm. There was no road to the Barry household, only a track with a few wild gooseberry bushes and a verbena growing along it. The family lived in a house partly built from stone from an old Franciscan abbey which we passed. It had almost fallen down and there were still huge lumps of dressed stone which had lain about in the long grass by the river since the abbey began to crumble some hundreds of years before. It had had its heyday before the days of Henry the Eighth. He had fallen out with the Catholic Church over his divorces and persecuted the abbeys and monasteries. After him Cromwell had done more, and worse.

The abbey was a beautiful shell, the vaulted rooms now courtyards open to the sky. In what once must have been the chapel there were crypts broken into and full of bleached white bones and skulls. A tramp known as Paddy Gaddy slept in a crypt on top of the bones. He kept a blanket and a billycan inside the tomb, which had a Latin inscription cut into the stone on top of it. One would need to be brave to sleep there, I thought, as we walked along. At night in the great deserted place with only a glimmer of moonlight, it would have been eerie alone, with just the noise of the Blackwater River a few yards beyond.

Recently the government had decided that the abbey should

perhaps be a national monument and had got John Joe Fitzgerald in the village to shore up the pillars and patch up the stone window arches with new grey cement. It didn't really destroy anything because he had only a short ladder so couldn't reach the high windows. Most of them were high and they looked beautiful – curved, delicate and empty of glass, framing the green vistas beyond and the blue of the Galtee Mountains.

The nettles stung our legs wickedly on the path by the abbey and I wondered idly who had planted the old gooseberry bushes; whether it was perhaps a monk, or whether that would have been too long ago.

'It's very wild, this place,' Breda said, rubbing her nettle-stung legs with the juice of a handful of dock leaves to soothe the stings. We sat down for a moment beside a holy well and pulled sorrel and chewed it and sucked the honey out of clover flowers. We were in the shade of a tree growing over the holy well. People passing had tied pieces of coloured rags to the tree and hung holy medals on its boughs. You drank the well water from a tin mug hung on a crotch in the tree, or took the water in your cupped hands, asking Bridget the Saint for a wish. We both drank and wished. Neither of us had rags and I had no holy medals, so I tied the belt of my cotton dress to a branch as a libation to Saint Bridget.

When we got to the house, Mrs Barry came out. She wore extremely large men's boots without laces, a long black dress and an apron, and had forgotten to put her teeth in. Inside the cottage there was very little furniture – just the dresser, a picture of the Sacred Heart with a red light burning in front of it, two chairs with string seats, one on either side of the fire, and a fire wheel you turned to make the turf glow.

Mrs Barry took off her wedding ring. It was a big thick gold one. She rubbed it over my warts. The clock ticked on the dresser. It was cool and dark in the cottage. The window was small and the floor, made of packed earth, was smooth.

She shut her eyes and I shut mine. She rubbed the ring on my hand, muttered something, a prayer or a charm, saying that the warts would go by sunrise. Then things came back to a normal conversational level. The hound puppy, fat as a bonham, nosed through the door and we had soda bread for tea and apple cake, treacly and delicious, baked over the fire on top of the three-legged pot.

'I have a grand present for you,' said Mrs Barry. 'May God be good to you, I have indeed. It's riches I'm giving you – a clutch of guinea fowl's eggs.'

We admired Mrs Barry's enormous yellow dahlia growing next to the manure heap.

'It's as big as a hat. Honest to God, I think I'll wear it on my head going to Mass.' And then she gave me, as we left, the present: five guinea fowl's eggs, a sitting, for myself. 'You'll get a good price for the chicks when they are hatched. God be good to you now so,' and we were off home again.

A few evenings later Breda's mother hired a car driven by a man who looked like a petrified weasel, by name of Patsy Flynn. She arrived at the house as night was falling. The preparations in the Servants' Hall for her arrival were tremendous. Molly had an apple cake and baked barmbrack; bacon, eggs and sausages were cooking, and Breda was flying round like a scalded cat.

I was spending rather a dull evening reading old Duhallow hound lists dating back to 1906 to Grandfather, who was dozing in his armchair in front of the smoking-room fire upstairs.

'Dempster out of Dairymaid sired by Duhallow Dreadnought.'

'A grand old hound … grand,' he muttered sleepily. 'Go on.'

'Frailty 1910. By Docile, sired by Flagstaff, of the Funcheon Vale Hunt.'

'She ran a grand hunt,' he nodded, 'that Frailty. I remember her in one hunt out of Ballygliff covert. Hounds casting. Not much scent, when I heard Frailty's voice. She was speaking, she was on to him.' He fell asleep again.

I switched hound lists to 1935 and shuffled through the 1951 bundle, when the door opened and one of the maids put her head round it.

'Mrs Barry's below for you,' she hissed. 'She's reading the cards.' The head vanished.

'Havelock out of Duhallow Dainty, sired by Humble,' I intoned. There was no response. Grandfather was snoring gently in his pea-green plus-fours and I tiptoed out, leaving hound lists all over the floor.

Downstairs was really jumping. Steaming cups of tea and a strong smell of bacon frying. There was a porter cake thickly sliced in the middle of the immense table, the wireless was blaring forth and a cracking game of '45' was in progress, punctuated by roars of laughter.

The only person who was not participating in all this gladness was Patsy Flynn, the driver of the hired car. He was sitting bolt upright in the corner clutching his cap with his eyes shut. Every now and then he opened them and exclaimed hopefully, 'Come on now. We'll go home so.'

To which Mrs Barry replied, 'Whisht will you. Haven't we all night before us?'

Espying me, she gave me a great welcome. 'Sure it's yourself, growing into a grand young lady, God love you. Sure it's big you are now and your life before you. Will I read the cards so?'

'Shuffle them there now,' she instructed me, 'and cut twice.'

The whole roomful of people, even the card players, leaned forward to hear my life revealed. Patsy Flynn woke up again and muttered, 'Come on now so. We'll go home now.'

'Don't mind him,' said Mrs Barry, annoyed. 'The place where he is not is always more potently attractive to him than the place in which he is.' She leaned forward and sucked her bottom lip. The clock ticked in the silence. Someone turned the wireless down.

'I see you going across water,' said Mrs Barry. 'Across water to a far country. When you get there, I see blood all around you.'

'Sure God help us,' said Molly gloomily.

'There's blood all right, but she's out of it. Men all around her and the blood is between them and others. She'll marry a fellow with brass buttons on his uniform. He's in the pay of the King and he drawing his money by cheque.'

This final accolade was received well by the assembled company and the game of '45' resumed. It was not taken very seriously, least of all by myself, unaware that within six months I'd fly to Africa and live in the very heart of the Mau Mau troubles in Kikuyu-land, leaving behind me for ever hound lists, whisperers, banshees and horses, and live a life so different I'd wonder if I were still on the same planet.

Molly, true to her ideas of what was proper, was to sew holy medals into the lining of my coat for the journey and to bake me a four-pound porter cake to keep me from starving on the way.

'Africa,' she had said gloomily, 'is terrible far away and full of blacks.'

Oddly enough it was that evening that was to come back to me so clearly so many times in my life, because, in a strange way, nothing was quite the same after that.

– 16 –

Things were changing. A violent storm had blown down the two beautiful old copper beeches near the house, leaving ugly yawning craters. Then suddenly, just before harvest week, John Joe's body was found in the wood near a river. I missed him, but nobody else seemed to care.

'That dirty old fairy!' Moll had said scathingly. Then there was talk of Ned retiring. His daughter in America was sending him a cheque every month, so there was no need for him to work. He was getting old, he said, and his bones ached from the damp.

Moll had changed too. These days she was not herself. She had always been a tower of strength, but now she was moody and not inclined to talk. In the past she had boasted to the current governess that she had 'reared' me, as if, I had thought sulkily, I was one of her turkey chicks in a box near the Aga. It had embarrassed me then, but now I missed being her dote and being fussed over. I was growing up and not the centre of her world any more. Lately she had taken to saying, when I hung around the kitchen, that my place was 'upstairs'.

'You are big now, a young lady,' and she would turn her back on me to knead soda bread without another word. But upstairs required a different persona, where you said what you were supposed to say and not what you thought. It was dull and there never seemed to be anyone about, only garden visitors raving about plants.

Gran was well over eighty now and retired earlier and earlier to bed. Grandfather, who was much younger than she was, salmon-fished until late at night on hot summer evenings. Sometimes he came home after eleven when it was dark, so, more alone than before, I mooched across the parkeen, hands in pockets, with the dogs, or wandered through the gardens until I heard the sound of the dogcart and saw a glimmer of the carriage lamp through the trees signalling Grandfather's return from the river.

He fished the Blackwater, pulling out enormous salmon which lay on the freezing floor of the larder until Moll cooked them. Sometimes we ate them cold with new potatoes and Irish mayonnaise and baby peas fresh from the garden, followed by apple pie, the pastry flaky and gold, held up by an egg cup, and the apples, sweet Irish peach from an old tree in the garden. Only the Irish would have apple trees called after peaches!

If Grandfather caught sight of me on his way to fish he would make me walk a piece of the road with him beside the dogcart because of an old Irish superstition that if a foxy-haired girl walks with you when you go fishing you'll have a grand catch that day.

As well as being a keen fisherman he was Master of the Hounds and at that time a great gardener and a countryman to his bones, which this story demonstrates. It's probably apocryphal, but typical of him!

In a conversation with a visitor he enquired, eyeing the man warily, 'Do you hunt much?'

'No,' said the visitor.

'Fish much?'

'No,' said the visitor.

'Shoot much?'

'I can't say I do.'

'Garden much?' The visitor was becoming a trifle demoralised.

'No.'

'Well, what the devil *do* you do then?'

He had absolutely no conception of the ins and outs of earning a living.

'Strange chap,' he would say of some top and well-known industrialist who had come to visit the garden or fish with him. 'Fella spends his time crouching in an office.'

And then, as an afterthought: 'Not a bad chap though. Tells me he ties his own flies,' and he would wander off into his private world of rare shrubs and lilies.

There was a summerhouse in the walled garden created by Grandfather's spinster aunts that I used to love, but now I found it depressing. Grandfather's grandfather, the old General, had died at Annes Grove in 1849 after fathering seventeen children and more, it was said, in the villages. Some of his daughters had never married and had whiled away long days lining the interior walls of the summerhouse painstakingly, twig by dried twig, stick by stick, in intricate patterns. It must have been complicated, fiddly work, and time-consuming – but then time, I supposed, had been the least of their worries. Standing in the doorway of the summerhouse I could picture them, if I closed my eyes, down the Crows Walk near the house, tramping through the rainy woods, long tweedy skirts damp from the wet, spending dreary hours picking sticks. Surely, I thought, looking at the little gazebo with its borders of lavender and the year 1860 picked out in twigs, they must have been suffocated with boredom after a while; but perhaps that was only a projection of how I felt that summer.

Sitting in the green dusk one summer's evening near the fox covert at the farm, I watched a tumble of russet fox cubs play under the golden gorse, the vixen stretched out to suckle the smallest one. I had sat without moving for such a long time that they had not noticed me. Outwardly as I sat there, knees drawn up to my chin, I was as still as a statue, but inwardly I was grappling with a turmoil of churning emotions and feelings that I scarcely understood myself. I was not the pliable girl of a year ago, but rebellious and bored.

'After all your Granny has done for you!' I could almost hear Molly saying, but I was seventeen that year, feeling differently about everything and waiting for something to happen.

Ungratefully, I thought that if one more garden visitor told me how lucky I was to live in beautiful, romantic Annes Grove I would scream. And yet I loved Annes Grove, knew every part of it and almost every tree, so what did I want? To see the world? To fall in love? Mostly, I thought, someone of my own age to talk to and some sort of work. The social life allowed to me involved only the Anglo-Irish houses, or hunting, and most people of my age were over in England in any case.

Grandfather once received a letter from Gerald Annesley at Castlewellan suggesting that I come out with his daughter, but that was tossed into the wastepaper basket with a snort.

At last an invitation came for me to a ball at Byblox, a huge house only a few miles from Annes Grove. A rich English family with two daughters had rented it for the summer and the dance was for them before they left for London.

I was amazed to be allowed to go and was driven over by Doyle in the dogcart in his bowler hat with pipe clenched between his teeth. The rain was teeming down, ruining my hair which had been ringleted by Molly into terrible corkscrew curls. I clutched tightly onto a dress box in which reclined a hideous blue taffeta dress. It had been sent on approval by Dowdens in Cork. It was far too large in the bust, with awful droopy sleeves.

I had been to Byblox often enough in the past but now, as we drove in, it seemed alien, much grander and far more imposing than before. The door with its Georgian fanlight was opened when I rang by one of the daughters, her hair cut very short in a cap of red curls the same colour as mine. She was Georgina and as we went upstairs she, carrying my dress box, said, as though it were perfectly normal, that she had had her dress made by Worth in Paris. It hung in her room, a cloud of grey tulle, with a stole to match, fringed in green. A parure box lay open on her dressing table displaying real emerald and seed-pearl jewellery. She held up the long earrings to her pierced ears and pirouetted.

Dressing gloomily in a centrally heated bedroom, I looked disparagingly at the blue taffeta lying on the bed and even more disparagingly at my reflection in the mirror, and wished I had never come. A maid pressed the crushed blue dress and pinned my petticoat straps with little clucks of dismay. She even tried to harness the drooping sleeves with a needle and thread, which made it look a little better; but going down the curved staircase to supper I caught a glimpse of Georgina far below me in her grey Worth dress and thought that my appearance really didn't matter. She was stunning and so was her sister. Downstairs there was champagne cup to drink, banks of flowers and the band tuning their instruments. The dance began at nine.

I was shy, gauche and all feet when I danced, a country bumpkin, hating the blue dress and the silver shoes Gran had lent me. The evening seemed endless, enlivened only by a man I watched playing noughts and crosses with the waiters on the back of ten-pound notes until, maddened with whiskey and in a flurry of bank notes, he threw a large flower pot through the conservatory window.

The band stopped playing for a split second and then pounded on. The glass was rapidly swept away by minions and in the hubbub I escaped to search for my bedroom, where a white card with my name on it was pinned to the door. I tore off the horrible taffeta dress and lay awake hearing the thump of the band below, feeling plain and inadequate, until the sky was streaked with dawn. Doyle's arriving to collect me in the trap next morning was like the relief of Mafeking.

It was the first and last ball of my teens.

Molly's moodiness increased. She had turned down a suitor who had wooed her for years. He was called the Hacker because of his prowess on the hurley field and now, with her mouth drawn down at the corners, she spent the afternoons darning socks in stony silence in the Servants' Hall. She cheered up when a letter arrived from my aunt in America, who came every summer to Annes Grove bringing with her a whiff of New York and never fewer than twenty pieces of luggage. Molly was her devoted slave and so totally taken up with her that my nose was well out of joint.

When the *Queen Mary* liner came into Cobh my aunt was on board and there were two cars waiting to collect her and her luggage, with Jerry Owen-above-at-the-Pump driving one car and Grandfather at the wheel of the other.

The Blue Room was her territory and she transformed it. Furs, dresses and dozens of pairs of shoes, bottles of scent, clouds of tissue paper and glossy magazines littered the room. Grandfather, amazed anew every year at the amount and size of his daughter's luggage, enquired why she never wore any of the clothes she brought with her. She was always dressed in dark-green tartan wool pants, a cream silk shirt, flat brown moccasins and a hacking jacket. Her scent filled the house when she was in it, but apart from arranging huge brilliant cascades of flowers she almost immediately departed to buy rolls of Donegal tweed to be made up by Tailoreen at the crossroads. Tailoreen, a quiet bespectacled man who sat cross-legged on his kitchen table stitching for the village, braced himself when he heard she was coming.

She whirled into his dark little cottage like a cyclone, armed with pattern books, bales of tweed, buttons, zips and dresses from Lord & Taylor she wanted copied. From there, usually with me in attendance, she drove at a terrifying speed to the dressmaker in Ballyhooly for more measuring and altering.

She had a knack of inspanning everyone in her orbit to do anything and everything for her, so, if one percolated into the Blue Room, Molly would be ironing her blouses, and someone else putting laces into her shoes, sewing on buttons or merely opening or closing a window as she ordered. I would steal past her room hoping not to be heard and allocated one of her inexhaustible lists of jobs, but she had ears like a bat, so if a board squeaked and she heard you, you were doomed.

She was often down in the Servants' Hall, skirts drawn up to the heat of the stove, drinking tea and gossiping with Moll, who adored her. She called her 'Your Ant', the Cork way of pronouncing Aunt, and was around her like a satellite.

'Your Ant,' said Moll, 'is the pick of the bunch. The best of the lot of you.'

Once, driving along in the car, crushed in amongst bales of tweeds and linings, I plucked up the courage to ask her about my father. He was after all her brother and they had grown up together. She looked at me out of the corner of her eye as if sizing me up before she said guardedly, 'He wasn't a stuffed shirt, I'll say that for him. Poor old Mickey Malone!' We cornered in a shower of gravel, missing a donkey cart by inches.

'Mickey Malone?'

'That was my pet name for him.' She put her foot down flat on the accelerator and rocketed towards the crossroads and Tailoreen, and that was that.

Somehow, with all the comings and goings and the focus on my aunt, I wanted to hear someone praise my father. He couldn't have been all that bad, but Moll, when cornered in the Servants' Hall, was dismissive.

'Ah, he was always wild,' Molly said. 'Always wild. Sure he would never listen to anything. The poor Mistress! He used to drive her mad with his carry-on. He couldn't do anything right.'

'He rode well,' I said defensively. 'Doyle told me.'

'Not as well as your Ant.' No one in Molly's parlance could hold a candle to my aunt. 'She was a picture in the hunting field. A picture!'

She turned the heel of a sock, needles clicking. A smell of hot blacking rose from the doors of the stove. The old corgi yawned at her feet and put his nose between his red and white paws. Molly looked up at the clock and shouted at the kitchen maid. 'Breda, have you the chickens drawn?'

'I have.'

'And the scullery scrubbed?'

'I have so.'

'And the bread out of the oven?'

'I have.'

She was counting stitches and not in the mood to talk, but I did not want the conversation to end.

'He is good-looking in the pictures upstairs,' I persisted.

'Ah, but not like your Ant! *She* was a picture! And full of fun! The night before her wedding, the carry-on! She told me she did not know if she should marry your uncle or the best man! The Mistress was fit to be tied when she heard her.'

'So *she* made Gran go mad as well?'

'Not like your father, the poor man, God help him. He made her *pure* wild. "He should have died young, Molly," she said to me once, "and that would have been the end of him and his bothers."'

It seemed a rather extreme statement to make.

'And I would never have been born,' I said bleakly.

The thought did not seem to have occurred to Molly, who was counting stitches, with her bottom lip thrust out.

'And my mother, did you ever see her?'

'Ah, she wasn't right at all. Not for this place. I never seen her nor your Ant never seen her,' – the inference being that if my aunt had never seen her she couldn't have been much.

'Did Gran?'

'They saw her in London, your Granny and your Grandfather. They went over. "The best place for her is Africa," the Mistress said. She wasn't right for this place at all.'

'How not?'

'Don't bother your head with her. Your place is here in Ireland but don't give trouble now.' She looked at me over the top of her glasses. 'When your father was here from Africa there was always fighting. Here's trouble, I'd think, when I seen him coming. A funny sort of colour he was too, from the sun in Africa.'

She sniffed. 'And one time he come home with a beard. "You'll shave that off, Michael!" the Mistress said, "before you eat a mouthful at this table."'

'What did he do?'

'Started laughing. But up he went and took it off up in the green bathroom. "You are like Queen Victoria!" he said when he came down, "like Queen Victoria."'

'What did she say?' Having a beard hardly seemed a crime.

'Nothing. Only put her mouth so.' Molly pursed her lips. 'The way she was when a person vexed her. God help her! The poor Mistress. But she was good to you in spite of him.' The needles clicked and Breda came in with a tray of things from the scullery.

'I wonder if I'll ever see them. My parents, I mean,' I said, pulling at a loose thread on my jersey.

'No! And better off without them. Your mother did a terrible thing when she left you. Your Ant told me.'

'A terrible thing? What kind of thing?'

'Ask no questions and you'll be told no lies. Why and what all day long!' and she slopped off to the linen cupboard for a tray cloth.

Anything personal to me seemed surrounded by troubles, and one could scarcely have anything more personal than a parent. My father gave trouble and my mother had obviously given trouble, for which I felt unreasonably responsible. Probably by the very nature of being in Ireland I was giving trouble too, but there didn't seem to be much I could do about it.

Was there no arena in which either of my parents could have shone? They weighed heavily on me, made me feel I must compensate and please. Why couldn't they, I thought with a degree of sourness, have stayed together instead of leaving me to shoulder the burden of their shortcomings while they were swanning about in Africa? My mother could have been dead or alive. She never wrote, or perhaps she did and the letters went into the wastepaper basket. My father wrote, but his missives from Kenya meant absolutely nothing.

'We went to Lake Rudolph,' he wrote, 'and saw crocs on the north shore.'

In his last letter he had done a badly executed pen and ink drawing of a crocodile which swam across the flimsy airmail page. Looking at it, in the pouring rain of a winter's day, it seemed inconsequential and unlikely.

'Shot guinea fowl today on the Northern Frontier of Kenya,' he wrote, and in another letter, 'Gerry and I camped out near Buffalo Springs.'

'Well for you!' as Molly would have said. 'Well for you to spend time in such frivolity,' while I mollified Grandmother, pacified Molly and was forced to ride ponies I couldn't control.

'Don't you wonder about your mother?' Maria said once when she bicycled over for lunch. Free from Miss Maiden, she was at college outside Dublin, sixteen now and home for the holidays.

'Wonder what? I expect she's dead by now.'

I wanted no further demands made on me by my parents,

not even wonder. We were lying on our stomachs on the grass, pinching clover heads between our fingers and sucking droplets of honey from the flowerets. The flavour, mixed with the scent of clover and hot green grass, was lovely. Overhead, bumble bees, cross at our pillaging, trundled in take-off like overloaded bombers.

'I meant, wonder where she went to,' Maria said. 'I mean, do you miss her?'

It seemed a stupid question to me. In our sort of life children were brought up by nannies or governesses whether their mothers were there or not, and often sent off to boarding school as young as the school would take them. Parents had other priorities. Not like the village mothers, whose young clustered around their skirts, fingers in noses and never boarded at school. The fact that my mother had vanished, simply disappeared, gave her a slight interest value to people outside the family, but that was all.

'I *know* where she went,' I said. 'To Mozambique. She went with a man called Peter who had a scar on his lip.'

'How do you know?' Maria sat up, startled.

How did I? Sometimes little scraps of knowledge, tiny torn pieces of remembrance, swam into my mind from somewhere far down, but like dreams, if I tried to grasp and discipline them, they were gone, skittered away, blown by the winds of the here and now. I had been conditioned to disapprove of both of them, which set up a double bind in my mind. Easier not to think of them than struggle with it.

'Will you go? I mean to Africa, one day?' asked Maria.

'I don't think I'd ever be let.' The thought of free will was so alien that it was impossible to consider it.

It was on a morning when I was nearly eighteen that a postcard came from my mother. It was addressed to me. It was Molly who told me. She had sent it up with the mail on the breakfast tray.

'From your mother,' she said conspiratorially, half titillated, half disapproving. "Love, Mummy" it says, bold as you like. At the bottom. I don't know what *they'll* say. It's from some place in Africa. I put it with your grandfather's letters.'

I went up to the breakfast room, dragging my feet. It was a study in Victorian bad taste – the wallpaper of glassy-eyed owls swaying on the banks of overblown mauve tulips clashed with a Persian rug. Heavy furniture dominated the room and the masks of foxes in their death throes were mounted on wooden plaques.

The postcard was lying among a pile of envelopes, a splash of colour. It was a picture of some African town, aqua sea, blue sky and a cliff dotted with white houses. All eyes swivelled as I sat down, picked it up and read in silence.

'Lovely here,' it said. 'Such beautiful views of the mountain!'

Grandfather's eyes bulged.

'Your mother wrote that?'

'Yes.'

'Then why don't you say so?'

The obvious answer, 'Because you have already read it,' would be thought impertinent, so I buttered my toast in silence.

'"Lovely here!"' he snorted, picking the card up between finger and thumb. 'It looks perfectly damnable to me. Some housing estate stuck on the side of a hill.'

It was the first communication I had ever had from my mother.

Strangely, almost the next day, a letter with a Uganda stamp came from my father. This was to bring even greater changes.

'Your father's written from some mad place in Uganda,' said Grandfather, looking at me over the top of the *Irish Times*. For once he didn't sound angry or tense when he mentioned my parent's name.

'Seems to think he has struck gold or tantalite or some such damn thing. Could be, of course.' He went back behind the paper, to emerge a few minutes later. 'He wants to pay your fare out to have a look at him, or for him to have a look at you. First damn time he's ever paid for anything.'

Stunned, I tried to look nonchalant. 'Can I go?'

'Depends. Walter Trench is over at Castle Oliver in Limerick for the summer. He's got some ranch out there in Kenya. You can't fly out alone. I'll speak to Walter. If he's going out, then he can take you and keep an eye on you. Wouldn't trust your father to keep an eye on anything. Suppose you could be based at the Trenches.'

He had great faith in Walter, who was by way of being my father's trustee, a job that nearly drove Walter mad over the years as the financial go-between. When my father wanted to manipulate his trust fund, Walter was supposed to stop him. The Trenches had an 8000-acre farm in Kenya and huge red-brick Castle Oliver in Ireland with a hundred and ten rooms. It was an ice-cold edifice with no electricity, and bathrooms about two acres from the bedrooms. Staying there once, I spent half the night trying to find one, down freezing passages with only a candle stump for light.

I opened my mouth to speak but the telephone rang and Grandfather lumbered off to answer it. I could hear him bellowing at the steward. When he came back I sat as still as a mouse, afraid to broach the subject or seem too keen. Keenness was the death knell of any suggestion to him. But there was a small ache in Grandfather for Africa – if he'd ever had to earn a living or branch out alone instead of inheriting estates at eighteen, he would have been up and off. He had an ache for the bush he'd never seen, plants which grew at altitudes unknown, flowers in some far-flung place unpicked, unseen, uncatalogued. On the rare occasions when there had been amicable dialogue between him and my father, it was always about trees or shrubs or plants in Africa.

'Lobelias ten foot high on the slopes of Mount Kenya,' my father would tell him, and however enraged or high Grandfather's temper, a flicker of interest sparked in his eye.

'Your father,' he growled now, 'thinks he can restore family finance. You've never seen such a letter as he wrote. Whole lot of codswallop if you ask me. Still, he may be onto something. He is supposed to be working for some damn American trading company out there. Instead, he's prancing around near the Mountains of the Moon and got all the damn fools he's working for to put up the money.'

'Money for what?'

'For mining this tantalite stuff. It's three thousand pounds a ton, according to him. They seem to use some spin-off from the elements in atomic power plants or jet engines or something. Can't make head or tail of the letter.'

'Can I go?'

'It depends on Walter. If he's going, yes. Otherwise no, and I don't want any trouble if you do go out there. Marrying some damn counter-jumper or anything like that. Had enough trouble with your father.' And he lumbered off to tie salmon flies in the smoking room. It was amazing that I was allowed to go. Amazing to fly halfway across the world with Walter.

More amazing still when I got there.

I had never seen my father in any milieu except Ireland, where, with a face too brown and foreign from the African sun and in suits hung so long in cupboards upstairs in his absence that they looked as if they neither fitted nor belonged, he shrank in dimension under the cold disapproval of his parents. When I got off the plane at Entebbe, the tall sunburnt man in khaki and a bush hat took on a new identity in my eyes.

– 18 –

He seemed so right in an African setting. An Arab at the airport in Ireland the day before had stood out in the crowd of travellers like a glum reveller from a fancy-dress party, but when we reached Cairo he got off and blended into the scene there like a chameleon. It was the same with my father: he belonged here.

As we walked towards the Land-Rover he moved with an assurance I had not known him to have. It was my first intimation of the freedom the African bush gave those who belonged to it.

Driving away towards Nairobi, he peppered me with questions about home, commented on my pink and white European look, and teased me about my neat pink and white dress. He obviously couldn't wait to get out of a town environment. The dresses I had bought, the high-heeled sandals and little white handbags were not going to be unpacked that month or the next, but at that time I didn't know it. I had an inkling of it, though, a week later, driving through the uncluttered space of the African bush towards Uganda. Birds stalked on the tawny plains, a feather effect behind their ears like Dickensian clerks with quill pens.

'Secretary birds,' he said. Later we slowed down to let giraffe with young cross the road in front of the vehicle. The country was growing wilder and wilder as we literally penetrated into remote parts of Uganda. He talked of subjects which had never crossed my path or hearing ... of pegmatite, tantalum, niobite, columbite ... of Seychellois and Walloons, panhandling and fool's gold. Meanwhile, we met fewer and fewer cars.

We stopped for the night at a rest house, where little transparent geckos ran across the ceiling in the room where I slept. Outside the door strelitzia plants grew like something from the Land of Oz, not quite real. Pawpaw for breakfast and tea with condensed milk and we were back jolting in the Land-Rover, while my father told me about prospecting and we drove deeper and deeper into what appeared to me to be uncharted territory. Behind us a backcloth of volcanic mountains, ahead an endless winding road. He described and named every hill, every mountain, every fork in the road with the same loving familiarity that my grandfather showed towards Annes Grove when he took people round the gardens or the estate. The difference here was that it was not some twenty acres of garden, but wild immense Africa not far from the Congo border.

'That's Schandl's Camp,' he said, pointing to a lightning-blasted tree stump near a rock, with a track beside it. 'He lived there when he was trying to conduct the Muhavura stream down the mountainside to Kisoro village.'

'Did he succeed?'

'No, he was a bit dimwitted. He led the stream over volcanic ash, which soaked it up like blotting paper. There's a lake up that track to the mountain. Full of fish. I pull them out occasionally. Not many people around here, so nothing's ever fished out.'

'I'd imagine,' I said, hoarse from shouting against the thumping of the Land-Rover as we were thrown from side to side by the ruts, 'I'd imagine there wouldn't be.'

'Wouldn't be what?'

'Wouldn't be people much around here.'

'A lot of gorilla though. Especially on Muhavura Mountain.'

It was wild and lonely, not a single human in sight. No house and the track we bumped along hardly deserved the title of road, when suddenly he said, jerking a hand from the wheel as we started to descend into a valley, 'Well, here we are then. I got the boys to build you a mud and wattle house. Cool in the heat and warm at night. Digging the foundations gave me a chance to look at the earth and rocks. Place is alive with minerals.'

Now I would be horrified. *Then* it epitomised all I felt Africa to be. The mad drive through the Mfumbiro Mountains with its secretary birds, giraffe and volcanic lakes just jumbled into an enormous exhaustion from the journey. But I felt conditioned to this crazy sunbaked world already. We had got up at dawn to drive while it was cool, through places I hadn't imagined could possibly exist – enormous mountains, crystal volcanic lakes seen fleetingly as we jolted up roads that, boulder-strewn, were like dried-up river beds. And now, below us, on top of a small hill on a valley floor, were curious beehive huts daubed white with the local clay. I felt a sense of total unreality as the Land-Rover slowed down and stopped near a few Africans who were digging pits nearby.

'What do you think of it?' he asked.

'Like something out of the *Boys' Own Annual* come to life,' I said. 'Who's that down there?' I pointed at a spiral of smoke just below us.

'Just Africans – porters, labourers – and there is a Seychellois chap called Joe in the valley. The boys say he's found a pocket of cassiterite. I think I'll try to buy his claim for the company.'

He took me for a walk to stretch my legs and pointed out tantalite. One piece weighing roughly fifteen pounds was just lying about on the hillside. We walked down to see Joe, who was panning beside a small stream which rose in the heart of a scooped-out volcanic mountain called Kihimbi. The Seychellois, panning with clear water from the stream, was looking for tancol crystals as well as jerking a container over a small fire to burn off the dross. There seemed to be deposits everywhere. He spoke of wolfram briefly with my father, who was more interested in a pegmatite ore body he'd uncovered which had contained quartz, beryl, mica and tancol crystals. Pegmatites were the result of molten matter being forced upwards through cooled granite by deep earth eruptions a millennium ago. When it reached its external destination it was called pegmatite and contained a lucky bag of various minerals. Exploding from ground to surface meant the component parts of these minerals got chucked about by impact, and everything, even the beryl vein, was patchy.

'Tantalite's the thing,' my father said. 'That's where I'll make it if my luck holds.'

'You should have been a geologist, sir,' Joe said. 'You've got a feel for it.' He smiled at me, white teeth in a brown, open face.

Days passed. I learnt about streak plates, bits of unglazed china on which you rub a mineral to identify it. Each mineral had its own streak colour. I watched Joe streak and I tried a bit of amateur analysis on some of the minerals.

This place was wild, it was beautiful. The Mfumbiro range made a backdrop behind us. Two of its mountains were volcanically alive. One of the volcanoes erupted that night while we sat over coffee by the camp fire, reddening the night sky. By contrast, another distant peak had a tablecloth of snow, and the nearest, Muhavura, hot and tropical, harboured gorillas which were fearless. Cowardice, my besetting Achilles' heel, loomed when they trooped out of a patch of deep shaded forest next day. Not many humans had come their way and they were far too tame for my peace of mind.

I was constantly amazed at my father's passion for the bush, for a life totally away from civilisation and, more than anything, his complete lack of nerves. I, far too imaginative, worried to death as to what might happen if the Land-Rover broke down or if one of us became ill. Miles to a town, no proper roads, no airstrip. The way he walked off into the bush or the mountains paralysed me. If he broke a leg, where would one start looking? How would one even know? But, as weeks passed, I realised that what seemed totally empty virgin bush had its own population. Amazing, fascinating, cosmopolitan people lurked in tents, in camps, prospecting, doing geological surveys, photographic safaris, studies of the gorillas. Never mind the fact that they were fifteen or twenty miles apart from each other, at least we weren't the only people, we and Joe and the diggers at the edge of the Belgian Congo.

Mr Swanepoel, the famous ivory poacher, was the nearest neighbour to our camp. He alone had a brick house on the periphery of the impenetrable forest. He affirmed that he was crowned King of the Pygmies and a close friend of the legendary Grogan. He had a horde of children of every shade, from pale lemon to coffee, was the unlikely partner of an aristocratic German baron who made a living killing crocodiles, and kept his children at smart boarding schools abroad, including Le Rosay in Switzerland. He was married to a Bugandan princess, as lithe and beautiful as a cat, who spent most of her time in Kampala.

We drove over to the White Fathers' Mission one afternoon to see their wolfram mine. They manufactured cigars on the side and packed them in banana leaves. My father bought a few boxes and then sat talking till dusk with one of the Irish Fathers from Cork. The Mission where they were was at the top of a totally perpendicular incline. We'd climbed in the Land-Rover like a fly on the wall to the building on the summit. I hadn't dared to look down, or sideways, at the abyss below till we parked outside the thatched, whitewashed structure.

The Mission was haunted. 'Not one little ghost,' the Irish Father said, 'the place is thick with them. It used to be a rest house once. People died and so forth, but I don't mind the odd ghost if he is quiet.'

We left carrying their warmth and good humour with us into the night.

Halfway down, on a particularly bumpy bit of road, the engine started playing up on the way to camp. It limped along, and after we'd tinkered with it for half an hour by torchlight it was still not running properly. There was a bad bit of road between us and home, so we turned and went back to Mr Podopolis's camp, which we had passed earlier. I hadn't met him but my father had known him for years.

He came out, large, potbellied, Greek and hospitable, in an immaculate white tropical suit, a gold tooth gleaming in the light of the small hurricane lamp he carried. I liked his style. He had opened a small mine and struck a rich seam. He spent a lot of time gambling with his profits in Kampala and had a host of well-trained African servants in camp and a large fridge run on a tinga-tinga engine. He was expansive and delighted to have company. 'You eat, you drink, you sleep. We feex the car inna morning.'

So we ate antelope meat roasted with dried fruit and drank excellent icy-cold dry champagne with it in his canvas mess tent. When I was shown to my sleeping tent at midnight, there was piping hot water for washing beside a canvas basin, a chair, a paraffin lamp, and another bottle of champagne and a glass beside the bed. 'Inna case you get thirsty in the night.'

Taking off my dusty shoes, I splashed my face with water and lay drinking Moët under the mosquito net. Outside in the African night the cicadas were sending out their curious science-fiction spacecraft bleeps. It was a far cry from Ireland and, with more than three-quarters of the bottle untouched, I fell asleep and dreamt of gorillas and Schandl's Camp, with the murmur of Podopolis's and my father's voices in the background, a smell of dust, and strange African noises in the distant forest.

'If I don't strike tantalite in large enough quantities, mining it won't be a viable proposition,' my father said the next night when we were back in camp. We were sitting on a log by the Muhavura stream drinking coffee laced with brandy to keep out the night cold. It was the first time I had heard a note of pessimism in his voice.

'Then bang goes seeing Annes Grove again and the conquering hero image falls away.' He sounded sad. 'My parents are such hypocrites. I don't know why I care; partly them, partly the place. Money is a dirty word to them. You've got no breeding if you talk about it, so my mother says … but if I make it I can go home. A lot will be overlooked. How they justify that attitude, I don't know. Left over from Queen Victoria's reign. That lot were a bunch of hypocrites if ever there were.'

'They didn't like your last marriage,' I said, stirring my coffee and brandy with a twig. 'You know how Gran goes on about being entertaining, how one must sing for one's supper, etcetera. That imperious way she has of waving her hand when she is bored, saying, "Entertain me! You are being dull!" When they got your last letter about your marriage in South Africa, she was really angry. She said, "Your father's married a bore." I thought she meant someone dull. I didn't realise that she meant Lisa was Afrikaans, a Boer.' Lisa, his second wife, was living in Nakuru with their two small children while he prospected.

We had spent the evening before with three Flemings who had camped on the other side of the mountain, where they had pegged a claim for a Belgian company. My father had been able to communicate with them and be understood by them in a kind of pidgin Afrikaans which he had picked up in Johannesburg. Afrikaans is a derivation of Dutch and they, from Antwerp, spoke a curious Dutch patois.

He fired their minds with prospecting fever in his inimitable style so that, as the evening wore on and their glasses clinked, they and even I began to see the bare Ugandan hillside as an Aladdin's cave. One of them, of solid farming stock, was not so sure. He was more inclined to think of farming the rich land over in the Belgian Congo than of nebulous mining schemes. A Walloon on safari joined us during the evening and I spoke to him in my bad French. He was on his way to Élisabethville, a place which had always fascinated me.

We got to bed late as the embers of the fire were dying. The hyraxes were making their winding-up-clockwork noises in the valley and the moon was hanging blood-red in the sky. It was a romantic place this, but a man's country. I was not at all sure that I was cut out to be a pioneer.

The mine where my father had pegged the company claim was showing a profit. It was justifying itself. But more equipment and firmer promises were needed from the directors in Nairobi. I got the impression from talking to him that he had stirred their imagination in this mad tantalite scheme of his much against their better judgement. That he had brought a breath of adventure and of the bush into their staid office lives, a whisper of a gamble which might pay off, but if left too long and without an injection of his enthusiasm their hearts might fail them. They might ask themselves what had come about to make such normally conservative businessmen like themselves embark on wildcat mining schemes. It certainly never had been the policy of their company to think along such lines.

'They must be kept on the boil,' he said, laughing, 'so we must go to Nairobi.' He described to me how he had first put the scheme to them in their panelled boardroom – he, so filled with enthusiasm that he had driven down from Uganda and, dusty and spattered, had stormed the office with a chamois leather bag of samples in his hand.

He had brought with him, too, a satisfactory report from a government geologist. They sat there, he said, in their pinstripes and silk ties with their mouths ajar, but they backed him. All the more incredible, it seemed to me, because he had no mining qualifications at all. But he, like Mrs Barry, could charm the birds off the trees.

It was a strange, fascinating world, but as a long-term way of life it wasn't for me. This never-never land, this fever pitch about minerals. Just as dawn was breaking we drove away and I knew that I would never come back. I no longer wanted to exchange one isolated way of life in Ireland for another in even more isolated Uganda. I wanted to see now what else Africa had to offer.

As we drove towards Kenya with the Land-Rover jammed with core samples in canvas bags, I felt acclimatised to the rock-strewn tracks and potholed roads. The landscape of thorn trees and baobabs was no longer strange. Africa was getting under my skin and I loved it already. My father sang as he drove. He had been pegging claims and labelling rock samples all week and was in high good humour, itching to fire up his directors in Kenya again.

It was clear that I could not camp in the bush indefinitely, he agreed. His mind was already on other things. So what was to be done with me? I could go with him to Nairobi for a few days or, he supposed, stay with the Trenches on their vast farm in the White Highlands, or perhaps go to the small upcountry town of Nakuru.

Grandfather had given my father some money for a small house, and he had bought fifteen acres of land outside Nakuru and put up a house on it. He called the house Ballyhimmock, the old name for Annes Grove – the place of the mound – presumably because of the barrow in the killeen. Lisa, his long-suffering wife, lived in it with their two small children. Long-suffering because he was always on the move, was hopeless with money, and half the time no one knew when he might return. Fortunately Lisa came from a family who loved the bush or the marriage might not have survived.

As I had not met Lisa and wanted to, I said I would stay at Ballyhimmock for a short time, just until I found something to do, so he took me there. It was not a success. Looking back, I feel it was a sad thing that Lisa and I, in the way sometimes of stepdaughter and stepmother, found in the end our relationship was strained. Things were not easy in her marriage and she saw me as a part of Annes Grove. There were people there that she could not forgive for their rejection of my father.

I, for my part, felt I had suffered enough as a child because of family feuds, so I had no sympathy in the matter and was sulky and withdrawn from her. The situation was tense, and my father, passing through again on his way to Uganda, could see that all was not well and was easy to persuade when I told him I had found somewhere else to live. His mind was on rocks and mining, not on relationships, and he was anxious to be gone.

– 20 –

Just before I left Annes Grove, Grandfather, feeling that I should have some serious preparation for life before I went out to Africa, had taken me for a drive down the Castle Avenue in his blue van. Parking it near his famous Chinese coffin tree, he cleared his throat and looked solemn. Dreading what might come, I gazed into space, while he struggled with his pipe, tamping down the tobacco and lighting match after match while he chose his words.

'There are good chaps and bad chaps, as you will find when you get to Kenya. Some chaps are damn bounders.' His eyes bulged at the mere thought of them. 'So keep clear of them.' He glared at me. 'Think of your upbringing and all that. Stick with your own sort.' And thus by a momentous effort having prepared me for the wicked world and instructed me on its pitfalls, he looked immensely relieved and drove home with a weight off his mind.

In reality, nothing that he could have said would have prepared me for upcountry Nakuru, which seethed with activity and was dominated by a rugger club, the Kenya Farmers' Association, wild men, polo and racing. But I loved it. I loved the Indian shops with their cascades of glittering sari material; the old settler ladies, ancient straw hats tied on under their chins, driving in to do their weekly shop in dusty pickup trucks; and the farmers like Black Harries, who was so enormous he kept his corduroy pants up with rope.

Sunburnt men in khakis and aertex shirts came in from their farms to buy feed and spare parts, and on race day there was *style* – high heels and pretty hats and pink gins at the Rift Valley Club.

Away from Ireland and drunk with freedom I saw life as an enormous glittering Christmas tree and myself with *carte blanche* to take what I liked from it. Adventures on offer appeared to me numerous and exciting. Dozens of opportunities flashed tempting signals all around me, like neon lights. I was out of the goldfish bowl that was Annes Grove and into the wide blue ocean of life. Everything in this new free world seemed so heady and exciting. I felt like Rip Van Winkle. I had fallen asleep in Victorian Ireland and woken a century later in 1950, in magic, permissive, sun-filled Kenya.

I had to earn some money, so I tried nursing for size at the Nakuru War Memorial Hospital, where there were almost more nurses than patients. There were no training schools for nurses in Kenya, so the idea was to try your wings before you set sail for South Africa or London to train. Of the five of us, three were settlers' daughters from the White Highlands. One, called Peedle, brought her own personal servant with her, who dossed down in the hospital labour lines, unbeknown to the authorities.

When it was Peedle's turn to make the mandatory ten beds every afternoon, she went to the veranda, put her fingers in her mouth, emitted a piercing whistle and along came Maritime, who had hung around during the day in case she needed him, just out of Sister's sight. Peedle's afternoon bedmaking was during the Sisters' tea break so no one was any the wiser and Maritime made half of the men's ward beds.

With the four Kenyan girls I arranged bowls of flowers, answered bells and chattered. The patients said that just looking at us in our butterfly caps and white linen dresses cheered them up. There was only one really large ward, the rest were private or semi-private. I weighed the new babies before and after they had been fed, and carried them, cocooned in white flannelette, to their mothers. They had pink screwed-up faces and tiny hands like little starfish, and smelt delicious.

'Tell us about Ireland,' the maternity ward patients urged, bored in the gaps between feeding their babies. They never seemed to tire of hearing about it and I couldn't understand why. Kenya to me was like a glass of champagne, everything to me was festive and exotic. Blue skies, jacaranda trees, giraffe and elephant even on the roads, the space, the people, the soda lake below Nakuru pink with thousands of flamingos, and all that endless sunshine. Servants padded about in long nightshirt-type kanzus with scarlet sashes. Everything was magic, even the huge stars over the Longonot Crater behind the town.

Work was not too arduous. We were on wards from six a.m. till two p.m. one day, from two until six the next, and then had a whole day off. We started our day off with breakfast in bed, when a houseboy in a red fez and kanzu padded into your bedroom with a tray laden with bacon and eggs, pawpaw, toast and hot coffee. All the nurses' bedrooms opened onto a veranda with steps that led off it into a jacaranda-filled garden, so no one knew when we came and when we went. We were not expected to sign in or out, but in spite of this no harm came of it and we kept reasonable hours.

Although Nakuru was small, the staff at the hospital had a hectic social life. Many of the English sisters (mostly in their twenties) were from St Thomas's or Guy's in London out on two-year contracts, and were soon snapped up by the Kenya bachelors and married.

On Friday evenings the nurses went out to supper at the local hotel with various escorts, for mulligatawny soup, tilapia fish and fruit salad. No variation! Or to a spluttering film at the local cinema where the cast seemed to swim in the fog, making it hard, as you ate your Rolos, to follow the plot. Occasionally the film snapped in two from old age and we trooped back to the hospital to raid the kitchens. We perched on the metal-topped kitchen tables and devoured everything we could find that was edible in the fridges. Junket, jelly, food labelled 'Diabetic' or 'Special Diet' were all grist to our mill and the catering staff had to start all over again the next morning, but no one ever complained.

On my birthday a Kenyan called B.J. invited me out. He farmed a thousand acres of wheat. Not sure of where we would go, I put on a white lace dress with a string of pearls. He appeared in a checked shirt and khaki trousers and opened the passenger door of his car for me, nodding affably without uttering a word. The venue turned out to be a place called the Prairie Inn. Well off the road, it was festooned with fairy lights. A sprinkling of brooding characters crouched over drinks. The band was deafening, which didn't create a problem, as B.J. was not into small talk. He seated me on a barstool, fetched me an iced tomato juice and a beer for himself, then lapsed into silence. Occasionally I shrieked a platitude above the noise of the band and then we both stared into space. He seemed to take his territorial dominance very keenly, glowering balefully at a young pink-faced Englishman in a Charterhouse tie who had unwittingly strayed where, as several people agreed, no 'Pom' had any right to be. Several other young farmers swaggered in as if they owned Kenya, ordered drinks and glared round suspiciously for no discernible reason.

It was like a frontier town in a film, and even more was to come. I had spilt some of my tomato juice on my white dress and was dabbing at it, the farmers were shouting to each other about night-ploughing with lanterns over the earsplitting sound of the band, when suddenly the double doors opened and a man, aged about fifty and armed to the teeth, came in. He was thickset but walked lightly on his feet, swaying slightly from the weight of two huge guns on his hips. I had never seen anyone like him before. He had a cauliflower ear, a broken nose and a habit, I soon discovered, of grasping your hand in a bone-snapping grip.

He had been one of Al Capone's bodyguards in Chicago in the twenties, someone explained, and he was about to become a legend in Kenya, Malaya or the Congo, or for that matter wherever there was trouble.

'A good man,' opinion around me agreed, 'to have in a tight spot.'

He was in fact a mercenary.

He walked up to my barstool, surveyed my white tomato-spattered dress with some surprise and, stretching out a hand the size of a small leg of mutton, said, 'Davo Davidson's the name, Cobber! Put it there!'

Later in the evening he repaired with a crowd to an outside veranda where a table and chair had been lined up to face the wall and a large facsimile of a playing card with five or six pips had been pinned up on a stand behind them. Davo sat down in the chair with his back to the stand and, at a roar from the crowd of 'Now, Davo!' put his feet on the table top and, kicking the chair over, somersaulted and came up in a crouch, guns blazing, shooting with deadly precision through every pip on the card. The smell of cordite at such close range was acrid. The noise was indescribable and, having earned a drink, Davo went off to be fêted at the bar.

This, I thought, is a strange place.

'Kenya is beautiful,' I wrote to Annes Grove. 'There are some amazing plants here,' and even more amazing *people*, I could have said, but I stuck to the flora and fauna. How would they react to a description of Davo and his six-shooters? Or to the Italian who had come into my life at the local rugby club and was swearing undying love? It seemed better not to mention either of them, or the fact that Walter had left for his castle and that my father had vanished into Uganda again in search of God-knew-what.

Not that I was sorry. I was off the leash and as free as air, answerable to no one except dear old Matron McDougal at the hospital. She had beaming brown pop-eyes like sucked humbugs and said that as we were still very young we must not be exposed to anything that upset us.

But upset I had been a day or two before, when I had begged Theatre Sister to be allowed to see an operation. Unfortunately the combination of heat, blood and smell of ether had proved my undoing, much to the icy fury of the surgeon.

'Get her out of here! Who let her in?' he shouted, as I staggered out into the scrub room, gulping and retching.

The Italian, whom I had left out of my letter home, had appointed himself my knight in armour and was exactly twice my age. Vincenzo had black curly hair, white teeth and curious knee-high laced boots which he never seemed to change. He dogged my every step like a gaoler when I was off duty. He collected me from the hospital and watched me like a hawk. Oddly, for someone who said I was perfect, he seemed to disapprove of almost everything I said or did. Unconsciously perhaps, I saw him as a father figure. At any rate I put up with him even when he was being particularly irritating and given to lectures, having somewhere got the idea that he was my custodian. He was also insanely jealous.

'Why do you talk to that man?'

'Where you go last night?' and, more frequently and querulously, 'Why do you keep me waiting? Why you never on time?'

After a dance one night he took me to a romantic, beautiful hill overlooking Lake Elmenteita. It was a warm night, the smallest breeze in the air and the moon, still up, hung like a halved golden *spaanspek* (melon). It was not yet dawn. The Italian carried a bottle of champagne and two glasses from the car on the road above, and we sat for hours in the African moonlight listening to the staccato bleep of the cicadas and the call of bushbabies down near the water. Below, as faint fingers of light touched the lake, the wings of hundreds of sleeping flamingos made a rose-madder mist which blurred with the dawn sky.

This, I thought, is fairytale country.

Two or three flamingos rose and flew low, necks outstretched. At the same time Vincenzo, digging in his pocket, brought out a sapphire ring. As I watched the sun come up, I said 'yes' to his proposal when I should have said 'no'.

My only excuse was lack of coping skills. It seemed less bother to say 'yes'. Refusing him when he had gone to so much trouble seemed ungrateful. Like Grandfather, he liked one to be in agreement with him.

Overjoyed, he drove me back to the hospital, and as we passed the night watchman at the gate, hunched in an army coat over his brazier, Vincenzo, full of enthusiasm, was listing plans for the future. *His* plans, I noted uneasily. I heard him speak of Brazil, of buying tracts of farming land there and opening them up. Thousands of virgin acres untouched, unfenced and remote. Warning lights began flashing in my head, and after that night we seemed to be fighting all the time.

It was he who put the announcement of our engagement in the *Kenya Weekly News*, which I read in a detached sort of way. Grandfather, however, six thousand miles away, hearing of it through Walter, was not so detached and responded cholerically. A furious diatribe arrived at the hospital in a bright green Irish airletter, peppered with heavily scored phrases. I could see that a strong line was being taken.

'Most unsuitable liaison! Consider your background!' he wrote. 'Is the man Catholic?' And, as a parting shot, 'Your allowance from me, let me remind you, may be stopped at my discretion!' and 'Your father must be very worried.'

Fortunately he seemed blissfully unaware that I had not seen my father for months.

The next objection came from the Catholic priest at Nakuru, who arrived at the hospital and for some reason didn't appear to think it was a good idea either. Vincenzo, he said, was a lapsed Catholic, far too old for me, and how could I know my own mind at barely eighteen, and so on. He was Irish and didn't like to be argued with either – I wondered who had alerted him. I suppose I might, perversely, have tied the knot and gone to Brazil with Vincenzo, to sit forlornly in the middle of nowhere while he fenced his virgin acres, but somehow I had a core of sense and knew it would never work.

Fate at this point intervened. Rushing to get ready for an evening with Vincenzo, while he sat scowling in his motorcar because I was half an hour late, I hung his sapphire on the metal spur of the bath tap. The bathroom window was near the drive and I could hear him hooting impatiently. As I flicked my bathtowel over my shoulder, it caught the ring hanging precariously on the tap. It dislodged, fell into the empty bath, bounced against the side and vanished in the last swirl of water down the plughole. It was an archaic plughole, huge, with a one-bar grid. I leaned over the bath in a panic, gazing down the round black space where Vincenzo's investment had vanished without so much as a gurgle. He was passionate about the ring, which seemed to me to be more his hard-earned investment than a symbol of love, and he was given to gazing at it from time to time with satisfaction.

He hooted again, and with no time to investigate further, I threw on my clothes and breathlessly arrived at the car, where he was tapping with impatient fingers on the steering wheel. I managed to keep my hand out of sight for a while, but Vincenzo, longing as usual to gaze at the ring, picked up my hand. Sadly, I had to confess that the equivalent of thousands of yards of fencing wire for his Brazilian dream farm lay somewhere in the bowels of the hospital drains.

His Latin rage rose and fell like heavy seas in a storm. Banging his hands on the table and shouting with anger, he went from total disbelief to castigation.

Later, pipes were unscrewed and a grating in the bath drain removed, to no avail. Bravely he told me he was prepared to forgive me but I had sensed he wanted to mould me to his will, which would have been no easy thing and would not have suited me at all.

Now that the ring was gone it seemed to me a good time to say 'Goodbye,' and soon afterwards I decided to go to Nairobi.

As I'd had no communication with my father for some
months, I thought I should let him know I was leaving
Nakuru. Lisa was now with him and no longer at
Ballyhimmock, and my father and grandfather were not in
contact at that time because of bad feeling between them.
News of their quarrel came from Walter, who had come back
from his Irish castle and was striding about on his Kenyan
acres.

My father, Walter said, had it in his mind to build a game
lodge on a piece of no man's land between Uganda, the Congo
and Rwanda. From there he planned to take tourists on safaris
to see the mountain gorillas near Schandl's Camp. He had
asked Grandfather to fund it in return for a half-share. For
some reason this talk of camps and gorillas drove Grandfather
wild. He had never seen a gorilla in his life and could not see
why anyone else would want to, or why he should put up the
money for what he described as 'a lot of half-baked tourists
to goggle at apes', so acrimonious letters had passed between
them and no money sent.

But my father, who had the bit between his teeth, went
ahead with his plans anyway and built a lodge on the misty
no man's land between the three countries. He called it The
Travellers' Rest and, full of enthusiasm, gave up prospecting
for the time being.

The concept was brilliant. He was, in fact, years ahead of

his time; and although Grandfather considered the project completely crazy, nowadays people travel thousands of miles to see the mountain gorilla in the wild. He was a wonderful ideas man, but the trouble was that, as in most of his schemes, there was a great lack of planning.

For instance, Lisa was supposed to be in charge of the food, but – brought up in Africa – she had never even boiled an egg, nor cared to do so. Her idea of catering was to hand the cook supplies and instruct him to prepare them. Unfortunately the Rwandan cook spoke no known language, so disaster struck and meals were inedible.

'What ees these?' a mystified Belgian guest was heard to enquire, poking at an unidentified offering on his plate. But no one seemed to know.

The guests, sick of tinned food and brick-hard bread, were not at all mollified by my father's helpful suggestion that, as there was good duck-shooting nearby, perhaps they would like to shoot for the pot.

'I may be a bloody Dutchman, but I pay for my food, I don't catch it!' an irate guest told Lisa who, by now thoroughly bored with gorillas, guests and thick mists, had taken up painting.

At the height of all this someone remembered that there were tilapia in a nearby lake and a 'fishboy' in a banana-frond hat was appointed to sit on the banks from dawn till dusk pulling out the fish, which were delicious.

But this was not the end of the dramas. My father ran out of petrol twice on his way to collect parties of earnest gorilla viewers. They were not amused. Bits fell off his car at crucial moments, pit latrines collapsed in heavy rains, and water mysteriously dried up in the home-made shower when guests were covered in soap.

Nor was my father often at the seat of custom, but some miles away clearing land for an airstrip, which was his latest idea. It occupied his time for months, clearing away vast boulders of lava and pumice stone and levelling the ground. The idea was that plane-loads bulging with guests would land and disgorge tourists, who could then be driven to the camp. He had even designed a brochure showing happy package-tour people waving and smiling on their way to The Travellers' Rest.

'Little do they know, poor things,' said Lisa, yawning.

But in the end only one ashen-faced pilot landed his Tiger Moth, heart in mouth. There were too many mountains in the line of approach for safety and the aviation authorities refused my father a licence.

'If you would like to move a few mountains we could reassess,' they told him. 'Great place for an airstrip if you are into kamikaze.'

Sadly, the logistics at the camp were eventually too much for everybody. The Travellers' Rest had become a travellers' nightmare! It was time to move on and it was sold soon afterwards to a man from Johannesburg called Baumgartel, who turned it into a viable concern and became well known.

I have a diary of my father's written in those days before his Parkinson's slowed him down. It is full of optimism and descriptions of journeys to remote parts of Africa. There are prospecting sagas, accounts of cars breaking down or people driving into them in godforsaken places. Projects come and go in the diary with reckless enthusiasm. Malaria, and once blackwater fever, caused temporary hiccoughs and then you turn a page and find him off and away again, prospecting for tantalite or columbite, starting a company called Purposes, drilling boreholes or fighting in Ethiopia. He was one of those people you think of as lovable when you are not with them and totally infuriating when you are.

– 22 –

Robin, the man whom at this time I had not yet met but whom I was to marry, dreamt for years, when he was at boarding school in Scotland and had never been to Africa, of Colonel Ewart Grogan's lands at Taveta on the Tanganyika–Kenya border. On awakening in the freezing Scottish dawn he would, groggy with sleep, remember vivid dreams of great baobab trees and fishponds and narrow red roads, of lions roaring and a curious landscape which he didn't know then was the African bush. When circumstances eventually took him out to Africa and he one day set off to work for an unknown Ewart Grogan on a remote East African farm, as he rounded a curve in the rutted road he saw with a sense of homecoming the place of which he had so often dreamt.

I had never dreamt of Kenya but I had the same feeling when I first saw it, of a place familiar to me and loved, to which in the natural course of events I had come. I was happier now than I had ever been.

The Kikuyu people, who predominated around Nairobi at that time, were to me fascinating. What I liked very much was the descriptive way in which they spoke of things, illustrating with hand and tongue a thing that had happened, so that it came alive. One spoke to me once of years passing, and conjured up a picture of a great fig tree, the leaves falling, each leaf another year of his life. Usually, as a tribe, it was more customary to speak of each individual year not as a number but in a very descriptive way.

There was the Year of the Iron Snake, the Year of the Red Dust and the Year of Many Black Cattle. Each year had a name of its own, and the events in it then fell into place like pieces of a jigsaw puzzle. During the Year of the Many Black Cows the Kikuyu had become rich and bought new wives and increased their shambas. 1897 was the Year of Many Sweet Potatoes, 1808 the Year of the Jigger and 1900 the Year in which there was Much Hunger. During the Year of the Iron Snake the Europeans had organised a railway from Mombasa up to Nairobi. Men from the coast had worked on it with the Indian navvies, and Asmani, an aged Swahili friend, described to me once lions circling round while he and some of his friends cleared bush for the railway.

'I was good at this job, memsahib,' he said simply. 'At this job with the Iron Snake I was *mzuri sana* [Swahili for 'very good'] but I did not stay.'

'Why not, Asmani?' I asked.

He explained to me that a friend of whom he was particularly fond had been taken by a Tsavo lion whilst he slept beside the railway track at night. As he lay in his kikoi on the ground with the night sky bright with huge stars, the lion had come, roared once, and taken him.

'It seemed to me then,' said Asmani bleakly, 'that it might well next time be I who was taken by the simba.' So he wisely went back to Mombasa, which was too built up for lions and safer. However, there was no doubt in his mind when this had all happened: it was in the Year of the Iron Snake.

In my memory, the year coming was to be the Year of My Engagement and it was also to be the Year of the Mau Mau and, as it happened, the Year when Grandfather Died.

'What are you going to do now?' Walter Trench asked. He had come down from his farm to see me and was sitting opposite me in Nairobi's favourite Kenya nightspot, the Travellers' Club in Government Road. Having brought me to Kenya he felt responsible and would report back to Grandfather, I had no doubt.

My enthusiasm to sample life made him nervous. A week before he had talked me out of yet another adventure, a job I had been offered on a huge plantation in the Belgian Congo. I had been interviewed at the Norfolk Hotel by a dark Frenchman, very *soigné* in a linen suit. He was the East African agent for a Monsieur Trouilles, who had detailed him to sift applicants for a job near Élisabethville. I had been all set to go. I was to have been flown to Entebbe in Uganda, where a small private plane belonging to the plantation would meet me and fly me on to the Congo. The salary seemed enormous and all I apparently had to do was to teach English to a little Belgian girl, or not even teach it, come to that.

'You just speak to her in *l'Anglais toujours*,' said the French agent. 'There are no lessons.'

But Walter had intervened. 'You can't possibly accept that,' he said firmly. 'They are miles from anyone you know. No way out perhaps, except in their plane, and no one knows anything about them either.'

I wonder what my life would have been if I'd gone. Cables had been flying to and fro after my interview and my seat to Entebbe was booked, but Walter stopped it. At that time I thought him very boring, but he was technically my guardian and took the responsibility seriously. He had even driven down from his farm and taken me out for an agitated lunch; and pointed out so many pitfalls that I had cabled the Trouilles and said I couldn't come.

So here I was, still in Nairobi and sitting at the Travellers' Club, the pulsebeat of the town, having dinner with Walter. While we were talking, men from the Kenya Regiment were clattering up and down the stairs of the nightclub, handing in their revolvers and Sten guns at the desk to be locked in the safe by an amazing middle-aged lady in a sequined fishtail dress, before moving to the dance-floor. The Mau Mau was at its zenith. Most of the soldiers in uniform had just come down from fighting around the Aberdare Forest.

'So what are you going to do now?' asked Walter again.

'I am going to join Ethiopian Airways as a hostess,' I said, picking the olive out of my martini.

'You're going to *what*?'

'Join Ethiopian Airways as a hostess.'

'But you don't speak any languages!'

'I do. French, and a bit of Swahili and some Gaelic. And Alec,' referring to a Greek airline director friend, 'has arranged it all. The uniform is green, my favourite colour. I'll be based in Addis and paid in American dollars.'

'The chances of an Ethiopian speaking Gaelic are pretty remote,' said Walter, laughing, but I ignored him. 'Their aeroplanes are held together with bits of string.'

'Rubbish!'

'They look like a Chinese kite, or cassata ice-cream or something – all those colours!'

'Very exotic.'

'Their pilots are as black as your hat.'

'Striking a sober note with the ice-cream colours, no doubt.'

'I have never heard anything so stupid!'

'I think it's tremendous,' I said. 'It's exciting. I'm young yet – why not!'

But somehow that fizzled out too.

23

An adventure cropped up later purely by chance in the early 1950s. MGM were in Kenya to shoot *Mogambo*. They had just about taken over Nairobi, and the New Stanley Hotel was their stamping ground. Clark Gable was constantly in the foyer, grinning with a 'Look at me oh!' smile. Ava Gardner had been in the Travellers' Club dancing in her stockinged feet. Grace Kelly was about. Frankie Sinatra had flown over briefly to see Ava. And somehow in the extraordinary way things just seemed to happen in Kenya, a double was wanted for Grace Kelly because Pippa Brue Smith, who had been doubling, was ill.

So I was roped in! I didn't really qualify in looks or height, but doubles are scarcely ever identical twins. Being told to take taxis everywhere and charge them to MGM, and told to buy myself a heap of safari clothes at Whiteaway Laidlaw and the film company would pay, was heady stuff. On top of that, to go on a safari down to the Mara, where America millionaires went after elephant and where the bulk of the shooting was taking place, seemed better than almost anything. It certainly made Ethiopian Airways pale into insignificance.

However, it was a peculiarly impersonal world, and once the glamour and excitement of the idea had worn off I wasn't so sure it was all it was cracked up to be. Two very unpleasant men had argued over my head as whether I had blonde or red hair, with me sitting awkwardly between them, ignored except for my tresses by both. In those days of being brainwashed by the potential glamour of films, one thought oneself lucky to be involved in however minor a way. Otherwise, stared at like a heifer in a cattle mart, I would have walked out.

'You're on!' one of them said laconically at last. The other patted me vaguely on the shoulder. He was the one who thought I would do. Demoralised and cross, I went up to Wardrobe.

'Doesn't matter much what colour your hair is,' said Gerda Williams, the wardrobe mistress. 'Most of it has to be pushed under a huge Bombay bowler anyway.' She threw a prickly browny-beige divided skirt over me to try for size, and a white flannel shirt with long sleeves. An orange scarf to be knotted tightly around the throat was the next item; not over-comfortable at seven thousand feet, it was going to be murder in the Mara on the plains.

'The problem,' Gerda said, demoralising me further, 'is going to be shoes. Grace Kelly has long, elegant feet.'

Mine were short, size four and a half, and stubby. However, her feet were very narrow and because the leather of the shoes was soft and supple, my feet ended wedged about an inch from the toe, so *that* was all right.

At Wilson airport next morning with a suitcase full of Horrockses cotton dresses, mosquito spray and two hundred cigarettes, I clocked in. There were a dozen people sitting around smoking, who looked as if they had had an all-night party. One enormous man, who was Clark Gable's double and had once been a hairdresser, sat beside me. He took off his white felt Stetson and showed me, engraved in the lining, 'From Clark Gable to Arthur – the best double ever.'

'Gave it to me himself, he did,' he said. 'You don't need those fags, nipper, you'll get a hundred free Camels a day in camp.'

We flew up to the Mara where there was an airstrip in the middle of nowhere, the only sign of life among thorn trees and barren Africa. The tsetse flies were up and about in evidence and biting strongly as we got out of the aircraft. Before we landed, while we were still circling over the airstrip, I had seen a puff of bright ochre-red dust travelling at great speed and faster than a dust devil. This materialised into a Land-Rover with hood down, driven by two men stripped to the waist and burnt nearly black by the sun. With enormous black beards and ochre-red from the dust, they screeched to a halt beside the Dakota.

'Trucks coming to fetch ya,' said one laconically.

More clouds of dust, and a few safari trucks with no roofs and open sides churned up alongside. We were crowded into three of them, two more were for wardrobe, cameras and baggage, and we were off to camp, red dust churning chokingly into our throats and nothing to be seen – just the narrow track and fever trees whose branches grazed the sides of the trucks, and a few Thomson's gazelles leaping out of the way, and bush and more bush, and boiling heat. The tsetse flies were biting ferociously now.

Nipper seemed to be my new name: "Cos you're just a kid, see.' There were an inordinate number of Cockneys on this unit, technicians mostly, and they mixed amiably with the Yanks.

Suddenly we rounded a corner and there was the camp. Row after row of tents, some under trees, with a big clearing alongside the Mara. There were streets of tents. A huge dining marquee, an entertainment tent, a Red Cross tent, an enormous ping-pong table, a few mobile homes, and a film screen strung across two vast trees. People were thronging everywhere in jeans, shorts or swim trunks – white hunters, advisers, continuity girls, black cooks, bearers, film people, technicians, nurses and a doctor.

'Food's flown in from a Nairobi 'otel every day,' said someone Cockney.

'You get free Camel cigarettes and as much Coca-Cola as you can drink,' Arthur told me.

''Oo's the nipper?' one of the cameramen asked, jerking his thumb at me.

'Doubling for Kelly, on a month's stint,' Arthur told him.

The canvas tent I shared with a Greek girl who was doubling for Ava had a bathroom area divided off by a flap from the two camp beds and canvas table. Africans tottered to and fro with *debis* (containers) of water boiled over a bonfire. We needed it to get rid of the dust. I looked like a Red Indian and my hair was definitely red now. The trouble was that there was prickly grass under the canvas of the bath, so when I sank voluptuously down into the water I was jabbed.

I wanted to see Grace Kelly – she was leaving soon.

I saw her briefly, sitting with a book outside her tent and wearing large spectacles with tortoiseshell rims. She was reading about African birds and had binoculars on her knee. She wore no make-up and looked a thoroughly nice girl – young, pretty and serious. We spoke briefly and I liked her. We, the minions, had moved into camp and the stars were leaving.

The camp was full of talk. Stories of the stars abounded. Frank Sinatra had flown in to Nairobi, adding fuel to the gossip that he was madly in love with Ava Gardner. One day Ava decided to shower mother-naked out of doors to 'feel the African sun on her body', and everyone in the vicinity in the camp had to lower their tent flaps and their eyelids while she indulged in her ablutions.

Up next morning while it was still dark and mercifully cool, I had a thick layer of Max Factor make-up applied to my face with a wet sponge. When it hardened, my face cracked if I smiled. The topi was wedged on so tightly that

my forehead ached. The tsetse hadn't started biting yet –
count your blessings! The day's shooting as it applied to us
was explained over a loud-hailer.

'White hunters in safari cars will circle the area and drive
the game towards your truck. You'll start up then and drive
through it while the cameras roll. Idea is virgin Africa, see.
Masses of game parting before yer truck like the bleeding
Red Sea before Moses. Light's got to be right though.'

We set off in convoy down the narrow track as day broke.
Truck after truck. The Red Cross wagon full of Disprin and
snakebite kits, the lunch wagon refrigerated and full of five-
star food flown in from the New Stanley, the camera crews
chewing gum, the directors, the technicians, the white
hunters, Land-Rovers with cameras mounted on them – and
us, with various hangers-on.

Each truck churned up its own quota of dust, and there
were no sides, no window glass, to our safari car. The heat
was unspeakable. My face, varnished with pink Max Factor
pancake, itched like crazy and the tsetse flies woke up and
began biting in earnest. The game didn't co-operate. There
was a lot of Africa for it to run through without coming
straight at our truck. There were hours of sitting ahead, plus
a lot of ripe swearing and a lot of swatting at dudus,
swallowing dust and wondering why the hell one was there
in the first place.

The English contingent were playing cricket and I had
smoked so many Camels out of boredom that I felt kippered.
I had decided that all Americans were rude, especially
Americans involved in making a film. They used four-letter
words like vowels, thickly peppering their conversation, and
the more the big game skittered across the horizon, the more
tempers frayed around the edges. Mercifully, as the day broke
and the sun came up, the animals weren't going to be around
but lying down during the heat of the day, so we wound our
way back to the camp, swallowing dust like vacuum cleaners.

The real adventure was a couple of days later. Driving home in deepening dusk after an evening session of trying to get the game to do their Red Sea bit, we were churning up the dust which lay in the headlights on the narrow track, fenced between two lorries full of equipment and a couple of safari trucks ahead. The VHF crackled and someone called up from the front, 'Pride of lion on your right! Nine of them and two lionesses! It's right alongside the road. Can't miss 'em.'

The lorry in front stopped and turned off the engine for everyone to have a look or take pictures. We couldn't see very well, but the lionesses were angry, a certain amount of tail-lashing was going on, and our safari car was the genuine 1912 model, for film use, so it had no sides. The ignition key turned in the truck ahead but the engine didn't turn over, it just shuddered and died. The lionesses were getting angrier. One got up and started padding forward, eyes green in the headlights. We could go neither back nor forwards ourselves. Panicky, someone radioed the white hunters' car.

'Have broken down, pride of lion alongside. What do we do? Over.'

Bunny Allen's voice came over unmistakably: 'This is Africa. No panic. Don't get your knickers in a twist! See you in camp! We'll chill the beer for you. Over and out!'

The lionesses and young gazed at us unblinkingly, their eyes green in the truck lights. One growled.

'Helpful bastards those white hunters,' one of the Cockneys said bitterly. 'What are they supposed to do then,' someone asked; 'shoot the bleeding lot to save your skin? This is a game sanctuary, this is.'

'Yer, and wot abaht us?'

One of the technicians in the safari car behind intrepidly jumped out, went to the lorry bonnet, lifted it and fiddled around. The truck spluttered into life eventually, but it was a long half-hour and a longer drive back to camp as, now we were out of convoy, the leading truck took a wrong turning.

The days dragged. I went out to look for elephant on foot with a lecherous white hunter. You live and learn. We found steaming elephant droppings and heard their stomachs rumbling and he told me a lot of tall stories about elephants charging. 'Hang onto me, sweetie, and you'll be fine.' Time passed in a blur. The camera crew shot yards of film daily and we drove further and further afield, earlier and earlier in the morning, looking for game which hadn't yet been scared by the Red Sea Round-up. Ava Gardner's double had an appendix scare and had to be flown back to Nairobi for an emergency operation at the Maia Carberry.

Kippered with Camels as I was, and gassy with Coke, the routine was losing its charm.

24

The last week, coming back in the evening and parched for a drink, one of the cameramen told me there was a cable waiting for me in camp. I knew instinctively before I opened it that Grandfather was dying. Standing with it in my hands, I could hear on the track behind me the shouting of Africans coming in to prepare the evening meal. There was a smell of red dust, and a few spots of rain on dry earth. I knew I had to go. There was a heart tug in that cable. The same old 'I hate … I love' feeling. Ireland and Annes Grove always hit me below the belt, and he to me was Ireland and undoubtedly Annes Grove.

It was strange standing there, holding the telegram in that African heat, slapping at the tsetse fly on my bare legs, and being pulled emotionally and mentally halfway across the world.

'Elephant herd just below camp!' someone said to someone behind me.

'Howzit, Nipper! Bad news?' a white hunter asked me, but he didn't really wait for a reply. Dust-streaked, he wanted a beer and a shower. It would be late winter, early spring now in Ireland. Grey, still days, snowdrops coming out. Molly in the kitchen or in the Servants' Hall mending socks in her rocking chair. Where would he be? In hospital or at home? Home more likely. Hospitals spelt an invasion of privacy. He'd always said that *if* he died – not *when* he died of course

– he'd die in his own home, with his dogs around him. In spite of the great lump that seemed to be shaping up in my throat and making it hard to swallow, I couldn't help smiling. Not his family about him but his dogs! So typical! Animals before people. To die in the hunting field was the family's acme of the right way to go. Preferably on one's own land of a broken neck, with one's favourite hunter cropping grass nearby, but this (it would have saddened him) was not happening to him. The cable said 'a stroke' and that made sense. Memories of him roaring, red in the face with rage, of Gran saying, 'You'll die of a stroke with that temper!'

Slowly I folded the cable, shoved it back into the orange envelope and went to Continuity to say I would want a seat on the early-morning bumpy little plane which flew over the Mara to Nairobi. I'd have to see my father who, never recovering, seemed now moribund in a small house on the lip of the Great Rift Valley. Faint stirrings of hope. Would bygones be bygones at this late date? The feud dropped? Could he have been asked for as well?

'Dangerously ill, and asking for you. Come at once,' my own cable read, but when I got to the Rift Valley farmhouse, I knew before I spoke that my father's cable had not said that at all. He was sitting up in his wheelchair, his face rigid from the advanced Parkinson's that even El Dopa, a drug derived from velvet beans, did little to alleviate. It was difficult for him to speak, and when he did, it was in that hollow computer voice, the hallmark of his Parkinson's.

'It's all too late, it's all too late.' It *was* too late.

His father's attitudes had been set in a mould in the 1880s and everything that he had assimilated since that time was laid on those foundations. My father's marriages had shattered him; and the money he had asked for and taken to Africa, an outrage. To Grandfather, the financial problems of an individual could not be used to dissipate a heritage.

In a small family context it seemed harsh, and I, who was

to see Kenya change and go from white-ruled to black, was particularly aware that land and homes were at all times vulnerable to political change or financial necessity. People, emotions, family ties seemed to me much more important at that moment when I kissed my father goodbye.

I took his messages and also some bougainvillaea cuttings for the gardens in an old cigar case, which he put into my hands as if he were sending his own small piece of what was Africa to Ireland.

Flying, sitting alone on the last lap across the Irish Sea, I felt for him.

Ireland was the same. The same startling viridian green of the fields below, as the plane banked, was easy on the eye. I had the feeling of timelessness again that Ireland always brought.

Things had changed although the house had not. Grandfather was lying on a high bed downstairs when I went in. The piano had not been moved. The clock on the mantelpiece looked exactly as it had four years before. The hands still pointed to a quarter to twelve. The French porcelain lady in floating pink draperies surmounted by her clustering cherubs still leaned on top of the French porcelain clock, and around and above were bleak sea scenes in gilt frames that my grandmother had liked so much. Cold seas, enormous threatening waves, here and there an oil painting of some dismal ship floundering in a storm. This had never been my favourite room, nor was it now.

He lay on the high bed and his face, except for his great jutting nose, had sunk, and I saw with unbearable shock that suddenly he was now only a little old man with a collapsed face, and the authoritative presence had gone. He recognised me and spoke in a whisper. A nurse lurking in the shadows tiptoed out. I sat and took his hand beside the bed. He asked about Africa and, as the shadows fell, I sat in the cold room and talked of zebras running before the lion in the sun, of wildebeest grunting like frogs as they crossed the Serengeti in migratory lines. I talked of buffalo, and maribou storks planing on the thermal currents, and when I paused because his eyes were closed, he opened them and said, 'Go on.'

When at last he slept, I sat holding his hand, looking once again onto a grey Irish day and thinking of impala running before the wind, then of my father.

Next day it seemed to me that he was further from us. I brought snowdrops and put them by his bed to herald the spring, but he was not to see it again. When he died it was a grey Irish February day, mild and bland. When I was told, I went alone to the rhododendron garden, a quarter-mile from the house, as if to find him there. In the past if he could not be found for telephone or guest, it was where he often was, a small figure in his green plus-fours, dwarfed by some great exotic rhododendron from a Himalayan slope. It seemed even now that the whole garden was full of his presence.

From America there came my Irish aunt, I remember, in black in a French *curé*'s hat. He would have smiled because she was his favourite of us all. He loved her hats and style and yen for clothes, and swore that at the Last Trump she would be at the dressmakers.

Meanwhile he was laid out, his nose still jutting just above the sheets, in the drawing room on a high narrow bed, and there he lay embalmed for more than a week. From time to time the bell rang and people came and stood by the bed to say a prayer.

The day of the funeral, fighting with the lump in my throat, my thoughts again were with my father. Letters addressed to him, as the eldest, were handed to me to read. Letters hoping he would take as much interest in horticultural societies, preservation of shrubs and financing of Himalayan expeditions for rhodos, plants and ferns as had his father. Letters expressing condolence and offering sympathy.

In the sadness I felt for him and Grandfather, it seemed

then that it would be better that he stayed for ever in Africa, where, in its space and dusty plains, there was no mirror to the green past. He would have loved the estate but he would have ruined it and spent whatever little money there was like water; and, to all of us, to destroy Annes Grove would have been like a murder. I knew this and was happy that it was now in good hands, his brother's hands.

25

I flew, Fokker Friendship, on an Aer Lingus flight to London and on to Kenya, where I spent some days with my father. I rang Walter Trench from Nakuru.

'What now?' The hospital where I had been so happy seemed an answer. I needed a stable environment and I needed it at once. Walter, sensing my thoughts, said just that.

'You've taken to Africa like a duck to water,' he said. 'Stick on that butterfly nursing cap of yours. There's a lot of life out there waiting to be lived.'

I thought of Grandfather's querulous letters to me in the past when I had been sampling life, moving around Kenya and trying something new every few weeks. Exasperated by the changes of address, he'd write, 'What the devil are you at?'

And I would write back 'Catching the devil by the tail!' which meant keeping one jump ahead of my problems. So what the devil was I at now, mooning, sorry for myself and indecisive? I made a quick decision, and when Walter came down to see my father I told him I was going back to the hospital.

The hospital was even nicer than I remembered because it was small and friendly, and the wards opening onto wide open verandas gave a feeling of space. Below them in the garden, blue jacaranda trees and flowering shrubs splashed colour against the sky. The patients, mostly farmers and their families, all knew each other, so the atmosphere was more like a club or an English cottage hospital than one in Africa. The rooms were comfortable, the food delicious and the nursing sisters, mostly from the older London hospitals, brought high standards with them from places like Bart's or Guy's or St Thomas's.

It was a happy atmosphere, if a hospital can be happy. Certainly the maternity ward was, and I wandered about, in love with Kenya all over again, answering bells, weighing babies, rolling bandages and dispensing trays of delicious food. Lady Mountbatten came to visit us and we all lined up in a row and bobbed. She was in a Queen Alexandra nursing uniform, wore too much brown suntan make-up, and looked as if she were in love with Kenya too.

There were only two general wards. The rest were private or semi-private and, because it was such a small hospital, each patient got time and attention. In Ward 3 there was a witty, delightful Noël Coward type, who was being dried out. He didn't seem to suffer severe withdrawal symptoms as he was well supplied with whiskey. His private room had a French window leading onto the open veranda and, as the sweepers who cleaned the sluice rooms were not averse to money for running errands for him, he could get what he wanted. The more whiskey he had, the more charming and witty he became, so it was almost a pity to stop him. Once or twice I was sent by Ward Sister to see, in the politest way, if I could spy a concealed whiskey bottle anywhere in his room. This always made me nervous, as – however nonchalant I pretended to be – he always rumbled me.

'What are you looking for, darling?' he said, amused on my second visit. He was sitting up in bed in a delicious brocade dressing-gown, smelling of some exotic aftershave. 'You look like a frightened rabbit.'

'Well, nothing really,' I said nervously, feeling like one, and leaning against the wall, my eyes swivelling from side to side in their sockets like a chameleon. Sister had found two empty whiskey bottles in the rubbish bin that afternoon, so the game was up. I saw the neck now of another bottle among the wood chips in the grate. His eyes followed mine and he twinkled at me, wrinkling up very blue eyes.

'I'm sorry – Sister says, well it's not good for you, you see,' I said, feeling a kill-joy as I removed it. I could hear him laughing at me as I scuttled off. It was a bottle of Scotch with a still unbroken seal but I knew it was only a red herring and that he probably had a half-dozen more which were better concealed. By the next afternoon there was another empty bottle in the wastepaper basket and he was flirting outrageously, in his silk pyjamas, with one of the St Thomas's sisters when she went in, crisp as a meringue in starched white, to reason with him.

'We are here to protect you from yourself,' I heard her saying as I went past with a bowl of daffodils. 'Do you want to kill yourself, Mr McKenzie?'

'Ah, to die in your arms, Sister, would be a pleasure!'

26

In the men's ward there was a dark young man, a Scot called Robin, with a bad go of malaria. I didn't know at the time that it was this young man that Mrs Barry had seen in the cards, nor did I think for one moment that I would marry him. I rubbed his heels and elbows with methylated spirits and played chess with him when I was off duty, perching on his bed and slithering off it when Ward Sister came round the corner. I made him laugh with scandalous stories about the hospital. Because this was more like a hospital in the Home Counties, no one seemed unduly concerned that I was usually to be found perched next to Robin, my white butterfly cap on the back of my head.

Robin was working for an amazing man called Colonel Ewart Grogan, the Grand Old Man of Kenya, now known as the Legendary Grogan (see *The Legendary Grogan* by Leda Ferrant). Stories about Grogan were legion and all true. He had walked from the Cape to Cairo to win his future wife's hand, and written a book about it with a foreword by Cecil Rhodes. He had fought in the Matabele Wars, been attacked by a cannibal tribe called the Balekas on his journey north, had shot a dozen of them and escaped without so much as a nibble out of him, to marry Gertrude, who was later immortalised by the Gertrude's Garden Children's Hospital in Nairobi.

Grogan, to expurgate a clause he felt unreasonable in the

statute book, got the Kenyan government over a barrel. He dug up a main street in Nairobi which, unfortunately for them, he owned, impeding the flow of traffic and inconveniencing Nairobi considerably. When asked why he dug, he said it was for gold. When asked whether gold would be found, he said, 'Unlikely.' When asked further by the apoplectic Governor if he would stop drilling, he replied, 'Possibly. Under certain circumstances.' And so, after several days of dust, and when the noise of drilling had driven the Nairobi-ites to near insanity, he won his point and the clause was expurgated.

Robin told me all this while I pretended to roll bandages to keep Sister at bay, and I was extremely impressed that he should be part of the entourage of such a famous and colourful pioneer. Everyone knew Grogan, who could be seen holding court at Torr's or the famous Muthaiga Club, ringed by his admirers over lunchtime gins. He had a rather exotic look about him and was very brown with a white beard and large eyes. He was irresistible to women, who were drawn to him like pins to a magnet. He didn't look Irish at all, although in fact he was.

In return for racy tales from the other wards ('Bag any bottles today?') or my descriptions of swooning in the middle of a hernia operation ('Yards of gizzards – gruesome!'), Robin described his own adventures on Grogan's estates since he arrived in Kenya a short time before. Not for him the humdrum round of sales targets and office meetings. He lived in a perfect welter of lions, pythons, king cobras, elephants and bubonic plague on Grogan's ranches, sprawled down at Taveta somewhere on the Kenya–Tanganyika border. Grogan didn't live there all year round, but launched himself from Nairobi from time to time with a lady known as the Marmalade Cat, to keep his finger on the pulse of his Taveta estate.

His house at Taveta was known as Grogan's Castle on

Girigan Hill. Robin described it as totally amazing, absolutely enormous and reinforced with aeroplane struts. It stood on 120,000 acres, with snow-covered Mount Kilimanjaro behind it, and was built on the lip of what was left of an extinct volcano. When Grogan arrived, he set off almost immediately to cover distances of up to twenty-five miles a day on foot, a mere bagatelle to him after his walk from the Cape to Cairo.

He had a theory that the tsetse fly could fly only short distances at low level, and believed that if one burnt large areas of tsetse-fly-infested bush they might be got rid of. With this in mind he covered miles on foot, hurling lighted matches over his shoulder, leaving spirals of smoke and fires in his wake and wreaking, so he hoped, death to the tsetse fly.

On one of these fire safaris he succeeded, unfortunately, when the wind changed, in burning to the ground a large modern school, an expensive dispensary and labour lines which he had just built at considerable expense for his African labourers and their families. He had come down from Nairobi to open them himself, only twenty-four hours before, and the labourers, joyfully celebrating his munificence, were a little disturbed to find a huge bush fire, ignited by their benefactor, roaring towards both them and the complex, demolishing buildings and leaving only cinders and a blackened plaque in its wake. No wonder that Grogan often said that farming in Kenya was an 'optimistic path to bankruptcy'. But in spite of everything, his tremendous zest for living and his love for ladies remained undiminished. His illegitimate children were legendary and the tales of 'Grogs' were legion.

Most of Grogan's ladyfriends had red hair, and the Marmalade Cat was no exception. She had a room in the tower of Grogan's Castle at Taveta especially for her clothes, and its walls were lined with cupboards full of marvellous things for her to wear. When she walked about she carried a white Pekinese and, in her own way, was quite as well known as Grogs.

Robin found the whole scenario of Taveta rather bracing after Scotland, and enjoyed his working days with a Polish baron called Stanaslowski as his mentor. This eccentric Slav stalked Taveta with a gun, waging war on the hordes of marauding pelicans which hovered over the Taveta fishponds. Both he and Robin had extremely uncomfortable houses close to what is now Tsavo West, which was then teeming with lion. In fact Robin, writing a letter by the light of his petromax one night, had a curious feeling of being watched. Looking up, he was disconcerted to find a lion standing on its hind legs peering through the mosquito wire gauze with an interested look on its face as it watched the pen move across the page. As his hand moved, so did the lion's eyes. He chucked a shoe at it and it casually strolled away. I was pop-eyed by all this; it was a far cry from green and misty Ireland.

A few months before Robin's malaria attack, he told me (this time I was making swabs), he had been batting at a fast pace on his motorcycle down a rough track at Taveta with a canal on one side of him and a bank on the other. In the heat haze ahead he saw a king cobra upright on its tail, swaying, its hood extended. Going too fast to stop and with no room to swerve, he closed his eyes, accelerated and, just as he got alongside, put his feet on the handlebars. He got through this circus act intact, but diced with danger a week later when photographed wearing a dead python round his neck like a Hawaiian lei. The python had been killed by the farm workers in the lucerne sheds, where it had curled up to sleep, full of rats, and was supposed to have been clubbed to death by the headman but was merely stunned! It revived shortly after being removed from Robin's neck, fresh as a daisy, on the back of the farm truck.

All these exotic African dramas seemed highly

technicoloured to me, and when Robin left the hospital I went with this interesting fellow twice after guinea fowl through Hell's Gates to Crater Lake, an extinct volcano hollowed out and green with lush vegetation. We sat on the rim, our legs dangling below us, where lava had once bubbled up. There was a green lake down in the heart of the hollow with rhino grazing beside it. It was like sitting on the rim of a huge teacup.

We danced at the Prairie Inn near Nakuru. It was here that I had met Davo, Al Capone's ex-bodyguard. It was like the Wild West, this Kenya, and at the same time magic, sophisticated and unique.

I saw Robin when he came to Nairobi. I had gone to work at Gertrude's Garden Children's Hospital and he sometimes came to see me when he could reluctantly wrench himself away from Taveta and the Baron and bush fires. He was not a city lover, but to me Nairobi was great fun. The safari trucks rolled in from the Northern Frontier District. The white hunters checked their guns and their stores outside Ker & Downey Safaris. Americans like Bob Maytag and Robert Ruark were in the Travellers' Club. Film units were on location. Members of Persian royalty, dressed in safari gear, ate next to us at the Stanley Grill, and all this in the tiny town made it seem like a film set in its own right.

But change was coming, bit by bit. More and more men were seen in the streets in jungle green and bush hats. The Mau Mau, not yet taken seriously, were beginning to pose a threat. The Kikuyu were in rebellion, and Robin wrote to say he was joining up, growing a moustache, and being sent off to the Aberdares and Mount Kenya with the Kenya Regiment. His letters were not about lions now, or the great tawny plains of Taveta, but about the moorland and the bamboo forests where he was with 'B' Company, about patrols and encounters with rhino and Mau Mau. I missed him a great deal, and the days his letters came were red-letter days. There was no proper mail delivery, so several weeks could go by before I heard from him, but when any of 'B' Company in the Kenya Regiment came down on leave they always brought some letters with them to distribute to wives or girlfriends. The mail to the forest was dropped by Punch Bearcroft, a one-armed pilot who flew food drops in for the army in his Cessna, alarming elephants as he swooped dangerously low over camp.

I lived for Robin's letters, which were written on any piece of paper that came to hand, and gave accounts of icy nights near the snowline.

'We are now high up on Mount Kenya,' he wrote, 'and are moving into the bamboo forests. The bamboo here is thirty or forty feet high, and thick. We had some shocks when we burnt dead bamboo for firewood. Half the sections were full of water, built up steam and went off like gunshots. Made the chaps very jumpy.'

And later, writing from ten thousand feet up: 'We are on the moorlands. Cold, wet and mainly treeless, but we have seen several leopard at this altitude. Strangely, they are almost totally black.'

'We are following mainly game tracks now,' he wrote from the Aberdares, 'as the animals have a special feel for firm, dry ground. Beard frozen stiff when I woke this a.m.'

And more prosaically, 'A lot of rhino around. They have bad eyesight but a great sense of smell so the platoon pee around the perimeter of the campsites to mark the territory, and it seems to work.'

From time to time he appeared, red-eyed and weary but keen for the fleshpots, so we would go off to the Travellers' Club to dance. It was small and almost pitch dark inside with a pocket-handkerchief dance floor and red velvet banquettes. Ava Gardner had sung there barefooted with the band in *Mogambo* days as well. Robert Ruark and half the Kenya Regiment and a lord or two frequently propped up the bar. I loved the Travellers'. In a green satin backless dress made for a song by a Sikh near the mosque, I drank icy martinis like cold electric shocks making my skull tingle and my eyes pop, and Robin and I talked and danced.

More often than not, a taciturn Swede who suffered from depression would slide onto the banquette opposite us and stay late into the night. It never seemed to occur to him that we might like to be alone, but Nils was old and sad, and we were twenty-one and happy, so we let him be. Robin, who had only met him once before, did not know him well, but in any case neither of us minded. He spoke little, drinking broodily till he fell asleep, his pale head resting against the red velvet banquette. He became so much the background of our love affair that we would write of him to each other:

'I saw Nils in Government Road.'

'Nils was at the New Stanley.'

Or, if for an evening when we were there and he didn't appear, 'Where is Nils?' When after a while he disappeared completely and we did not see him again, we almost missed him.

When Robin came down on leave from the forest we got engaged. We were both twenty-one. As there were no older people to help plan our wedding or advise us, we planned it all ourselves.

Robin's parents came from Rhodesia three days before the wedding and Walter drove down from his farm and gave me away. My father was not in the country, so Walter did the honours.

Molly wrote from Ireland, very pleased. She had shown Mrs Barry one of the wedding photographs and there was Robin in regimental blue, complete with brass buttons, exactly as predicted.

'Mrs Barry was asking after you,' wrote Molly, 'and she'll read the cards again for you when you come home.'

27

The Mau Mau situation now began to get ugly. Murders were reported more frequently, but however one looked at the situation of Kenya, it was difficult to find hatred in one's heart for the Kikuyu. They seemed to me to be a people of great depth and charm, with a sense of hospitality which extended to their minds – a people who were more prepared to share the thoughts of Africa than any other African tribe that I have met, whether in South Africa, Swaziland, Tanganyika or Kenya. They were thinkers, these Kikuyu, and at the same time lovers of their land, their children and cattle. The thing which was so endearing about them was their wit and sense of humour. There may have been any number of dour Kikuyu about, but the ones I knew were not humourless at all, and had great character of their own.

I had become involved with many of them as servants and friends, and they stood out in my memory for many years afterwards as total individuals, living their lives in a manner that they felt to be right. In a curious way which I cannot totally define, the ambience they created reminded me of Ireland. There was the same craving for land, a closeness to the soil, and the laughter, wit and love of talk which I associate with my own country people.

Kikuyu legends, too, held a peculiar fascination and seemed so appropriate to the beautiful countryside. Mount Kenya, for instance, believed by them to be the place where Gikuyu and Mumbi, the black Adam and Eve of Kikuyu Genesis, were created by God, was in itself a Garden of Eden. There was a magic triangle below the snowline, of which it was said that no two reports and no two photographs of the area ever tallied. This great snowline, so unlikely on a mountain on the equator, had, far below it, endless moorlands covered with tussocky grass where plants grew to amazing heights. The giant groundsel up there stretched up fifteen feet, with thick stems blotting out the sky and horizon as one climbed. Under these, cross little rhinoceroses often lay, snoozing away in the hot afternoons. A surrealistic animal under an Alice in Wonderland plant.

Then there were areas in clearings where bright damp moss lay sprinkled with yellow buttercups and other tiny wild flowers over which orange and powder-blue butterflies hovered. There were sunbirds and giant lobelia and elephants drinking from rivers beside crystal waterfalls – such a magic wonderland of snows, leopards, giant bamboos, flowers and birds that any writer of a children's fairytale, pushed for ideas, had only to percolate a little up Mount Kenya to find a world which was not quite real. You could only applaud the Kikuyu for choosing such a magical mountain as their sacred place.

It was not always so when storms blew up and rain descended like a shutter. It could be menacing, but then Africa too, sometimes benign, loved and enchanting, could suddenly show one a face of such savagery, such unbridled ferocity, that one almost fled for cover to Europe crying, 'Not for me!'

Once I opened one of Robin's files lying on the desk. It was clearly marked 'Confidential' but I opened it nevertheless. The report in it was in Kikuyu, but I saw photographs of a massacre of Africans by Africans in Lari, which gave me sleepless nights, nor were the accompanying descriptions of the Mau Mau oathing ceremony any less horrific. Yet, whenever I left Kenya and returned to it from Europe, there was always that feeling of homecoming, always that affinity with the Kikuyu.

Still, Mrs Barry was right about the blood. Remembering that night in the Servants' Hall at Annes Grove, and now sitting up in bed at midnight in Africa, I thought of a favourite remark of Molly's: 'I never thought I'd live to see the day.'

I had never thought I'd live to see the night that I would be looking down the barrel of a gun and hearing someone actually say to me: 'If they come to kill, aim low. You're not a good shot, so it's your best chance. If they're outside and trying to break in, take the pin out of one of these hand grenades, throw it through the window and then run like hell for the bathroom and lie on the floor.'

In fiction the brave colonial wife in a tight corner in Africa is clear-eyed and unwavering and very, very supportive. She grasps her gun, checks her ammunition while respectful porters and bearers wait for orders. Here and now there was no bearer and no porter, only me in spotted Marks & Spencer's pyjamas and a husband about to go on a sweep through the Maguga Forest. It was now the time of the Mau Mau in Kenya and a band of guerrillas had been apprehended in the Maguga Forest in an area a few miles below our house. Robin, a district officer for the Kikuyu Guard, was on call to lead the sweep. We were a long way from other people, right on the lip of the Great Rift Valley. There was nowhere to leave me except at home on an escarpment overlooking the terrorist-filled forest, so he'd just picked out two hand grenades and given them to me.

Viewing them as if they were gaboon vipers, I said nervously, 'I don't even know how they work!' I wasn't really sure how I lit flickering paraffin lamps in the room either, if they went out, and there was no electricity in the house. The thought of pitch darkness, two hand grenades and a gun, and possibly a posse of bloodthirsty Mau Mau wasn't calming.

'I mean, what I mean is, how do they work? Do you *have* to go?' Silly question. That was why we lived there.

My husband was checking his Sten gun and looking for his bush hat, but he generously paused to show me.

'You pull the pin out, count ten and then throw it. Run like hell as soon as you've chucked it.'

'Run like hell? Where to?'

'Into the end bathroom. The walls are thickest there and you always have a certain amount of shock afterwards.'

'And the gun?'

He gave me a quick kiss.

'Look, I've got to go. See that red spot? The safety catch is off now. That means it's ready to use. I'm sure I've explained all this to you before. I gave you target practice last week, remember? Anyway, you'll be okay. They won't mess around blotting people [a euphemism for killing me] when there are so many of us in the area.'

And he got into his Land-Rover and drove away.

The Mau Mau didn't come that night or on other nights when I sat quivering on my bed with the hand grenades within reach. Hyenas knocked the lids off the metal dustbins in our twelve-acre moonlit garden and my heart jumped into my mouth. Ten acres of wattle beyond the garden, twenty acres of potatoes, and then a sheer drop down to the Maguga Forest where they said General Cargo, freedom fighter, terrorist, call him what you will, had moved in with his gang. There is nothing as noisy as silence when you're lying in bed listening. The thump of my heart sounded like a water ram. Paraffin lamps flickering made shadows grow large and move with a life of their own. I lay in my bed with an eye on the hand grenades for most of the night, and when the sun came up and Robin still wasn't back, I fell asleep from sheer exhaustion.

Ironically, did I but know it, there was a high-ranking Mau Mau not a hundred yards from where I slept, someone with whom I had conversations every morning and whose company I enjoyed. At that time I was alone a good deal and I often idled in the kitchen listening to his stories of great meals he had prepared. His name was Kenyanjui and he was our Kikuyu cook, a white-haired patriarch who had arrived with superlative references as a chef a few months before. Someone, I can't remember who now, had brought him one morning while we were eating breakfast on the veranda. He had said that he only wanted eighty shillings a month to cook for us. Of course I engaged him on the spot, although it was rather like taking on Michelangelo for a small painting job, as amongst his references was one from a famous German, Prince von der Schratz, a white hunter. Prince von der Schratz in his day had entertained the Prince of Wales to dinner way back in 1929. Kenyanjui had had a free hand in his kitchen, judging by the fact that everything in our house thereafter was cooked swimming in butter and cream, but penury was worth it and we sat down nightly to delicious dishes of chicken *suprême*, *médaillons de boeuf*, and puddings straight from the illustrations in Mrs Beeton's cook book, like *crème brûlée*, apricot soufflé, featherlight omelettes and blissful tortes.

On clear blue Kenya mornings, discussing menus with Kenyanjui in the kitchen, the conversation often turned to the evils of the Mau Mau.

'God will surely punish them, memsahib. *Kwele*, truly, God will punish them for their wicked ways.'

With this philosophy in mind, he could not have been surprised when a posse of police drove smartly up to our house one day. They arrested and handcuffed him.

I was more than surprised; I was furious.

'He is absolutely innocent,' I said, standing by the police vehicle. 'All our servants have been screened.'

I defended him until the last document, which gave irrefutable proof that not only was he a Mau Mau; worse, not just a senior official in the hierarchy of the Mau Mau;

but, more terrible still, an oath administrator, one who instigated and recruited. The difference between a user and a pusher.

'He's a loyal servant,' I said weakly. 'I'm sure there's been a mistake.'

'They all say that,' said the police sergeant without rancour or sympathy, shoving him into the back of the Land-Rover.

When Kenyanjui came back to us some time later, having been through an oath-cleansing ceremony and with his name now at last off the black list, I lectured him on his hypocrisy.

'Every morning we spoke of it together, you and I. When you heard of the Lari massacre you yourself cried, and all the time you …!'

'It was better that you did not know of this matter, memsahib,' he said simply, tying on his apron and whipping up mayonnaise for an avocado mousse, 'for if you had known that I was a Mau Mau you would have been very much upset. Very upset, memsahib, and anxious.' The fact that what he said was perfectly true did not mollify me very much; nor the sneaking suspicion that even if I had known I might not have handed him over.

Meanwhile at night, during all this, we continued with a Kenyan custom without perceiving the irony of it. Kenyanjui cooked his usual inimitable dinners and the two houseboys brought in the dishes and laid them on the sideboard or waited on us as we sat. The fact that this necessitated having guns loaded at the ready, beside our plates, to be ready to shoot if there should be any suspicious movement outside or on their part, seemed no reason to change the domestic routine. It was a colonial custom that dinner was served by the houseboys in their long white starched kanzus and red fezzes, and the fact that one might be murdered while one ate was no reason to serve dinner oneself. You simply kept your gun ready with the safety catch off and locked the dining-room doors between courses.

– 28 –

At that time there seemed to be a lot of Mau Mau activity near us. Driving back in the Land-Rover from a weekly shopping excursion to Nairobi, we took a newly bulldozed road through the African Reserve. It was a beautiful afternoon, peaceful and sunny as we drove along, with here and there a francolin crossing the road and once a small mongoose, when suddenly, rounding a corner, a young European district officer flagged us down.

'Got your Sten, Robin?' he shouted. 'There's a part of Cargo's gang on the ridge. We flushed them out a few minutes back.'

Left guarded by a tribal policeman, I sat in the Land-Rover trying to concentrate on ticking items off my shopping list. There were sporadic bursts of gunfire. Africans started to run across the road. Two were shot down right under the wheels of the Land-Rover. They threw their arms up, fell, and died at once. I had never seen anyone killed before. I blocked off thought and went ice-cold.

It seemed like a bad dream, made almost more nightmarish because nothing earth-shattering followed the brief burst of violence. After a few minutes bird song started again in the trees, a goat with its spancelled companion resumed its cropping at a tuft of grass, and the bodies were loaded into the DO's Land-Rover. They were to be taken to the police station for identification. One was a wanted man.

'*Watu mbaya amikufa*, memsahib,' said the tribal policeman cheerfully. 'The bad people have died.' It was all in a day's work for him. I noticed with a sense of chill that he had quickly taken a pair of boots from one of the dead men and had slung them round his neck, the laces knotted together. A useful souvenir for him of the affair.

A few days later, while I was still jumpy from the shooting incident, it was decided to go into what was then a prohibited area and visit an indecisive Kikuyu chief known as Chief Muthaya. At that time Muthaya was unable to make his mind up whether to support the Mau Mau cause or pay lip-service to the Crown. He was sitting on the fence. This was known from information brought in by the tribal police, so it was considered expedient to pay him a visit and to take gifts for his wives, which might very well make him look at us in a more friendly light. For Bwana DO to visit him and make a small *baraza* with him would show that he was an important man.

So it was because of this arrangement that I found myself shopping for dress materials for Muthaya's wives. It was a problem because I was not at all sure of the protocol involved. Was there a first wife and then varying grades of wives, or were they all treated equally? As it happened, the head wife had no superior authority over the others at all and was respected only for her seniority in age. But I did not know this and agonised over the bolts of materials in the shops. There were some rainbow-coloured silks and some cheap shiny satin which might be suitable for a senior wife, but then, when I came to think of it, none of the pieces of material seemed ideal for a mud hut in the Kikuyu Reserve. It occurred to me that most of the Kikuyu ladies I had seen in Kikuyu-land were not at all *femmes fatales* but quite bald, with heads like little brown billiard balls, not a great many teeth, and were barefoot and dressed in brown cottons or woollens, so I turned reluctantly away from the satins and silks.

'I want some material for the wives of a Kikuyu chief, for a present,' I told the Indian shopkeeper in the bazaar in Nairobi. 'A Kikuyu chief with five wives, not a *mutu* of the Scots Presbyterian Mission.' The Kikuyu who had been educated by Mr Smith at the Kikuyu Scots Mission only had one wife at a time – in theory at any rate.

'Kikuyu are liking very much blue colour and also orange,' said Mr Patel, smiling. When he smiled the sun caught his gold teeth so there was a blinding flash much like a laser beam. He was obviously curious as to why, when the Kikuyu were in rebellion, a white girl in blue jeans was buying presents for five of them.

Later that evening I sat perched on the seat of a jeep next to Robin, clutching paper parcels full of orange and blue dress lengths. We were on our way to see the chief and his wives.

'This visit, we hope, will bias him towards us,' Robin said. 'He knows a lot more of what's been going on in this area than he's telling. Maybe he'll open up a bit. I hope so. They're bumping off just too many people around here.' The jeep lurched about on the rutted Kikuyu roads, the dust pouring in through every aperture in a thick red murram cloud. Drive for long on murram roads in these newly issued jeeps, and one looked like a Red Indian.

It had been a long, dust-oriented day. In the early afternoon, cattle that had been found grazing repeatedly in a prohibited area were put up for auction. Robin was the auctioneer and I the auctioneer's clerk. We had corralled the cattle into a veterinary department boma and I, sitting literally on the fence post, like Matthew at the seat of custom, had taken the money. The bidding was brisk. The amounts reached over two thousand shillings in some cases, and grizzled old Kikuyu, naked but for a blanket, with snuff containers round their necks, bid and bought, producing great wads of twenty shilling notes. The money raised was handed in to the tribal courts, and now we were on our way to Muthaya's boma and dusk was falling.

His kraal was circled by a moat, a trench ten feet deep in which wooden bamboos were planted, razor-sharpened ends pointing upwards. Mau Mau sympathiser or not, he was taking no chances. The stakes had been singed in flame to harden them so that an enemy attacking in the night, if he fell, would be impaled like a kebab.

Charming! I thought, clutching my brown paper parcels. A drawbridge of poles was lowered as we arrived so that we could cross into the kraal.

It was eerie inside, only firelight flickering and one or two dim paraffin lanterns. The talk went well as we sat surrounded by the peculiarly African smell of animal fat and wood smoke. The chief was affable but inscrutable, and I smiled at his wives and they at me while the men talked. They seemed pleased enough with their presents but there were long silences in their conversation. They did not speak Swahili, only Kikuyu, a language punctuated frequently by long-drawn-out vowels like 'Eeeeeee.' They murmured among themselves for a long time, fingering the coloured cotton and saying 'Eeeeeee' from time to time, or occasionally, seemingly for variation, 'Aaaaaaa.'

Suddenly here was a tremendous scuffling and shrieking and bursts of laughter. The smile vanished from my face. It was now almost pitch dark except for the flickering light.

My God! I thought, my nerves jumping. The whole lot of them are probably Mau Mau and here we sit in the middle of them in an isolated kraal miles from anywhere, talking earnestly about the *serakali* (government). I looked at Robin, who was engrossed in talk with the chief. The noise got more and more deafening and at the same time nearer. It sounded as if a heavy object was being dragged along the ground.

At that moment, into the circle of firelight appeared three villainous-looking Africans and an enormous dirty woolly sheep which two were pushing and another was dragging on a piece of rope.

'It is a present,' the chief said slowly and very graciously, 'for the memsahib. My wives would like very much for her to have this sheep.' A piece of cotton was one thing, but as a reciprocal gift a colossal and unattractive sheep quite another. But there was nothing for it but to smile equally graciously and accept. The chief beamed and the sheep, by this time on its back and smelling vilely, kicked and maa'ed.

At least we hadn't been murdered, I thought, relieved, and thankfully it was time to say our farewells. The sheep was heaved into the back of our open jeep by a posse of Kikuyu youths, a collar put round its neck with a length of rope attached, which was handed to me. Still waving and smiling, I with one hand clutching the rope, and the sheep leaping, tugging and defecating, we drove off into the night.

I seemed at this time to be pleased most by the fact that the weeks had passed, the nights alone in the house above the Maguga Forest and the days out on safari in the Kikuyu Reserve, without us being murdered.

But we were under a lot of strain without realising it. Robin had received two or three anonymous ill-spelt letters on cheap blue-lined paper over a period of a few weeks. All of them said he was a marked man and would soon be murdered. They were obviously from Kikuyu and were hard to decipher, but their general drift was clearly threatening.

'People get them all the time,' he said vaguely, throwing them into the wastepaper basket.

But I was pregnant now and everything made me jumpy, even the fact that our house did not have electricity. With the baby soon due, the thought of groping around with matches and paraffin lamps at night in a lonely house in a wattle grove didn't appeal very much, particularly if Robin was out on a forest sweep. A Mau Mau murder had happened in a farmhouse not very far away where a woman who was heavily pregnant had been slashed to ribbons with a razor-sharp panga. Her husband and three-year-old son had been killed by the servants after her murder. It had been done in a particularly hideous way and the media had given it publicity.

I dreamt one night that Kenyanjui stood by my bed, a panga in his apron, and looking apologetic.

'It is as well you didn't know I would kill you, memsahib,' he said sadly, in my dream, 'because if you had known you would have been very upset, memsahib, very upset and anxious.'

And so things which hadn't bothered me now seemed to be getting to me, and when Robin went out on an ambush one night I asked him to drop me at the Njogo Inn while he was away. I didn't feel like being alone these nights, but all the same, sitting sleepily for four hours in a deserted bar drinking warm Coca-Cola with only the Jaluo barman for company was dreary, even if it was safer. Things improved when an army battalion moved into the area and was based at a farm down the road.

I had often thought of Mrs Barry and the cards during the months of my pregnancy. She had said that there would be 'men all around me' and at this time I saw little or nothing of my girl friends because we lived so far from Nairobi. Besides that, we were in a Prohibited Area. I saw plenty of the other district officers (Kikuyu Guard), however. They were all bachelors, who frequently stopped at our house for supper and a bath, so there was always company. A couple of the district officers lived in the bush and they particularly liked to call in if they were passing.

Once a month Robin took me into Nairobi in the OHMS (On Her Majesty's Service) jeep to see the doctor, a taciturn man who bred greyhounds and was far more interested in horses and dogs than in people. But he was from Cork, and I rather enjoyed him. He weighed me at each visit, and while he listened to the baby's heart he talked about the racing results and the superiority of Irish horses, occasionally making desultory notes in my file as he spoke.

I had no older woman to advise me except my bridesmaid's Aunt Mamie, who was in her late seventies and had never had children; but she was a pillar of support. I bought a primrose-yellow carrycot for the baby and I read Lynne Reid

Banks's book *The L-Shaped Room*, which told me more or less what to expect month by month, and betweenwhiles I read Grantley Dick-Reed's book *Childbirth Without Fear*. Robin was in agreement with Dick-Reed about natural childbirth. He said it was one of the most natural functions in the world, and pointed out that African women often had their babies under or behind a tree, never turned a hair, but strapped their newborns onto their backs and resumed weeding or picking tea or building huts or whatever they were doing when interrupted by the birth.

It all seemed very easy, and as Robin's father was a gynaecologist from Harley Street, now in Rhodesia, I had no reason to doubt this unconfirmed report. I went everywhere with Robin in the Kikuyu Reserve in a jeep which sucked in red dust like a Hoover, feeling happier to be with him than at home.

Ten days before Marnie, our daughter, was born, Robin's mother arrived from what was then Rhodesia and was horrified. She was horrified by our tribal policeman who sat in the passenger seat next to Robin on his way back from the airport, his gun slung casually over his shoulder with the barrel, she was convinced, pointing at her heart. She was horrified at the remote place in which we lived – on the lip of the Great Rift Valley with the forest below us teeming with gangs – and terrified by the hype she had read in the foreign media, which convinced her that we might all be murdered by the Mau Mau in minutes.

It worried me too, but I did not say so.

Nor did the guns beside our plates at meals reassure her much. Too reserved to tackle me, she tackled Robin instead, on the lunacy of allowing me to whirl round the bumpy dirt roads in his jeep at this stage of the pregnancy, in an area which was extremely dangerous. To me she simply said she would be glad if I would stay at home with her for company, and to Robin's aunts she wrote that, apart from two nightgowns, two vests, two jackets, nappies and safety pins, the baby when it arrived would be naked.

Of course she was not. After our daughter was born and I was in hospital with no inclination to weed or pick tea and thoroughly disillusioned with Grantley Dick-Reed, who for obvious reasons had never had a baby himself, friends deluged us with gifts for the baby; and the aunts, galvanised into action with their knitting needles, sent us so many garments that they were outgrown before they could ever be used.

Our daughter was called Marnie. She was enchanting, like a little doll, with slightly slanting navy-blue eyes and black hair. We took her home to the house on the edge of the Great Rift Valley and Kenyanjui baked a cake in her honour.

A short time later we moved to look after the district officer's house while he was on home leave. He was Robin's superior, a bachelor called John Campbell. He had been in Popski's Private Army and been awarded the Military Cross and bar for daring deeds. We liked him enormously and asked him to be Marnie's godfather.

His house, however, was a nightmare. It had an outside loo, and a parade ground flanked by offices, with the Union Jack flying on a pole in the centre of the boma. The offices were a hive of activity; streams of people came and went all day. Tribal police drilled on the parade ground and the dusty, minute garden was serviced by fifteen prisoners, who watered it by pouring water out of a bucket into cocoa tins perforated with holes. Even watching this soul-destroying activity drove me mad. There were no trees around the boma and it was always noisy as government Land-Rovers roared in and out in clouds of dust.

It was, in short, no place for a baby, so I asked permission to leave Marnie, between feeds, asleep in her pram under a giant fig tree in a nearby garden. Permission was granted and an armed tribal policeman with a gun occasionally guarded her. His name was Andrew Kamau and he did not feel it was the least bit beneath his dignity to sit next to her pram, sometimes bringing her little animals that he had carved for her out of wood, which she blinked at when he held them up for her to see.

– 30 –

The days flew past and the date set for our long leave in Europe grew closer. It was at this time, only a week before we left for England, that an extraordinary thing happened which affected me very much. When Robin brought the post from the office in Kikuyu, there was a letter for me in a hand I did not recognise. I was even more mystified by the endearments at the beginning. It appeared to be from a total stranger, because neither postmark nor handwriting was in any way familiar. When I turned the pages over and found the signature at the bottom, I was shattered. It was signed by my mother.

In it she wrote that she would be in London for the next few months and that she had heard, in a roundabout way, that I would be in Europe. Would it be possible for us to meet? We had never been in touch all these years, and as our lives had taken us to different parts of the world it would be a pity, she felt, if we were to miss this opportunity.

My reaction to the letter was strange. I felt not excitement but apprehension, as if whole areas which I had shut off in my mind would be opened if I saw her. I was not at all sure how I would deal with them, but all the same I knew that I would meet her in spite of this. I wrote quickly to say that we should arrange it for the day after we arrived in England. I suggested Fuller's and lunchtime, to make it more normal and humdrum, because however I looked at it there could not fail to be an element of drama in the meeting.

When we reached our London hotel there was a note from her at the desk, confirming the time and date, and my stomach gave a jolt when I saw it. For some reason I did not want Robin to come with me and I went alone to meet her, nibbling my fingernails with nerves and thinking how unreal it was to be meeting her like this at the age of twenty-three.

Waiting in the hubbub of the coffee shop I wondered idly what she would look like. I had absolutely no idea at all. Would she be dark or fair? Would she be old to look at or young? I worked it out on my fingers. She must be forty-two, not more, so she would be youngish, I supposed.

The glass door into the restaurant opened, letting in a gust of warm summer air from the streets and a dark pretty woman in a green dress came in, carrying parcels. She had shiny eyes and wore the high strappy sandals everyone was wearing in London that season. She looked about the right age. I hoped she might be my mother. But in the corner there was a group of people and one, patting a chair, called out to her to join them, so she obviously could not be. Meeting a daughter last seen as a baby, one would scarcely loiter to talk with friends – but then she was an unknown quantity; she might, I supposed, do anything. God knows, she seemed unpredictable enough from all accounts, skimpy as those might be.

At that moment it struck me as odd that I had not thought to ask my father what my mother looked like. It had never occurred to me to ask him, and I was not sure who in the family had and had not known or met her. Earlier, with the perception of childhood, and guessing it would not be acceptable, I had not brought the subject up.

Fuller's was becoming crowded. I fidgeted in my chair, and a waitress in a black dress and lace-trimmed apron came up and asked if I wanted to order. I said I was waiting for somebody. After twenty-odd years it would not kill me to wait a little longer, I supposed, although she was now very late. Had she taken fright, I wondered, or, like me, when insecure, gone to buy a new dress to buoy her up? I always bought something new to wear in moments of stress.

When she finally came in I knew, by the way she glanced uncertainly around the restaurant, who she was. She looked worried, bit her bottom lip nervously, stood slightly on her toes to see the far corner of the room. I felt absolutely nothing immediately, except a feeling of triumph. She *had* bought a new dress! It could scarcely have left the shop window an hour or so before. The pleats were pristine, the buttons glaringly new. Because I had guessed what she would do and why, I felt an affinity that she, too, was vulnerable, but no emotion besides that, just detachment. The dress was a thin cotton, striped brown and white. Her fair hair was shoulder-length. Dark eyes, a murmur in a faint Scots burr, and there behind her, hovering protectively, a man.

'Darling! I'd have known you anywhere – so like Norman! We're so late … the traffic … have you been here long?'

I wondered what it must be like to meet a daughter one had never known. Obviously a strain. As they sat down, she opposite me and he with his arm lying lightly on the back of her chair, she deferred to him constantly, drawing strength, and I felt irritated. Did she think if we were alone I might castigate her, ask her why she had left all those years ago? She was speaking again, quickly, nervously.

'She is very like the boys, Peter, very. The same eyes. Same smile as well, like Norman. *Exactly*. You never knew Norman, did you, Diana? Your half-brother?'

'No,' I said. She must be very rattled. Difficult, after all, for me to know half-brothers whose existence I had not been aware of until now.

'You'd love Norman. She'd *love* him, wouldn't she, Peter!' A pointless conversation, particularly as it transpired that Norman was in India.

I ate my limp salad and tried to visualise someone with

the same face as I saw in the glass in the mornings, only male, striding about India. Now presumably she could write to Norman: 'She's very like you, Norman. Same smile, same eyes.'

Would it interest Norman? I wondered. I doubted it. His existence meant little or nothing to me. I was trying with difficulty to assimilate a parent just met; a half-brother seemed superfluous at this point, and India and Oxford Street too diverse. I looked across the table and found her staring at me, prattling with forced gaiety. I had never felt more serious and wished I had Robin with me for support.

Thinking about that day, years later, I have tried to visualise what else could have happened – how that scene set in a London coffee shop might have been, given other circumstances. I suppose she could have opened her arms embracingly, or walked towards me with arms extended, but then I suppose I might have shrunk back. How to bridge with love a chasm that had separated us for over twenty years? It was impossible. How could I, with my own child so much a part of my life, warm towards someone who had walked away not just from me but from three other children?

Decades later I tried to explain her to Marnie, who said incredulously, 'Didn't she bring *any* of her children up?' I shook my head. 'Like Puss,' Marnie said round-eyed. Puss was her Siamese cat who, when her litter of kittens had become too much, took them in her mouth and dotted them around the house, two in each child's bed and one in ours, and then with a sigh of relief gone mousing. But at least, I thought wryly when Marnie asked, Puss had come back. This stranger had not.

'I had six children altogether,' she said suddenly, dabbing her lips with her napkin 'Two died, but you knew that – Susannah and Peter.'

'I didn't – no one told me very much. I wasn't supposed to write to you.' This last defensively.

'No, of course not. I knew that. And I didn't have a fixed address. There seemed no way ...' Her voice trailed off. She looked at Peter for support, crumbling her bread roll, and he came up trumps, on cue.

'We were always travelling, on the move a lot because of my job.'

'I loved Africa,' my mother said and I looked up, relaxing a little. At least we had Africa in common. We had both lived there.

'Peter loves Africa too, don't you, darling? I miss the African sun so much, and the Africans. I have this amazing affinity with Africans and you loved them too even as a baby.'

I smiled politely. The waitress brought our coffee, setting down the three cups carefully, and Peter asked for the bill. We had scarcely touched our food. And then suddenly, my mother, putting down her coffee cup and lighting a cigarette, began to talk, nervously, quickly, as if something had crossed her mind that she felt I should know. She fitted her cigarette into a black holder and leaned towards me.

'When you were small,' she said, 'about seven months old, we lived out in the blue, miles from anywhere, with no car; your father and I – and of course you. No one else. We just had this one African house servant, a man. It was during the Depression and we were house-sitting in this enormous house some miles from Pretoria. It had been vacant for months and was infested with spiders, that I do know. Huge ones.' She shuddered. 'It had an alabaster bath in one of the marble bathrooms. I felt like Cleopatra when I had a bath! It had dozens of bedrooms, so many that the boy never cleaned them properly; a billiard room and an enormous kitchen, but no telephone. It belonged to a man called Sammy Mann or Marks, I can't remember which.'

I was all attention now. The time she was describing was when we had all three been together, a proper family. A time never mentioned at Annes Grove. I glanced at Peter, who looked bored. He had probably heard it all before, but I was riveted. Putting down my coffee cup I listened, fascinated. She blew a smoke ring.

'Your father became very ill in this barn of a place. He was delirious with a high temperature. It turned out to be enteric fever.' She put her cigarette down in the ashtray, drank some coffee and continued.

'The old houseboy managed to get word to a doctor – you know how Africans are at spreading the word – drums or something.'

'Drums?' I said doubtfully. 'Surely not drums?'

'Well, anyway, bush telegraph, or whatever – eventually the doctor came. Just as well, Michael was half dead. He took me and your father to Pretoria to an infectious disease hospital. Not you, of course. It was no place for babies, but I don't think the doctor realised that we had no family to leave you with or that we knew no one nearby. Speed was of the essence, you see, because your father was at death's door.'

I was looking at her wide-eyed. She had my full attention now. She opened a fresh box of Gitanes, lighting one cigarette from the other.

'There was this tall African woman. It's all coming back to me now. I don't know what tribe she was, probably Xhosa, because she wore those long swinging skirts. She came from the huts, a kraal behind the house. I used to watch her some evenings when she crossed the field to draw water, carrying a gourd on her head – you know the way they do. Very graceful.'

She sipped her coffee while I stared at her.

'Anyway, there was nothing to be done. I saw her in the distance and called to her and she came towards me, very stately with a sort of folded-cloth thing on her head – "doeks" I think they call them – and you held out your arms to her.'

She paused and smiled at me.

'"Can you look after my baby?" I said to her. The old

African boy had to translate because I remember she didn't speak any English. Not a word. She must have been Xhosa. They speak with those amazing clicks.'

I nodded.

'Well, I took her into the house, showed her your clothes and your food, with the old man trailing along behind. When I came back a day or two later, there you were,' she said brightly, 'as right as rain.'

'In the house or in the huts?' I asked.

'I have no idea. It's years ago.'

She gathered up her bag and gloves slowly, and then, as if at a given signal, we got up, leaving Peter to pay the bill, and walked towards the powder room together.

It is said that we never forget, really forget, anything that has happened to us. Even the moment of birth can supposedly be recalled through regression. I searched in the recesses of my mind for even a fleeting image of dark huts, and wood smoke, to me as much the scent of Africa as rain on dust. Had I slept, comforted and lulled, against chocolate skin and drunk the milk of Africa? Who knew?

Outside, the London traffic roared in a darkening afternoon, and I thought of a tall black woman with swinging skirts reaching out her arms for a stranger's baby.

In the powder room, on impulse, I took the brown and gold beads I was wearing around my neck and gave them to my mother. They matched her dress, and we kissed briefly. Mother and daughter standing reflected in the mirrors.

'They match, they look nice! A small thing here for you.' She fumbled in her handbag, clearly uncertain, embarrassed without her husband, and gave me the package, a jeweller's box. It was a small nondescript brooch, like our relationship, without any sparkle.

'Don't think too badly of me. I did what I felt best for you. Your father's ...'

'No, of course I don't. And thank you for the brooch.'

Muttering excuses, regrets, inventing trains to be caught or London circumvented, we separated. There was so much to be said it was better not to start, better to back off from a situation neither of us could handle.

I never saw her again.

Back at the hotel, chosen in Africa from a newspaper ad, Robin said, probing tactfully, 'Was it awful?'

'Not awful, just dull. She kept talking about Norman all the time.'

'Norman?'

'A half-brother, apparently. She's married again. Her husband came with her. I wished you'd been there.'

'I would have, but you didn't ...'

'I know. I thought it would be – well, you know, warm, sort of emotional, but it wasn't. She kept apologising.'

'Bit late.'

'Twenty-odd years too late I suppose.' I suddenly felt a wave of emotion for the first time and wondered if she was sitting on the train on her way home, holding Peter's hand for support, talking about what had seemed to me a very strange day.

– 31 –

The British government had settled people in Kenya, relied on them to support and fight for a British colony – and now in 1959, unbelievably, was walking away from the situation, leaving what had been patriotic fervour as *de trop* as last year's newspapers. To us who had lost friends in the emergency, both African and European, it seemed in retrospect to have been a gigantic waste of lives and time. As well as this, we were angry about the Kikuyu Guard, whom Robin had worked with and who were now being publicly decorated for bravery and service to the Crown while at the same time the Mau Mau were being released daily from the detention centres. It was obvious that the Mau Mau would recognise the recipients of the medals from the British government as the people who had stood by it during the emergency, and target them.

Thousands of glib platitudes were being uttered in the media about bygones being bygones, about the new regime which would forgive and forget, but just the same one knew that there were many remote parts of Kikuyu-land, lying up isolated tracks and paths far from the main road, where, in spite of glib reassurances, retribution would be exacted from time to time, and old scores would be paid off and people murdered in ways that would not be traced.

It was a poor return indeed for loyalty to the Crown and, to the anger of settlers, the Mau Mau were beginning to be referred to as 'freedom fighters'. It seemed easy for our masters in Whitehall to be complacent about such matters from where they sat, but it was more difficult for us to be lulled into complacency when we knew the people involved as intimately as we did, on a day-to-day basis. This Kenya was a land that none of us took lightly. It was a country much loved, unique and magic. For it, we wished only the best.

This general unsettled feeling of discontent made an oil company's offer to Robin seem attractive. It had come out of the blue. Neither of us knew much about commerce. Robin's father was a surgeon in Rhodesia and Annes Grove was hardly the hub of the marketplace. But commerce had one advantage, it appeared. It lacked hypocrisy. People were in it for the money, and said so.

The terms offered by this oil company seemed dazzling to us, with the advantages of no dangers, no hand grenades or bumpy, dusty jeeps or night terrors. Instead it offered us a modern house with – hurrah! – electricity, a motorcar, and a generous salary. We reminded ourselves that at the height of the Mau Mau we had not been paid – through an error – and of another time when a clerk in the Treasury had forgotten to deduct our Widow and Orphans' Pension at source for a while, and had then snatched it back in one fell swoop, leaving us salary-less when we were about to go on leave. With the oil company, it seemed we were going to be wrapped in cotton wool and positively mollycoddled.

Our decision to move into commerce was not received well by our friends. Lunching at the Equator Club in Nairobi with some former district officers of the Kikuyu Guard, one said to me patronisingly, 'Do you really fancy being the wife of a petrol seller?'

'Yes,' I said without hesitation, 'I really do.' And I really did fancy it. Corpses, guns, mutilations, goat entrails in oathing ceremonies could be put behind us and, although I knew

Robin would miss the camaraderie and living out in the blue, the Mau Mau was a chapter that everyone wanted closed.

Our posting orders from the oil company, when they came through, were for us to go to a village called Nanyuki, a Maasai name meaning red-brown, in the foothills of Mount Kenya. It is not far from Isiolo, the frontier post into the torrid Northern Frontier District, which is a country of dry and punishing heat, Somali and Samburu tribes, camels and Turkana, running up to Somalia and Ethiopia. 'Running up' is hardly the word because the road was as rough as a boulder-strewn river bed, but picturesque for all that.

When we arrived at Nanyuki one clear blue day, there was a company house for us on the river, and far more to do than we had ever imagined. We went game watching on the slopes of Mount Kenya, drank gin and tonics at the Silverbeck Hotel in Nanyuki where the line of the equator crossed the floor of the bar, and I spent an afternoon with Raymond Hook, who caught cheetahs and trained them for maharajahs in India. This was all in the first three weeks, so I could see we weren't going to wither away from suburban boredom even though we were back in the white areas.

Raymond Hook's farm was an amazing experience. A friend's cattle had strayed onto his land, and as her husband was a white hunter and out on safari with Americans in the Northern Frontier District, she asked me to come with her, for moral support, to claim the bullocks.

'My cattle have broken his fences,' she said nervously. 'He's very eccentric and might come out shooting. He shot at our herdboy a few weeks back.'

This sounded a little alarming, but the huge gentle giant who towered above our car outside his dilapidated farmhouse was as courteous to us as if we were welcome guests. He wore an enormous filthy bush hat which, when he lifted it, bisected his face into a pink, shiny high forehead and, from the eyebrows down, into a mahogany-brown mask. Talking amiably, he led out his cheetahs on red dog collars and leads, describing how he had once taken several to England, to Harringay, to race against champion greyhounds.

'Did the cheetahs win?' I asked, looking at the huge faded sepia photographs on the veranda walls, of maharajahs with cheetahs, cheetahs on Mount Kenya, and cheetahs on an English racetrack.

'No, it caused havoc. The cheetahs batted the greyhounds, swatted them like a cat with her kittens if they overtook on the tracks. The greyhounds were worth thousands, so some of the owners were as mad as hell about it. Broke one champion's nerve completely,' Hook said. 'He never raced again with the same verve, d'you know? Always looking over his shoulder for one of those cats to close in.'

So would I, I thought. The greyhounds were not accustomed to such close proximity to the wild, Hook said, which seemed an understatement. Looking at pictures of them in their neat initialled woollen kennel coats, standing next to the aristocratic cheetah, the dogs looked nervous, as if they could sense before they started that the race wasn't going to be run by tried rules.

Hook showed us a most marvellous series of three photographs. In the first the cheetahs, semi-tamed but obviously not totally so, were being led out by their handlers onto an English sward. In the second, which was a blow-up, the action was clearly defined. A greyhound was closing in on the gap on the racetrack between itself and the cheetah, and the cheetah – a blur of speed even on a fast shutter – was still ahead. In the third exposure the cheetah had paused, his paw was still raised, then clouted the greyhound, which was seen as a crumpled ball, and had gone on to win.

'Harringay wasn't a success,' Hook said, which seemed a slight understatement. 'Hunting's the thing for the cheetah. The Egyptians, Assyrians and Hittites hunted with them. The fastest animal on four legs. Over a short distance they can clock seventy miles an hour.' He opened a book of photographs of ancient friezes and wall paintings, which looked Egyptian. There were the hunting chariots, drawn by magnificent horses and driven by tall Nilotic figures. Running beside the wheels of three of the chariots were cheetah, their eyes always on distant horizons.

'658 BC,' Raymond said. 'I wonder how they captured them, they won't breed in captivity. Ran them down with Saluki hounds, I expect. Lend you this book if you like and you can read about them.'

When we left, two Kikuyu were exercising three couples of cheetahs on leads. They looked aristocratic creatures, fit company for kings. Hook lifted his huge hat, bisecting his face into pink and brown again, and waved it to us as we drove away.

At the other end of Nanyuki, a few miles out of the village on the residential side of the town, was the exotic five-star magnificence of the Mawingo Hotel, now the Mount Kenya Safari Club, where Hollywood film stars usually stayed when they came out to Kenya. The windows of the bar framed twin peaks of Mount Kenya, and the luxury, the food, the roaring open fires in winter, and the sophisticated international jet-set people who stayed there made a dramatic contrast to the stark wildness of the Africa of just a few miles away.

The Northern Frontier District, where Robin went shooting guinea fowl, was only an hour's drive, and we watched game up there too. Herds of elephants with their calves were everywhere, trundling across roads or bathing in the Ewaso Ngiro, grey-black in the water among the doum palms.

How to describe the Northern Frontier District, to bring alive the fascination of what, on the surface, appeared to be just punishing frazzling sun and boulder-strewn roads, the miles of nothing but shimmering heat and scrub? Difficult to construct the total wonderful wildness of it all, but it got to you. It has left photo flashes of memory, of driving along what appeared to be the wilder parts of a moon crater and seeing ahead a solitary Turkana, elongated by mirage, loping along spear in hand at least seventy miles from home and hepped for his journey on a handful of miraa leaves.

Another flash is of the Anglican clergyman in his eighties, ivory-faced in a faded greeny-black cassock, whom I saw sitting in the back of an ancient lorry packed with spear-carrying ochre-plaited warriors. He was a scholarly Balliol man, fifty years in the Northern Frontier District, teaching nomadic tribes and journeying with them. He came into Nanyuki sometimes if he could get a lift on a truck and had a hot meal and a bath at the Anglican rectory. People had reported seeing him far up towards the Ethiopian border, trudging along, frail and white-haired, in the stark deserted scenery. He was always flanked by tall near-naked tribesmen who treated him with the deference due to a great *mwalimu*, or teacher, and he, in turn, regarded them as his flock.

I had in my mind's eye a picture of ochre-plaited Samburu listening while he spoke to them of the Bible. One could see that they would listen with great interest and relate well to the Book of Genesis, and to stories like that of Jacob and the spotted, speckled and ring-streaked cattle of Laban, because in just such a way would they themselves have behaved. You could see from the way they lived how simple it would be for them to feel a kinship with men like Abraham or Lot, caught up with the watering and grazing of flocks and herds in a hot dry country.

After the tension and fear of Kikuyu-land, I think I have never been as happy as I was in those days in Nanyuki. I made a garden, small but all the same charming, with Mount Kenya behind it as a beautiful and theatrical backdrop. Things grew so easily here in this beautiful climate that one didn't need green fingers. I planted moonflower outside our bedroom window, so that when I looked out of the house I saw the fragrant white waxy flower trumpets and, just above them, the snow peaks of the mountain.

The Nanyuki River ran at the bottom of the garden and there was a gate there with steps leading down to its wooded banks. Robin went down often in the evenings with a rod and caught speckled trout, returning at dusk when the fireflies were out. The river was ice-cold even when the weather was hot, and when we picnicked beside it we dropped our bottles of white wine, with strings tied round their necks, deep into the river depths to cool, and ate chicken legs and wild strawberries on the banks, with Mount Kenya towering above us. We had two children now. Hugh, our treasured son, conceived under Mount Kenya, had arrived, a little Piscean, the oldest and wisest sign of the zodiac. It was magic to walk safely with them without any of the nagging fears of the Mau Mau to spoil the blue and golden days.

Unfortunately a move to Tanganyika was becoming more and more probable, and although we tried to take an interest in the project, I sensed that leaving Kenya would be like the amputation of a limb. I knew very little about Tanganyika except that Dar es Salaam was the capital city, that it had a great Arab influence, and that the dhows still came to trade there from Arabia as they had done for thousands of years, bringing Persian carpets and dates. I knew that Zanzibar, where the Sultan lurked, was not far off shore, and the fabled Mount Kilimanjaro, once another magic Kenyan mountain, was within the borders of Tanganyika since Queen Victoria had 'given' it to the Kaiser as a birthday present 'because the dear boy is so fond of mountains'. She always had an imperial disregard for boundaries and for local ownership, but to have taken anything so lovely away from Kenya seemed sacrilege.

It was easy to push to the back of our minds the reality of a move, until one day a letter came, confirming that we were being sent to Dar es Salaam. Finally we had to take some interest. The continual feedback about Dar es Salaam was heat and more heat. Either it was very hot and humid or it was muggy and humid, so that clothes grew green mould. When they were drycleaned, someone said, the marks disappeared, but when the rains broke the marks reappeared in the same places. One's shoes, satin or suede, grew mould, and everything smelt of mildew. Hell, it seemed, would be a pleasure resort after a hot season in Dar es Salaam.

At this time I was running a nursery school for army children whose parents were stationed in Nanyuki, so I had no wish to go away, nor in fact ever to leave Kenya. To be ripped away from the cool winds of the snowline and the fascinating Northern Frontier District, and sent to a community teeming with oil company employees, townspeople, with all their rigours of rank and office hierarchy, was going to be a real drag. Our lifestyle until now had been idyllic and very free.

We were only visited intermittently by our superiors in Nairobi who, in holiday mood when they came to us, were free to fish the rivers, shoot guinea fowl and dine at the Mawingo between small bouts of business in the Nanyuki area. They were jovial and easygoing and on Christian name terms with us in spite of our junior standing. They always took us out to dinner at the Mawingo Hotel when they came up on safari.

They drank large amounts of gin and tonic on their expense accounts, clapped each other on the back and told tall fishing stories over their prawn cocktails. I met most of the head office people through the Mawingo dinners. Robin brought them home from time to time when he came to collect a picnic lunch, before whirling them off to visit clients on cattle ranches up towards Isiolo or down on Cole's Plains. Sometimes he flew with them in a small aeroplane as far north as Wajir.

With people like Raymond Hook about, the oil company's

clientele was colourful. Most of the people here were from pioneering stock and so of strong character, determination and decided views. They had a curious attitude to life and how to live it, which was, people said, a direct result of living at altitude right on the equator.

There was, for example, a retired naval commander who drove a vintage Rolls and had been known, when he parked, to hurl an anchor and chain out onto the kerb.

There was a wing commander who, displeased with the difficulties of getting through to the telephone exchange at night, swore to shoot the telephone operator if he didn't stay awake after nine p.m. Eventually a serious emergency arose and, having tried the telephone repeatedly for an hour, and being a man of his word, he got his gun and drove, roaring with rage, to the telephone exchange. The slumbering operator, warned by some sixth sense, woke up to see the headlights of a jeep approaching, driven as if at Le Mans; wisely he bolted the door, pushed all the furniture he could find against it, and crouched for safety on the floor behind a steel filing cabinet. The wing commander, coming down like a wolf on the fold, loaded his gun and, roaring loudly in Kikuyu all the while, loosed off several rounds which splintered parts of the main door of the exchange, broke one or two windows and, understandably, made the operator, traumatised by this intrusion into his slumbers, wish he was back in peaceful Kikuyu-land tending his goats.

By the next morning the whole area knew of the story, because some of the bullets were inextricably lodged in the old-fashioned switchboard and no calls could be got in or out until someone drove the hundred and thirty-four miles from Nairobi to repair it.

The Kikuyu, when he appeared as a witness in court, said he had not been harmed physically, but told the magistrate that he had decided to take early retirement from East African Posts and Telegraphs and work for the Nanyuki Butchery, where people were less likely, when vexed, to arrive shooting.

The wing commander, fined for being in possession of a firearm without a licence and for damage to government property, had public opinion on his side. Everyone agreed that the telephone service was appalling because there was no automatic dialling and the night operator never answered the telephone unless desperate measures were taken.

'Like shooting through a door?' enquired the magistrate, raising his eyebrows. One could see he felt that life in this district was very wild and very odd.

All this seemed curiously like Ireland to me. People were free souls and, although perhaps eccentric, at least there was no grey sameness about them, no dreary conformity. The tapestry of life was full of colour, and in the atmosphere of Kenya some of these settlers seemed larger than life. When they left Kenya, like fish taken from the water, their colours faded and the sparkle was gone.

When February came and we were due to leave in March, it was no longer possible to pretend that we were not going to Tanganyika. There was very little to pack because the company supplied fully furnished houses complete with china, linen, kitchen utensils and glass. In fact they were so comprehensive that, reading through the inventories, I was often baffled by some of the items. When we got to Dar es Salaam another company house would be waiting. The inventory would have to be checked and brought up to date for us, so we would only have to unpack. All the same, I had no sense of adventure about this move. My heart was heavy as lead, and the nearer the day of departure grew, the worse leaving Kenya seemed to me to be.

When we drove down the winding murram road past Karatina and the Nyeri–Fort Hall turn-offs, I felt as if a pigeon's egg was stuck in my throat. We stopped for tea for the last time at the Blue Posts in Thika. Elspeth Huxley's flame trees were in flower and the blue posts on the veranda had been repainted sky-blue. Afterwards, when we left East Africa for good, I could not read her *Flame Trees of Thika* because it made me so homesick.

– 32 –

We flew into Dar es Salaam in 1959, into the muggy heat we'd heard about, as opposed to the blistering heat. It was raining that day and looked dull, run-down and seedy, with grey seas and dripping palm trees. The few Europeans at the airport had washed-out yellowish tans, the paint was peeling in the immigration lounge and it smelt of mould. It was not a propitious beginning at all and the company house was a nightmare.

We had not expected anything like our Nanyuki house, but this was not even in the running. It was on a piece of land that looked like mud flats, was populated by hermit crabs, and had one huge coconut tree towering above it. It was next to a main road. It backed onto a creek and didn't even look towards the Indian Ocean, which meant that at no time of day would there be a sea breeze. Inside it had speckled hard white terrazzo floors which hurt your eyes in the glare, and the non-optional extra – mildew!

It had a boxy sitting room which smelt of mildew and a long corridor with rooms opening off it which smelt of mildew. The company sheets smelt of mildew and the towels smelt of mildew. Besides this, it was hotter than hell. In the dining room, which was totally airless and three times the size of the sitting room, were two cupboards which opened up onto washbasins. None of the bedrooms had basins and the bathroom was full of spiders and sugar ants.

Another feature was a flight of twenty-five stone steps which wound up and up in a spiral. They eventually ended up at the door of a tiny room, which in turn opened up onto a flat roof. This was strung with hideous multicoloured fairy lights and would have been an ideal place for a mullah to call the faithful to prayer, otherwise its use seemed limited. The tiny room, with its latticed peepholes, was the sort of room for an Arab Rapunzel to sit, combing her hair and waiting for a dhow captain lover. The steps leading up to it, I was to find, were constantly gritty with the creek sand, which blew through the windows continually.

There was no shortage of servants to clean them. The house, which was rented by the company from an Indian called Mr Mohammed Sulemanjee, came with three servants – Abdullah, Suleman Bin, and Ali – who were already incumbent when we arrived, had mapped out their lifestyle, and seemed a little inflexible regarding any changes I might have in mind.

Abdullah did the ironing and the garden and was as black as ebony. He usually burnt the ironing, and unless he polished the trunk of the solitary coconut palm for exercise the sandy garden would not keep him very busy. Someone told me that he was useful at killing poisonous snakes from the creek mangroves, a piece of information which started me off on a whole new and unsettling train of thought.

Suleman Bin, who was about four feet high, was very old and wore an embroidered cotton hat and a long white kanzu. He was the cook, he told me, and his speciality was lobster thermidor and curried prawns. He had a wall-eye, spectacles and a determined presence in spite of his size, and obviously didn't think women were up to much. How exactly he managed to get this across to me, I don't know, because he was always very respectful, always scrupulously polite; but he conveyed it subtly.

Ali made the beds, polished the floors, washed the terrazzo, waited at table, squeezed jugs of limes and fresh orange juice, and screamed conversations off the flat top roof to any of his friends who might be passing by on the road. Ali worked, in fact, quite hard.

I asked him why he didn't get Suleman Bin to give a hand in the long hours between boiling four eggs for breakfast and cooking lunch, when Suleman Bin didn't do anything except gaze in a trancelike state out of the kitchen window. It seemed a good plan, but Ali was horrified at even entertaining such an idea. He told me that Suleman owned a hotel in the native area at Kinondoni. Apparently Ali had a room there. He had been out of work before he found this job, and one way or another his hotel bill hadn't been paid, so he had a sort of deal with Suleman Bin to make life easier for him until he got square with his hotel accounts. It was going to take years, a lifetime, to clear his debts, he said, and where Suleman worked Ali had to be. So, over the years, Ali continued to wash up, scour saucepans and do all the work, while Suleman gazed out of the window at the palm tree, boiled eggs for breakfast and cooked the odd piece of fish for lunch. He was disappointed in our menus, but lobster thermidor and prawns weren't our idea of a staple diet.

Suleman really had to plug away for supper when we had two courses, but he managed to keep his strength up by supporting his weight on the kitchen wall for most of the morning and having a siesta at his hotel from two till six p.m. I would see him every evening, punctually at a quarter past six, a small figure in his long white robes and white embroidered cap, slowly crossing the right of way, ebony walking-stick in his hand, and nodding graciously to other figures in white hats and flowing robes who saluted him.

As a hotel owner, he had a high standing in the community. They were quite unlike the Kikuyus, these coast people, and I was not sure I liked them because I didn't have much rapport with them. They were a secret, brooding people, polyglots of coast Somali, Arab and African, and whereas the Kikuyu made you feel they were part of your life and you of theirs, these coast dwellers shut you out. They spoke a much purer and more dignified Swahili. They were more guarded in their manner. They were more lethargic, perhaps because most of them were riddled with bilharzia and malaria. So possibly it was not their fault, as the climate was against them and the heat not conducive to sparkle. But still, I missed Kenya and I missed the Kikuyu.

All was not gloom, however. When the monsoon changed at last and the dhows came down on the wind from the Gulf, the sea turned a brilliant aquamarine in the sunlight and now it was the cruising season and the harbour was full of liners strung with fairy lights. The yellow faces of the Europeans tanned in the clean sunshine, and the company's social life began to include us. Robin had a boat he had built sent down on a dhow from Mombasa, and we went to the Old Dhow harbour to collect it, and ate dates and drank Turkish coffee with the dhow captain, and tried not to think of the smell of rotting fish and the swarms of flies on the dates and coffee cups.

We spent days at the Yacht Club and sailed over to Honeymoon Island, mooring the boat beside a casuarina tree. Honeymoon Island was only a few miles offshore, small and deserted except for an old crumbling tomb with an Arabic inscription cut into the stone slab on top of it. For a long time I could discover very little about its incumbent, or why he alone was buried there. I was intrigued to find, when we sailed over on Saturday afternoons in Robin's *Enterprise*, a handful of marigolds or bougainvillea left on a low wall around the grave. They were always fresh, so I supposed it to be one of the fishermen who went that way in their ngalawas. It was a very old tomb and I resolved to try unravelling the mystery of it and learn a little Arabic. When I spoke to Ali, he said it was the burial place of a great Arab *mfalme* of long ago, an ancient Arab king, but who he was seemed lost in the mists of time.

There was a great deal that was new to discover here. It was different from anywhere we had been before. In spite of myself, I felt a faint flicker of interest stirring – it was very faint, but I stopped wishing quite so passionately that I was in Kenya and started to take an interest in the house and its surroundings, even in the land crabs, and applied to Housing for permission to buy striped cotton curtains and a new white sofa for the living room.

The main trouble with the house was the fine sand which coated every surface, and the sugar ants marching in columns. They, and the cockroaches and giant centipedes which bred in the humidity, seemed to be everywhere. The house was sandy, got dirty quickly and was a nightmare to clean.

I wondered how the oil company people who had lived there before us, called the Van der Walts, had coped. They had had the house for two years and had been transferred back to Holland just before we arrived. I asked Ali, who had been working for them, how Mrs Van der Walt had organised the house.

'She no organise,' said Ali, surprised. 'What she going to organise?'

'But what did she do with her time, I mean?' I said haughtily, opening cupboards teeming with insect life – cockroaches, beetles, silverfish and horrible little creepy-crawlies called Nairobi Eye. If you squashed one unwittingly, you came up in blisters in minutes, usually on your face.

'Morning she go to beach. Afternoon she go to sleep. Nights she go party.'

'Every night?'

'Every night,' agreed Ali. 'If she no go party, peoples come here.'

'Well, things are going to change around here,' I said. 'You and I are going to clear out these cupboards for a start, line them with fresh newspapers, spray them and put Epsom salts and mothballs into them.'

Ali was genuinely horrified. He watched me with a look of dismay and amazement on his face as I rolled up my sleeves.

'He bad, memsahib. Not good for memsahibs to work,' he told me, leaning against the wall with his white cotton hat tipped over his eyes and his arms folded.

I worked flat out all morning, with Ali in obstructive attendance, muttering to himself.

'Mbuya sana. Mbuya sana.' (Very bad. Very bad.) It was like a litany. My dress was sticking to my back, my hair soaked to the scalp with sweat, and I was seeing spots in front of my eyes. I had cleared only four cupboards when I had to sit down. Tottering to a chair, I called out to Ali to bring me some fresh orange juice and ice. Bootfaced with disapproval, he was cleaning the copper trays.

There wasn't a breath of air anywhere and what little wind there was had dropped. I struggled on for a few mornings, but by noon I always felt like someone recovering from a long illness. I had a prickly heat rash, sore and itchy around my neck, under my arms and at the back of my knees. On the fourth morning I almost fainted from the heat, and, looking at my face in the glass, I saw a pale grey ghost in the cloudy mirror which I barely recognised as myself. A scorpion with its babies on its back scuttled out of a cupboard I was cleaning and I started to shriek, but decided I felt too exhausted. It was beginning to dawn on me that in this climate, at the height of the hot season, servants weren't a luxury but a necessity.

'Ali,' I said faintly, handing him the spray and the dusters, 'I'm going to the beach.' Thoughts of cool waves and rustling palms floated in front of my eyes like a mirage.

'It is better, memsahib. Mzuri tu,' said Ali, cheering up. The whole spring-cleaning programme had given him a complex. He hadn't smiled for three days. When I put my bathing things into the car, he was his old cheerful self again. His face was wreathed in smiles as he waved with the duster from the rooftop. After that I joined the children, who practically lived on the beach, bobbing around in the rock pools in their rubber rings.

We had to go out a good deal at night and couldn't leave them, so I got an ayah named Fatima to live in. She didn't actually have a yashmak but she wore a black georgette kanga, and every time she saw a man would cover her face to the eyes with a corner of the black georgette and giggle. As there were quite a few men around, it took up most of her day. She spoke only coast Swahili and I spoke only upcountry Kenyan Swahili, so we couldn't communicate a great deal. She had small hennaed hands, wore thick red nail polish on her toe- and fingernails and smelt of very musky sweet perfume, but she washed nappies, giggled, held her kanga over her face and giggled, and sometimes sat with the children on the beach or walked them to the children's rock pool up at Oyster Bay when the temperature wasn't high enough to fry an egg on the tarmac road.

The heat in the house began to grow more and more fierce, the sun beat down on the flat roof day after day. When the monsoon came, the long rains would break and it would be cooler, people said. I noticed quite a few of the other staff houses were facing the beach and had a breeze most of the day, but we were unlucky because we had arrived last, after the expatriates had taken most of the better houses on the sea. Mr Mohammed Sulemanjee's house, most understandably, had been the least in demand.

So at night we tossed and turned under sweat-soaked sheets, with twanging mosquitoes flying up in their droves from the creek. The mosquito nets kept them at bay but made our bedroom more airless still.

It was when the hot season was at its hottest that deliverance came, in the form of a company cocktail party, which by now we were obliged to give in return for months of hospitality.

I battled to begin with, thinking, How, in this oven, can we entertain without our guests dropping like flies in their tracks from heat exhaustion? Then I thought suddenly, Why try? *We* had to live with it. It was a company house ... In fact the heat might speak for itself.

'Suleman Bin,' I said, 'we'll have curry puffs, sausage rolls, samosas – anything really spicy. We're going to have a party!'

I decided on lots of heavy sweet sherry to start with. We'd be sparing with the iced drinks. Ice melted anyway almost as soon as it was out of its trays.

'Sherry isn't very suitable for this time of year,' Robin demurred. 'The temperature is in the hundreds! Why not Pimm's or iced daiquiris or something cool?'

'Sweet sherry to start with.' I was sticking to my guns. 'Bristol Cream. It will help make the ice go round when people switch after their first drinks.'

The day of the party, the heavy-duty electric fan, which half-heartedly stirred the humid air, was on from early afternoon in the sitting room, but the windows were closed to keep the mosquitoes out, and when the guests arrived at seven p.m. they were ushered straight into a nice little ten-by-twelve oven. The sherry and cocktail food circulated on trays carried by Ali, looking very smart in a long white kanzu to his toes, with an embroidered waistcoat and his red fez with a tassel, and by Abdullah, who bore round a tray of curry puffs.

By eight p.m. most of the guests were drinking Scotch on the rocks and growing scarlet in the face. I noticed the personnel manager running a finger agonisingly inside his collar. Oil companies in East Africa at that time were very conventional and upmarket. Protocol was strictly observed, so no one was wearing shorts or open-necked shirts. Every man in the room was wearing a tie.

'Tell me,' said the personnel manager, gulping his Scotch and waving away a tray of turgid sherry, 'don't you find this house a bit hot?'

'Oh it's terrible,' I said bravely and then, sweetly reasonable, 'but there isn't another company house available, you see, so we just have to put up with it.' I trailed off, smiling bravely, and offered him a chilli-filled samosa.

'The Van der Walts used the roof a lot, made a sort of roof garden up there,' he croaked, but I pretended not to hear him.

Next day Robin came home at lunchtime and said he'd had the best news possible. Our house wasn't up to company standards and we could look for another near Oyster Bay and the beach.

I found another house in a cool garden full of mango trees and frangipani. It was big, with high ceilings, flagged floors and slatted Spanish shutters instead of window glass. It had an electric punkah in the sitting room and an air-conditioner in one bedroom. It was right in Oyster Bay, the 'in' side of Dar es Salaam, which always had a breeze blowing up from the bay.

Ali and Suleman Bin were delighted. They felt it was a step up the social scale to work in Oyster Bay. Besides, the cool breezes were a bonus to them during Ramadan. Ramadan was something I knew very little about before Dar es Salaam. If I gave it any thought, I suppose I knew there was a period when the faithful of the Muslim community went into retreat and didn't eat or drink until a certain time had passed.

I was somewhat taken aback one morning to rise and find Suleman Bin in more of a glassy-eyed trance than ever, eyes crossed, leaning almost perpendicularly against the kitchen wall. Ali was tottering round with a duster, flicking the furniture as delicately as if it were made of Dresden china. Both wore a look of pained resignation on their faces. Hamedi, the new gardener, was asleep in the shade of a large mango tree. Breakfast wasn't ready and the polishing wasn't done.

'Ramadan, memsahib!' explained Ali, resting against the edge of the dining-room table. 'Very tough time for Suleman, Hamedi and Ali. We drink only water. No tea. No food pass our lips for many days now till new moon come up!'

'No food at all?' I asked, aghast.

'Only when dark come. Sunset to sunrise we may eat. All day we have nothing and,' he said, shifting his weight slightly and holding onto the wall for support, 'too much work, memsahib, make big thirst.' He rolled his jelly-bean eyes and sighed.

'Well, you'd better find replacements for yourselves temporarily,' I said feebly, trying to get on top of the situation, 'and all go home until the fast is finished. Cut your hair, Ali,' I added, looking at his luxuriant oiled locks, 'it's waving down your back.'

'No cut hair during the fast,' explained Ali joyfully. 'Fast go on for many days, for many, many days, memsahib, and who come to work so hard for the memsahib as Ali? Ali good houseboy, memsahib, and good Mohammedan.'

For the rest of that month Ali and Suleman and Hamedi sighed and groaned, and rolled their eyes, taking a nap wherever possible. The house wore a neglected air. I felt a brute when I asked Ali to do the laundry or Suleman to cook an omelette. The new moon had not been sighted. They were all at the end of their tether and so was I.

Thick cloud covered the sky and we were beginning to watch as anxiously as the servants for the appearance of the new moon. Eventually it was announced on the wireless that the mullah had decided to take to the air to look for it above the cloud bank. Having hired a small aeroplane and accompanied by a European pilot in white shorts and a T-shirt, the mullah in his long white robes and little embroidered cap climbed into it. They were watched by hundreds of the faithful from the airport balcony as they soared high over the roofs and mosques of sweltering Dar es Salaam.

To everyone's relief the mullah was able to sight the new moon for himself and landed with the tidings to cheering crowds. Ali, Suleman Bin and Hamedi departed to feast and revel at Kinondoni, reprieved from the fast. The feast of Eid had begun. The whole occasion had been made all the more dramatic by the hiring of the little plane – there was great talk of it and shouted end-of-Ramadan greetings in the bazaar and marketplace. Ali and the others did not return for three days, and it took them many more to get their feet back on the ground, so little work was done for some time afterwards.

– 33 –

The children were getting older, and because there was a very pleasant school next to us at Oyster Bay, literally just through the Kei-apple hedge, I went to look over it to see what it was like. If I liked it, I decided, we would put their names down. It was the school for the Oyster Bay area and I assumed that they would automatically go there because it was not a private school, so I was somewhat taken aback when the principal told me there were no vacancies for the children. He was sure, he said, that I would find the same problem in any school in the area: no vacancies anywhere. Too many Peace Corps, consulate and army people these days in the sleepy little coastal town – Dar es Salaam Education Department just couldn't cope. It was not, they said, even worth putting the children's names on a waiting list at the kindergartens and primary schools. It stretched into infinity. Marnie, bored with the beach and longing for company, was clamouring to go to school. Hugh, happy enough to be in the rock pools, didn't care either way, but the time would come.

So I put an advertisement in the local papers which read simply: European mother with two children and large shady garden will endeavour to teach the three Rs to other children in the 4–5 age group. Interested people can ring 8384111.

As an afterthought, I added the word 'experienced'. I had just remembered the army nursery school in Nanyuki.

Having put the advertisement into the *Tanganyika Standard*, I wandered, in an optimistic frame of mind, down to the Indian bazaar and bought a blackboard and chalks, some alphabet books, counting frames and six slates – perhaps even a dozen, I thought hesitantly. I bought a dozen and got out of the steaming heat quickly and home to the bay and the breeze.

When I reached home Ali was on the steps, dressed in his canvas apron, doing a sort of dance on his thin black legs and waving a piece of paper. Through the open window of the car he handed me a list of thirty-five telephone numbers.

'What on earth?' I said blankly. Some of the telephone numbers were out of town.

'All want school, memsahib,' Ali said, beaming. '*Mingi, mingi.*' (Many, many.)

Within half an hour I had had another dozen calls and by eight that night the number was standing at fifty-four. In the heat, the incessant ringing of the phone was driving me mad. I almost unplugged it, but rang a friend to relate what was happening.

'Don't unplug it, you're in business! Come on. Down with coffee parties. I'll help you, and so will Di Knowles!'

'I've got no experience at that sort of level, with those sort of numbers!' I screamed. But somehow the more I thought about having an independent school, the more the idea seemed feasible. The house was large enough. One whole wing could be the school area. A load of white sand under the mango trees would make a sandpit area in the shade. We needed beakers for orange juice, poster paints for finger painting, and the British Council would lend us cartoon films. We could hire buses and go to the beach, to the museum, and find people to give puppet shows. There were endless things we could do. Two of the company wives came round next morning and over endless glasses of iced coffee we began to make plans and draw up lists.

'You realise it's going to be multiracial?' someone said.

'Have you any idea how to deal with African and Indian children?'

I hadn't, but I didn't have to wait long for the experience as, on the day we opened, an enormous black car, stretching the length of the drive and flying the country's flag, inched slowly down towards the house. Inside in the back sat a very venerable and portly African gentleman next to a slender Tanganyikan woman. Between them was a small and very frightened child. The venerable gentleman got out

At the very least he is a member of the cabinet, I thought. He was. He was Chief Fundikira, friend of Julius Nyerere, accompanied by his young wife and little daughter, Nyanzala Fundikira. He asked very courteously if he could book his daughter in, and I agreed. In any case it was more like a royal command. He looked round, nodded graciously and said he would confirm the booking, then stepped back into his vast automobile which, with pennant flying, slowly and majestically moved down the drive again.

'Well!' I said, 'that's a good start. Recognition in high places.' But I had no time to say anything else as the next to arrive was the Government House car with the British coat of arms on the door. The Governor's ADC had a little girl aged five and she was going to join us. A fast white sports car wheeled into the drive with its hood down, driven by the elegant wife of the German consul. She came in, leading her small boy in his lederhosen by the hand. A French child, Gabriella, from the French Embassy, Americans from the Peace Corps and the United States Information Department, a beautiful little Greek girl with gold and pearl earrings in her pierced ears, and children from the Seventh Day Adventist Mission with accents like brown treacle.

We were totally cosmopolitan and we were full to bursting. It had taken only ten days from the advertisement to getting the school off the ground. As nobody wanted to wait, they had urged me to open at once.

Chief Fundikira had not confirmed his daughter's booking and the waiting list was over thirty at one point, so I telephoned his office to ask what he meant to do.

A very superior Roedean voice answered, 'Chief Fundikira's office. May I help you?' He wasn't available so I looked up his number at home in the Dar es Salaam directory. He had five houses and I rang them one by one, but no one who answered appeared to understand or speak English. There were just gales of giggles. When I rang his office again the next day, I told the secretary that the Chief and Mrs Fundikira had booked their daughter into my school but had not confirmed the booking.

'Which Mrs Fundikira was with the Chief?' said the frosty Roedean voice.

'His wife,' I said patiently.

'Which wife?'

'Well, his own wife of course.'

'Chief Fundikira has four wives,' said the Roedean voice, with no inflection.

'Four?' I was floundering. 'Isn't that bigamy?'

'Chief Fundikira is the Minister of Justice,' she said, with a note of triumph in her voice, 'and he is also a Muslim.'

Nyanzala Fundikira came to the school duly and was the politest, quietest little African girl, who gave no trouble to anyone and never spoke above a whisper. She loved the school and when she left we missed her. She cried the day she went, but the Chief's most glamorous wife had been at a finishing school in Israel and when the course was over she came back to Dar es Salaam, groomed to take her place as the Minister's wife, so Nyanzala and her mother were sent back upcountry.

One morning the most enormous car yet nosed into the driveway with a gaudy flag flying on its bonnet. This one was driven by an African in white livery. The colours of the flag were repeated on his cuffs and on the band of his peaked chauffeur's cap. Lying in the back, or rather reclining in the back, clad in what looked like an off-the-shoulder lamé dress, with one shoulder bare, was a superior-looking African gentleman. He wore opulent jewelled sandals and in front of him was a newspaper holder on a mahogany stand. The sheets of the *Tanganyika Standard* were spread on it and he studied them languidly, turning over the pages with bejewelled fingers for some seconds before stepping out of the motorcar.

'Aha, Madame!' cried he, advancing majestically. 'Aha!' Not knowing whether 'Aha!' was a form of Ivory Coast or Gold Coast greeting – his outfit was definitely West African – I was uncertain whether to shout 'Aha!' in reply. 'You are the lady I have overheard speak of, and this no doubt is your little school? What splendid wark you are doing here. Really splendid wark! Aha!'

Bedazzled by the jewellery and the whole scenario, and uncertain whether to bow or curtsy, I suddenly spied, crouching in the back of his Pontiac, two identical children dressed in West African cotton prints with jewels hanging from pierced ears.

'These!' he cried with an expansive gesture and the air of producing rabbits from a hat, 'these are my twin children, Jean and Jennifer Tu Fu Mia and I – I,' and his face split into a really splendid grin, 'I am the High Commissioner for Ghana and I wish that they now come to your school.'

As if at a given cue, the twins stepped forward and chorused, 'We are Jean and Jennifer Tu Fu Mia.' The scenario was becoming more Gilbert and Sullivan every minute.

'Our father is the Ha Commissioner for Ghana and we are four yeahs old.'

This was in perfect English but it subsequently turned out to be the total extent of their vocabulary.

At this point in the proceedings my three-month-old puppy trotted into view. Jean and Jennifer stood transfixed with horror and then, giving a piercing scream in unison, they threw themselves into the back seat of the car, where they sat cowering and clutching each other. Their father, with a deep belly-laugh, reminding me more and more in retrospect of the Fon in Gerald Durrell's books, arranged that they should begin school the following day, adjusted his flowing robes, clicked his fingers at the chauffeur who was admiring himself in the car mirror, and glided away.

Jean and Jennifer, who were so alike I could never tell them apart, duly arrived in short pink silk frilly dresses and diamond drop earrings. We locked the puppy up but I forgot the two tame vervet monkeys, Nixon and Ndogo, who lived in the garden in the mango trees and came to play in the sandpit. They were a great drawcard normally, but Jennifer and Jean took one look at them and fled, shrieking, with me in hot pursuit.

I had succeeded in recapturing them when the cat came round the corner and, at this, Jennifer and Jean, who had had enough, took to the largest mango tree and shinned faster than lightning to the top.

'Come down!' I called, peering into the branches myopically. 'It's only a kitten. She won't hurt you.'

But from the depths of the tree came a chorus in accents of terror in the only English they knew. 'We are Jennifer and Jean Tu Fu Mia. Our father is the Ha Commissioner for Ghana and we are four yeahs old.' When the monkeys, bursting with curiosity at these phenomena, joined them in the upper branches of the mango tree, they came down, shaking, and threw themselves into my arms. They were terribly afraid and nothing would calm them.

Life with the Ghanaian twins was wearying for me and no doubt it was anguish for them. They were terrified of anything four-legged that moved or breathed. The sight of an ant threw them into hysterics for hours, and the monkeys had to be banished each morning on a long canvas harness to the shade of the frangipani bushes, in Hamedi's charge.

Every day the vast car glided into the drive and Mr Tu Fu Mia, in flowing cloth of gold, jewels and cotton, would languidly beckon to me through the window, and, as I could scarcely ignore him, I came panting crossly up to the car where, leaning towards me, he nodded and graciously said, 'What splendid wark you are doing, Madame. Really splendid wark!' And then, waving imperiously to the chauffeur, he drove slowly and majestically away.

Mrs Tu Fu Mia came to tea with me one day, also in flowing robes and beautifully patterned batik cotton, which she wore bunched in layers around her hips. She told me that she had eleven children but all except three were in Ghana, and she said she was 'dead scared of sea barfin'. I thought she meant some dangerous sea creature, but it turned out only to mean bathing in the sea. Apart from that she was all smiles and very intrepid, and she sat with me all afternoon, draped and splendid like a figurehead. Beaming beatifically and sipping her tea, she told me that she meant to buy two puppies for Jennifer and Jean. I often wondered whether she did and what they did, because soon after that they left Dar es Salaam. There was something expansive and exotic about the Tu Fu Mia seniors. I think he belonged to the West African set who enjoyed golden beds and thrones inset with semi-precious stones. He looked very much as if the blood of kings ran in his veins, but there was no doubt he was very gracious.

The school progressed and we met interesting parents and attractive children. The little Parsee children behaved beautifully. They were Zoroastrians and had exquisite manners. Their parents came from Bombay and were on a two-year tour in Dar es Salaam. We had dinner with them in their house filled with jade and china from their previous posting in the Far East. The Parsee women had magnolia skin and huge dark eyes that looked Greek or Italian, and had been 'finished' in Europe.

Dar es Salaam was, I had to admit, more cosmopolitan and exotic than Nairobi. We had befriended a shy Ethiopian First Secretary whom we found skulking behind a bookcase at a dull cocktail party and, through him and the Tu Fu Mias and others, we were on the merry-go-round of embassy functions, shaking hands with different high commissioners, ambassadors and trade commissioners every few weeks, or so it seemed. Half of them had no idea who we were. We were obviously, through chance, marked down as representatives of the business community, so we stood in lines, shaking white-gloved hands, among the strings of fairy lights in Karimjee Gardens and sipping champagne or gin and tonic with the Chinese, Indians, Ghanaians, Ethiopians, Canadians and so on.

The yellow and pink fairy lights and the palm trees had the effect of a setting for a South Sea Island musical. People mingled in saris or national dress, or some of the diplomats wore Chinese-collared white tropical suits. In the setting of the Karimjee Gardens one almost expected them to form up and break into a soft-shoe routine with chorus girls:

I am the High Commissioner,
He is my ADC
We celebrate our national day
Beside the azure sea.

There was an unreal, fun element to all these Dar es Salaam receptions. I think that that is one of the reasons one enjoys functions in African states: the colour, costumes and the settings; yet nothing ever turns out as seriously as planned. Somehow, among all the pomp, someone makes a mistake and saves the day. Perfection humourlessly executed is very, very dull.

– 34 –

My mother had taken to sending me intermittent missives, sometimes as much as two years apart, so I was not particularly surprised to receive a letter from her on my twenty-sixth birthday. It covered several pages and didn't tell me very much except for an excerpt, almost indecipherable, written up the side of the last page, which said, 'You will be interested to hear that Norman' – I was beginning to take an interest in Norman in spite of myself – 'who was in India when we met, has been moved by his company to East Africa. It would be lovely if you two met. You are so alike.'

She finished with love, in a feathery hand with lots of loops, and the information that Norman's address was Jamhouri House, Mombasa, that she had given him my address, and that he would contact me very soon.

Norman, my *doppelgänger*, was getting closer! I expected little from our possible contact as, after all, the London reunion had hardly been sparkling. It was as well that I did expect little, as Norman never wrote. It was to be two years after I had heard from my mother before I was in Mombasa again, or in fact thought of her or of Norman, not guessing that on that particular occasion I would meet him.

I went to Mombasa on the spur of the moment. Robin was on safari and the children in boarding school when an unexpected invitation came my way. I flew from Dar es Salaam to stay with two of my oldest friends in a beach house on the

Kenyan coast. The beach was cut off from the outside world by acres of sisal plantation. I had stayed there before and it was one of my favourite places. In front of the beach house itself were feathery palms and enormous great splashy bushes of bougainvillaea, and beyond that again the sea, unreal in turquoise brilliance, and sand like castor sugar, dotted with tiny apricot and mauve shells.

On the horizon of this paradise was the coral reef. The Kenyan coast always will be Utopia. One dresses in kangas wound round one's body and tied just above the bust, and one can potter on the reef in a stupor of sun and happy relaxation forgetting the rest of the world exists.

For the first week I was there we lived on fresh fish and lobsters off the boats. Fish we couldn't buy from the ngalawas was brought to the door in *kikapus* (baskets) by coast Somalis with huge grins, and weighed on portable scales as fixed as a crooked roulette wheel. Occasionally we had to leave the solitude of the peaceful beach, which we did with great reluctance and only when staples ran out and we had to drive down the tyre-ripping coral road to Mombasa.

One morning it was my turn to go with Pat to replenish stores; and on impulse, standing in the gloom of one of those huge, curry-smelling shops owned by Indians, it suddenly came to my mind to make a call to Norman. I was waiting for an order of tinned butter, condensed milk and curry powder to be executed, and revelling in the luxury of being away from the baking heat of Mombasa's streets and the cacophony of klaxon horns. The two Patel brothers who owned the shop were moving quietly about, unpacking boxes of tea. A paper Jamhuri (Independence) flag fluttered in the breeze from an electric fan and somehow the juxtaposition of the flag, the tea boxes and Mombasa brought to my mind, like a fish swimming up from the depths, the thought of Norman.

I asked one of the Indians if I could use the telephone,

looked up the company number and, dialling, waited with a slightly churning stomach. A Goan voice answered, very brisk. Norman had given up employment with the international company, the voice said, and was working for himself in a different field. She gave me the number where he could be reached and I scribbled it on my chequebook cover. I almost dialled it, but somehow the impulse passed. It seemed pointless to contact him, he hadn't written and we didn't know each other; and my order was, in any case, ready.

The two *kikapus* were full, plus tins of orange juice, bottles of tonic water and special curry powder for a fresh prawn curry, and one of the Patel brothers put a present of cashew nuts on top. We loaded the jeep in the glare of Kilindini Road and, stunned by noise and street heat, drove like maniacs for the ferry and home. Shopping in Mombasa was only bearable early in the morning when it was still cool.

That evening we sat, as usual, on the veranda of the beach house, shukas wrapped around us and Mylol applied against mosquitoes, sipping *waragi* (banana gin) and nibbling Mr Patel's cashew nuts. There was a crème-de-menthe sunset streaking the sky and a dhow drifted on the sea in front of us.

Mellowed with *waragi*, I idly brought up the subject of Norman and the call which hadn't come off, filling in the background of an unknown brother only a few miles from where we sat and whom I had never seen. Everyone recharged their glasses, ate cashew nuts and gave opinions. 'How *could* I not ring again?' they said. At least try once more and then leave it in the lap of the gods. Should Norman be on leave or have moved, then that was that – it wasn't meant. But at least *try*, they implored.

There was, someone said, a telephone in a small Indian *duka* along the beach and I could drive down and use it in the morning. It was not, however, until a week later, when we were lunching with friends south of Mombasa and only two days before I left to go home, that I went walking along the Tiwi Beach with Norman in mind. I had had a need to be alone all day, coupled with a curious sense of *déjà vu*, so when the others were drowsing after a curry lunch I wandered off in the direction of the Shanzu Hotel on the headland, whose only claim to fame was a public phone. It badly needed some sort of incentive to draw the crowds, struggling as it did in a series of palm-thatched buildings and looking so unappetising that one wondered who would choose to stay there; but I found myself drawn towards it as to the focal point of the beach.

Sounds of wailing music floated from the door and blond hippies were listening to transistors in pup tents in a coconut grove below. A couple of vervet monkeys, examining each other's hands earnestly like palmists doing a reading, scattered on the *makuti* roof as I scuffed sand from my flip-flops. Normally hotels were crammed with German package tours, but this, for sure, was no German tourist mecca. There was a deserted air about the place in spite of the music and in spite of the hippies.

The three or four Sikhs who came up from the sea towards me made me jump. Without their usual neat turbans they looked shockingly wild, all waist-length hair, beards and hooked noses. I walked gingerly into the hotel and realised that I had been there before, years ago, in the heyday of colonial orderliness. It had been full, then, of upcountry settlers and their children. The area where I stood had been the dining room, with neatly typed menus, waiters in their white kanzus and tarbooshes, tablecloths and morning tea trays. Now there appeared to be no sign of a dining room at all, just a smell of stale pot and hair oil. The past had vanished completely. No memsahibs in straw hats, no bwanas.

A notice, pinned up with two tin-tacks, flapped in the slight breeze in the foyer and was misspelt with the block letters crossed out and misspelt again. DON'T WALK NAKEED IN THE

HOTEL, it said. I hoped the instructions were being obeyed, because a naked Sikh with flowing locks would definitely not be acceptable.

In a glassed-off cubicle, lolling about under another notice, which said 'Receptionist', was a huge Jaluo African youth in crepe-soled Grasshopper shoes, picking his teeth with a matchstick. He indicated a manual telephone with his free hand when I asked. It was in an airless booth in the corner, and smelt of the Sikh's musky hair oil.

With the toothpick still in his mouth, the 'receptionist' explained, 'You must ring two shart and one long eef you want the exchange.' He went back to picking his teeth and I tried the phone as instructed, holding my breath against the sweet, cloying smell.

Every time I turned the handle a chorus of African voices on the party line shouted 'Allo! Allo!' The subscribers on this line either had no idea of their call signals or else, maddened with heat and boredom, ran as men united whenever they heard the telephone. Sometimes one heard a click as they picked up their receivers, followed by deep breathing. Whatever the reason, for me, suffocated with the smell of hair oil and bludgeoned by the heat in the booth, it was extremely irritating, but I persevered with the two short and one long until, with an interested audience on the party line, staccato giggles and 'Allo! Jambo!' and 'Habari?', I eventually heard a receiver in Norman's office being lifted.

There were butterflies in my tummy when his secretary asked who was speaking. Should I say 'His half-sister'? Might it be a shock?

So I said, 'A friend – a sort of relation,' feebly, and hoped he wouldn't be put off. He had had word of me before, after all, and had not made contact, so perhaps half-sisters were something superfluous to him. Not to me they wouldn't have been, but then I had had a solitary childhood.

His voice when he picked up the phone was very English, very guarded, but friendly.

'When you say "a sort of relation", I am not too clear.'

'Well, a half-sister really. We have a mutual mother.' What an extraordinary conversation, I thought, like a really bad movie script.

'The same mother? Oh, yes, I had vaguely heard, I mean I knew of your existence, but had no idea ...' Could I come to his offices?

No, not now. I was too far out of town.

Could I have dinner that night?

Not possible. I was committed. As a guest, my time was not my own.

He was a member of the Mombasa Club, he said, and it was cool there and pleasant, and so we agreed to meet for lunch in two days' time. It would be the last day of my stay so I would not crowd him. I was intrigued, longing to see him but nervous as a cat as well, and I imagined, although it was scarcely true, that he had sounded diffident on the telephone.

The day of the lunch I went to as much trouble with my appearance as possible. Not easy with the sweat rolling my make-up away in pink drops and my hair sticking to my head in the heat. Mombasa in December was terrible and so, shiny-nosed, my cotton dress crumpling, I climbed the steps of the Mombasa Club into pure Somerset Maugham country.

Peacock-tail wicker chairs stood under the slowly revolving punkahs, and an African in a red-and-gold embroidered waistcoat and starched drill suit moved forward to take my order. I was parched with nerves and longing for a drink, but, not being a member, it wasn't possible. Here it was chits only. There were small groups of people drinking pink gins, the sound of hushed well-bred English voices, copies of *Country Life* and *The Illustrated London News*, all unbelievably British.

There did not appear to be anyone who was waiting for a guest when I first glanced round, but then I saw in the corner a bloated young man with a red face and greasy curly hair, too long at the back and thinning on top, sitting in a pink shirt and drinking a Tom Collins. My heart sank. I gazed at him out of the corner of my eye and, sure enough, his eyes unmistakably flickered to the clock.

He sighed, fished in his shirt pocket for a squashed packet of Clipper cigarettes and settled back in his chair. If this is Norman, I thought, I'll make an excuse and bolt for it. Nonsense, of course I couldn't! I'd have to stick it out. After all, I had instigated the meeting. I fidgeted in my high-backed wicker chair, just out of his line of vision. He fidgeted in his chair, blew his nose noisily and ordered another Tom Collins.

I was about to break cover and approach him when I heard a voice say, 'I think you must be my half-sister!' And there was Norman, slim and golden-haired, with brown eyes, in white shorts and silk shirt, looking shyly down at me.

The first thing that struck me about him was that my mother had not exaggerated. He really was like me. It was as if I were looking at my own reflection in a looking-glass. His eyes were not the same colour as mine and he was taller, but these were superficial differences. It was an almost eerie feeling to sit opposite one's male counterpart.

He ordered two Tom Collinses, stared at me with lively curiosity, and after a few minutes said, 'We could scarcely avoid recognising each other, could we! Even in a crowded room. I'm sorry to stare, but it's uncanny – the likeness, I mean!'

I shook my head. 'Not so amazing really, I suppose. We are half-brother and sister. It's just that I'm very like my father's side of the family and yet, when we sit here side by side, we could almost be twins.'

It transpired that he had been in Kenya before and at one point had been a mere twenty or thirty miles from where I was during his training. There was no feeling of tension between us at all. No awkwardness or strain, as there had been when I had met my mother. Perhaps when I met her she had felt nervous and guilty and on trial, and I had felt nervous and on trial, whereas with Norman, he and I owed each other nothing. It was as if two strangers, amused to find in each a carbon copy of the other, had arranged to meet.

But as we talked on, I found there were undertones. When we had finished our talk of Kenya and our marriages and children, we inevitably had to touch on our mother. I wanted to ask him about her, as I felt I knew and understood her so little. The fact that when we met she had not come alone had made intimacy in that short time impossible. But when I asked Norman about her he veered away from the subject, not once but several times, until, taking the bull by the horns, I said blatantly, 'What was she really like? Are you close?'

He shook his head. 'No, not close.'

'I met her in London. She kept talking about you all the time. When did you see her last?'

'Long ago. I scarcely knew her. I was brought up by my father's family.'

'Like me?'

'Like you. Only I had a brother and a sister and we shared everything – experiences, schools, everything. We grew up together.' He looked ruffled, but I had to ask one more thing.

'Were you angry with her?' I wondered. 'I mean, would you rather have been with her, been brought up by her?'

There was a pause and then he said, 'I don't know exactly how I do feel about that, but I know that I don't ever want to see her again. I was a little boy of about eight perhaps when she left.' He fiddled with the swizzle stick in his drink and changed the subject.

'My sister, your half-sister, lives in England. You'd like her, everybody does. She is the youngest and the closest really to our mother. Was brought up by her till she was about ten.

I'll write and tell her we met. Give you her address. She has no hang-ups about our parent. None at all.'

When we left the club and walked out to his Mercedes, I thought that if I'd been able to choose a brother he would have been high on the list, that I liked him very much, and that the telephone call had been worth it. Another thing I felt was a bond, inasmuch as I had not been the only person my mother had left. I felt at the same time regret that she would probably never see him again, which was sad, because he was a very nice person.

35

When I got back to Dar es Salaam from Mombasa, Ali was polishing copper trays on the veranda. He did not look well, but was full of news about a bloodbath which was to start any day now in Zanzibar. People were talking of nothing else in the market, he said cheerfully. Lots of Arabs were going to be murdered and blood would flow like water. He told me this with great relish, seeming in a very good humour at the prospect. He might just as easily have been talking about a football match.

'Many will die,' he said, polishing the trays with his hat tipped over his eyes and making sinister 'fwip-fwip' panga-slicing noises.

'The ancestors of these Arabs in Zanzibar sold our people as slaves and made money *pesa mingi*,' he said, scowling, '*mingi, mingi sana.*'

'That stopped a hundred years ago at least,' I pointed out, but it appeared to be a sore point and still fresh in his mind.

Zanzibar was only fifteen minutes by plane from Dar es Salaam, and people went over from the mainland to shop because Zanzibar was a duty-free port, ivory was cheap and carved in Zanzibar town, and the place fascinated. It lay like a small emerald in the immense blue of the Indian Ocean, fringed with palms and smelling wonderfully of cloves from the plantations. The airport building was like a small Arabian palace, the all-white turreted entrance to a magic island.

The Sultan of Zanzibar had a great palace outside the town and his white yacht, the *Sayyid Khalifa*, lay at anchor among the big dhows from the Gulf. The dhows, when they came down from Oman and Muscat to trade in copra and cloves, brought the Sultan gifts of Persian rugs, and his *Sayyid Khalifa* was in fact the means by which the Sultan escaped from the island during the coup which Ali had so accurately predicted.

Ali's information was impeccable. When the massacre occurred on the island, he was the one to bring the news that the coup was under way. The drums, which I often heard at night, had carried the news across the sea from Zanzibar to Bagamoyo and told of thousands of dead in the surf near the Sultan's palace.

Bagamoyo, once the main port in these waters, lay up the coast from Dar es Salaam. It had been the great slaving centre from where the slaves – Ali's ancestors perhaps – were shipped to the auction blocks in Zanzibar. You could see that island quite clearly from Bagamoyo Beach and the thud of the drumbeats from the island carried easily across the waves, or so Ali said, and then on from Bagamoyo down the coast in a chain of sound. It was through the drums that the news was known in the African market long before the newspapers carried the story.

I thought again of Mrs Barry and her predictions of bloodshed.

Ali at this time was not well. His face was a greyish colour and he grew thinner every day. I offered to take him to Outpatients at the local government hospital, and we went together in my car. He waited in a long queue of ladies in black shukas and I went off to do my shopping.

When I came back he was sitting under a mango tree in the hospital garden. He had been seen by the doctor and had a huge bottle of medicine. The doctor was Swiss and very thorough – I had been to him myself – but Ali did not seem to feel he had done him much good.

After the visit he took the medicine reluctantly, as if to please me, but he did not seem happy about it. It was not *kali*, he said (*kali* means fierce, bitter or nasty, and it can be used in many different contexts – for example, a lady who shouts at her servants is a memsahib *kali sana*). In Ali's opinion, any medicine which tasted agreeable rarely did one any good, whereas the more *kali* it was, the more efficacious he felt it to be.

At any rate, he continued to grow worse. His skin hung on his bones and in the end he became so seriously ill that I tried yet another doctor, who gave him several injections and a general-purpose antibiotic. In spite of this, it seemed that Ali was becoming weaker all the time. He staggered down the garden to work one morning, looking grey and emaciated, and was sent back to his bed.

A little later Suleman Bin came into the sitting room and stood with his hands folded in front of him and his head in its embroidered hat bowed. His wall-eye, which gave him a general air of gloom, settled on me.

'Ali is not well, memsahib,' he said at last. He was a man who liked pauses. Like a politician he often stopped at a crucial point in the conversation, adding an air of drama to even the simplest dialogue.

'Ali is not well, so it would be better if you gave him one hundred shillings.'

'One hundred shillings for what?' I asked. 'He has been to the doctors here. Now he must be admitted to the hospital at Magomeni for tests, and that has been arranged. If I give him one hundred shillings, he may go to a bad doctor for a bad *piga sindano*, and that sort of *piga sindano*, Suleman, is a waste of time.' *Piga sindano* was the Swahili word for injection. Africans in Dar es Salaam, who loved injections, would pay a fortune for one as a cure for anything from an ingrown toenail to a broken arm. Unscrupulous doctors injected sterile water into their veins and charged high fees, or so I had been told.

'The hundred shillings is not for *piga sandano*, memsahib,' Suleman said at last, after another long pause. 'Ali must go to the witchdoctor now or he will surely die.'

He stood, hands folded, courteous but implacable. He did not speak but had the air of a man who might remain there all day if necessary. Wearily I gave him the hundred shillings and he went away. He and Ali went down the drive shortly afterwards, got into a taxicab driven by a friend and were driven away. Suleman looked purposeful, but Ali looked weak and ill. He looked so ill that I felt in my heart he might never recover.

When they came back some hours later, the difference in him was considerable.

He walked with a springy step and already seemed better. It was quite amazing. He told me that the witchdoctor had cured him. He had held a Coca-Cola bottle full of boiling water over Ali's stomach and chanted, Suleman said. The evil spirits which were troubling Ali had gone into it and been burnt alive, and that had been the end of it.

'But you can't believe that!' I said. Suleman had always seemed a practical, sensible man to me.

'I am cured in any case,' said Ali simply, and he was. From then on he grew better every day.

36

The company policy was changing in Tanganyika. The oil company was Africanising its staff and all of us were to be posted. We were being sent to South Africa – to Johannesburg.

I closed the school and gave the monkeys away. We had tried to set them free over the ferry at Mjimwema, where there were colonies of vervet monkeys in the coconut groves, but they clung to the children, clutching them with their funny little black hands and shrieking and widdling.

Perversely, as the time drew nearer for us to leave Tanganyika, everything around us appeared more attractive and exotic than ever before. The rains had not broken and the sun shone every day. The sea glittered blue, and far out to sea Honeymoon Island, Sinda Island and Snake Island were just shimmering haze. Little ngalawas rocked in the creek at noon as they had done for thousands of years. They were dugouts made from coconut trunks and their owners lay asleep in the stern in the hot afternoons. They, like the coffee sellers with their tall brass coffee-pots, jingling handleless cups on the street corners, suddenly seemed picturesque instead of commonplace.

We had our last Christmas in Dar es Salaam and decorated a little casuarina tree with Japanese decorations from the bazaar. The angel on the tree was made out of celluloid and had slanted oriental eyes, and even the snowmen looked

Asian. The Christmas tree was droopy and garish in the sun, but this year, for the first time, we felt sentimental about a tropical Christmas.

Robin was offered a job in Zanzibar, but health and other services were becoming difficult. Mosquito control was lax and the water supply was no longer pure. Once, when I went to the hospital, I was ushered into a consulting room where a young foreigner sat in a white coat behind the Swiss doctor's desk. He was allowed, he said, to diagnose but not to prescribe, and there was no one else available that weekend. In a situation where one might need a prescription urgently, such a state of affairs could be impossible; with young children it would not be wise to stay on. Most private doctors had already left and their consulting rooms were let. Even the oil company doctor had gone back to Ireland.

The Sikh tailor came on his bicycle to our house to measure us for woollen clothes for our leave in a European winter. No one knew where he lived, but everyone trusted him with their materials and often paid him in advance. When he came back to fit us it was unbearable to feel the weight of the warm clothes and unthinkable, standing in the humidity while he pinned and tacked, that we should ever have the need to wear them.

Ali was sad that we were going, and the more so now no more oil company people would come to take the house.

'All the Europeans are leaving,' he said. 'Soon we shall have no work and we shall go hungry.' He was giving the big copper trays that I had bought in Zanzibar their last refurbishing with the juice of little bitter limes mixed with the special white sand he had made me bring from Leopards' Cove.

'Where now will you get the little limes to clean these trays if you leave us?' he said. 'Will there be sand like this where you are going?'

I would miss Ali, and I looked for another job for him at one of the consulates so that he would not be in thrall to

Suleman forever. I bought him an FM transistor, which he played all the time. The music made Suleman wince, but Ali, who was now quite recovered from his illness, liked it immensely. I imagined, with a certain satisfaction, the Beatles raving it up in Suleman's hotel in Kinondoni. Suleman Bin, who was a tyrant in his own way, would probably allow only Arab music, but meanwhile Ali could listen to 'Yeah, I need your love, Babe' and Nancy Sinatra in the long, hot afternoons.

The last weekend of our tour we drove to Bagamoyo and saw where Livingstone's coffin had been laid in the White Fathers' Mission. The very black Father who showed us around was charming. In the room where Livingstone's remains had been laid for a time, there was not much to see. A calendar, twelve years out of date, hung on the wall, and there was an old Singer sewing machine with a foot treadle in the corner and the inevitable geckos scuttling about on the whitewashed ceiling.

Bagamoyo was almost a dead town. It had been a great port on these coasts, difficult to remember now that it was crumbling away. Some of the little dark cupboards of shops had the most exquisite carved Arab doors. They were magnificent and made of heavy wood. We would have liked to have bought one that we saw hanging on rotten hinges in a ruined house, but the owner could not be found. Afterwards it became illegal to remove these doors from Tanzania.

We pottered about in the heat watching the fishermen and the ngalawas. Someone was repairing a small dhow and we walked down the crumbling concrete steps to the beach to watch. We passed a great plinth there, with a monolith in memory of the German soldiers who had died. It was overgrown with weeds, scrub had encroached, and lizards crept among the undergrowth. Part of the plinth was very badly smashed, so that one could barely read the names of the soldiers and soon they would be indecipherable.

Here and there one could still make out a word or two: 'Died courageously', 'Gave his life for' or 'Valour in the face of'. Would we, like them, I wondered, leave so little trace of who we were and what we had done? Would Africa, like a tide, wash all trace of colonialism away?

I knew, if and when it did, the palms would still rustle, the fishermen still sleep in their ngalawas in the bay. The real Africa, like Ireland, had this sense of timelessness.

I thought of the old Arab king sleeping in his tomb on Honeymoon Island, an Arab version of the Irish cromlech in the killeen, and wondered what changes of any lasting importance there had been on this coastline since his time. Not too many to sweep away.

Africa left its mark on men more than they on Africa.

From a purely selfish point of view I didn't feel sad at all, because Africa had given so many of us so very much more than we could ever have dreamt.

When we flew out of Dar es Salaam to Europe, Ali's was one of the embroidered caps bobbing at the waving base and somewhere there, too, was Suleman Bin, who had stepped down from his high horse to come and see us off. We had given him a watch and a new cap as a farewell *zawadi* (present), which he said was *Maradadi sani*. Ali would have his transistor and his three-year bonus, so perhaps he could pay off Suleman at last and be his own man.

Up soared the plane into the blue sunlit space, dipped towards Kilimanjaro in salute, and we were on our way.

37

'Is it true,' Abdullah had asked a few days before we left Dar es Salaam, 'that where you are going, memsahib, the black people walk on one side of the road and the people who are white walk on the other?' He seemed to be very amused at such a bizarre idea and had gone off laughing. I could hear him cackling away to himself in the kitchen while he shelled prawns for a curry.

Tanganyika was a United Nations trust territory and technically multiracial. By and large the races mixed, with only the occasional dissension cropping up from time to time.

'Filling it with little chocolate drops, are you?' one mother had said about my multiracial nursery school, promptly removing her child. But she was an exception.

Now we were on our way, sailing on the *Pendennis Castle* to South Africa, where multiracialism was a crime and where I could be closed down if I had children of colour in a nursery school.

We had been to Ireland to say our farewells and were bound for Cape Town. It would be a long time before I saw Ireland and Annes Grove again. The oil company in East Africa had given us paid home leave every two or three years, a month for every year served, but now there would be no home leave from South Africa to keep us in touch with the family.

Already there were many changes at Annes Grove. Gran had died quite a few years before, and her death had been the end of an era. She had been born in 1868. After her mother had run away, her grandmother the dowager had been partly responsible for her. The old lady had been nearly seventy when Gran was born, so the lifetime of the two grandmothers, hers and mine, had spanned one hundred and sixty-eight years.

How different things had been in Gran's day, I thought, remembering her in her eighties, riding side-saddle to hounds and soaring over huge Irish banks in her old blue riding habit. I remembered her driving the pony trap with its basket sides and damp cushions, in the pouring rain, wearing beautiful but filthy diamond earrings that were never cleaned, and a mackintosh that a tramp wouldn't thank you for. In my mind's eye I saw her teaching herself Irish with no idea how to pronounce the words, or sitting bolt upright in bed, her whiskey beside her, while she lectured Molly on Mrs Beeton and extravagant cooking. Moll was right – there would never be anyone like Gran again.

Listening to the throb of the ship's engines as we left Europe far behind us, I felt a rush of nostalgia for Gran and for Annes Grove as I had last seen it, on one of those twilight evenings that I loved. The grass was the colour of emeralds and the house looked much the same, like an old lady with a hat pulled down over her eyes. Moll was still there, still ruling the kitchen, looking much older now, her hair as white as snow, and still mourning Gran. She had promised to write to us often when I hugged her goodbye.

Watching the swell of the ocean as I leaned over the ship's railing, one particular night came into my mind. It was when I was with both of them, perched on the arm of the sofa at the foot of Gran's bed, with Moll brushing the Mistress's hair with a battered silver hairbrush. Moll often called her 'the Mistress', as we all did. The corgi was gardening away in its undercarriage under the bed. It was a night very much like a hundred others, except that Gran told us a story so uncharacteristic of her and so poignant that I saw her as a person I had never really known. She had been brought up to hide her feelings – 'Bad taste to show them,' she had often said – and she had always seemed to me eternally old; but as she talked that night I saw her not as a very old lady but as a young girl with thick mahogany hair, a Roman nose and brown eyes, riding near the sea with a man with whom she was hopelessly in love.

'I always thought of her as a person without feelings,' Walter Trench had once said. He was a little afraid of her, having been rapped over the knuckles once or twice. And sometimes in her dealings with my father I had thought so too, but then she was a soldier's daughter, schooled never to betray emotion.

That evening, when she and I and Molly were together in her bedroom, it was different. A fire was crackling in the grate and it was dark outside. There was very little light in the room, most of it coming from the flickering of flames reflected on the ceiling, which created a cosiness and an atmosphere of intimacy among the three of us.

'I almost went to Africa, to the Cape in the south,' she had suddenly said, staring into the fire. 'I was nineteen and madly in love with my cousin. He was my first and only real love.' She sounded wistful and lonely and unlike herself. 'He went out to South Africa with his regiment and then, when he came home on leave, he wanted to marry me.' She was looking into the fire and I think she had forgotten Molly and me. She was back, seventy-five years earlier, in a day still clear in her mind.

I looked across at her. She still had good bones and a strong nose and in the dim light she looked momentarily young again.

'His name was Patrick Macnaghten,' she said, the words slipping out slowly. 'We rode our horses along the beach at Portballintrae as we had done for years and he told me he had found a place where we could live out in the Cape. He didn't want to come back to Ireland because South Africa had captured his imagination. The place he had found was called,' she hesitated, searching for the name, 'was called Courtfan.' She described it to Molly and me as he had described it to her, and it was as clear in her mind as yesterday. It had blue mountains behind it, she said, and peacocks on the lawn and, for most of the year, sunshine.

'There were stables, and he said he would buy me an Arab mare so that I could ride across the flat land to the mountains. My father bred Arabs and I loved them.' Her voice trailed away and she sounded so sad that I thought he must have been killed out there.

'Did he die?' I asked. She had stopped talking and the silence had gone on for so long that I thought she had slipped into sleep.

'No, my father forbade the engagement and so did his. We were first cousins, too closely related, or so they said. It was the hereditary factor that made it impossible.'

I had never heard of this before. 'The hereditary factor? What hereditary factor?'

'When first cousins marry it is sometimes dangerous. Dangerous for their children.'

'So?' I asked with a catch in my voice. 'So he sailed to South Africa without you?' It was a story without a happy ending, and I wondered why she had not followed her heart and run away as her mother had done. Perhaps she had seen what a price had had to be paid. Her mother had never been allowed to see her sons again and both had died before the age of twenty-five.

I had seen a painting of Gran's mother once, at Dundarave. She was brown-eyed and creamy-skinned. In the portrait she had been wearing a low-cut dress overpainted with a hideous frill to hide her décolletage. It was a painting that surfaced after many years of facing the wall at Dundarave and I wondered vaguely what had become of it.

The more I heard about Great-Grandfather Macnaghten, the more monstrous his behaviour appeared to be. The evening that Gran was born he had expected a son – probably ordered one! Tar barrels all along the drive to Dundarave were to be lit in celebration, and a party planned for the tenants. When he was told she was a girl, he declared everything cancelled, and his wife, recovering from the birth, was alerted to her failure by the noise of tar barrels being dragged away.

As it happened, he was to lose both his sons, one of blackwater fever in Egypt with his regiment, and the other in India, and so the title passed out of his family. Perhaps it was fate's retribution. I have a copy of the letter their mother wrote, asking to be allowed to see the boys before they went abroad with the army, and the letter he wrote back refusing her request was brutal. When Gran was a little girl, he ordered her pet dog shot. He disliked dogs, but Dundarave was quite large enough for him never to set eyes on the animal. In the end a servant smuggled the puppy to Bushmills, where he was visited by the Dundarave children whenever they could slip away.

It was said of old Sir Francis that when he died and was buried in a nearby churchyard the villagers asked not to be buried anywhere near him, so fearsome was his reputation. They were afraid that on All Souls' Night, when the dead are supposed to rise from their graves, he might, as one old villager said, appear again as large as life.

And so Gran never saw the house near the blue mountains with the peacocks on the lawn, or Cape Town, which we would see for ourselves in a day or two when the ship docked. I think, knowing the sort of person Gran was, that she would have fitted easily into life in the Cape. She would have learned

Afrikaans and African languages, and the boundless landscapes of Africa would have suited her very well.

Decades later, when I was in the Cape Province, I tried to find a house called Courtfan which could have existed in 1887, standing somewhere near the mountains. I did not know where to start looking, but I found a wonderful place called Fancourt, as old as that, with blue mountains, and stables, and peacocks strutting on a sunlit lawn. It sent a shiver up my spine. But there was no reference in the history of the house to a young Lieut. Macnaghten ever having lived there or trying at any time to lease it.

Not so her grandfather, who had been out in South Africa in 1879. I had read two of his books on the voyage. He was William Howard Russell, war correspondent for *The Times*, who had made his name through impassioned dispatches from the Crimea. He wrote the truth unflinchingly about the hideous conditions the British troops endured and described how many of the soldiery were ill or dying, had frostbite and were bootless. In one dispatch he reported that when a cargo of boots was eventually shipped out, every boot was for the left foot!

Egged on by Florence Nightingale, Russell exposed blunder after blunder until the British public was outraged and the British government of the day fell under a torrent of criticism. As a result, when William got back to England he found himself famous. His friendship with the Prince of Wales blossomed and he became an integral part of the royal circle. For a red-haired brandy-drinking Irishman, not an aristocrat, he had come a long way, and soon afterwards went off to India as the Prince's personal historian.

Unfortunately my great-great-grandfather's South African campaign was not his finest hour. His sojourn there, once he had left Cape Town, was in fact a personal disaster. By all accounts he would have done better to have stayed cosily at home, chatting to Dickens and Thackeray at the Garrick.

Reading one of his diaries, I don't think he had any conception, before he came out, of the distances that he was about to travel. God had painted South Africa on a very wide canvas and it was across this landscape that William rode, complaining bitterly every trot of the way. Like my aunt, he did not travel light and had an absolute mountain of luggage on board with him when he sailed into Cape Town harbour. Boxes, bags, helmets, rifles, swords, trunks, decorations – including five orders in velvet-lined cases – three uniforms, five portmanteaux, dispatch cases, everyday clothing, boxes of papers and notebooks and a Gladstone bag, not to mention enormous cigar humidors. He was very fond of cigars. One can imagine the luckless servants staggering under all his paraphernalia and dragging it up the stairs to his quarters.

Then came the first shock to his system. Faced with the vast distances to be travelled, he was forced to ditch most of his belongings and auction off others, which didn't please him at all.

To begin with, everything was rosy. He had breakfasted with an old friend, Sir Bartle Frere, at Government House and set off with Sir Garnet Wolseley, the new Special Commissioner, and his entourage to Natal, where poor W.H.R. found it very chilly. It was July, the coldest time of the year, and his bones ached. His horse went lame and had saddle sores, and the weather veered from perishing chill to heat. The only bright spot seemed to be lunching and talking at length with Bishop Colenso, whom he admired.

Apart from the bishop nothing pleased him much, judging from all accounts, and least of all the Transvaal, where he was eaten alive by bedbugs and fleas and his digestion was in a frightful uproar from the food. To a bon vivant like himself, accustomed to dining with princes and the odd duke or two, or eating oysters at the Garrick Club with Thackeray, the diet of mouldy biscuits, terrible brandy and bully beef was the last straw. His litany of woes increased daily and he grew more and more dyspeptic.

Worse was yet to come. Fording a *spruit* near Pretoria in a thunderstorm his horse fell, trapping William's leg underwater, and he nearly met his Maker. Nor was he appeased when Sir Garnet Wolseley tracked him next day to a farm where he sat moodily sipping brandy and said, jokingly, slapping him on his painfully bruised back, that if the worst had happened he would have given Russell a jolly good funeral.

And so William went back to England thankfully and very cross, with minimal luggage and a sore leg.

It was his last campaign as a special correspondent and a disaster from beginning to end. He was nudging sixty, had damaged his leg (which had thoroughly soured him) and his controversial dispatches about bad discipline among certain of the British troops had ruffled a few feathers at home. It was one thing to plead on behalf of the British soldiers in the Crimea and quite another to criticise them. Not only that, but he was not sufficiently anti-Boer to please the British public, and, like Bishop Colenso, he disagreed with the imprisonment of the Zulu king Cetshwayo, whom he had previously met in Cape Town before he sailed. The Dukes of Wellington and Cambridge were now very cool to him for a time, while even his friend the Prince of Wales rapped him over the knuckles, refusing to believe that the British Army was anything but well-disciplined, and Lady Wolseley cut him dead for implied criticism of her husband.

By and large it was not a happy time.

I thought, as I closed one of his books, that I would like to have known my great-great-grandfather. He was a great character, a gourmet, good company and gregarious, writing feverishly to keep the bank and the Inland Revenue at bay, and then wining and dining his friends in style when he could least afford it.

Finally, years after his first wife died, he married an Italian countess who pampered him. He was knighted and a bust of him, cast in bronze, scribbling away in his notebook, was erected in the crypt of St Paul's Cathedral. The inscription beneath reads 'To the first and greatest of all war correspondents', which would have warmed the cockles of his heart. He had his detractors and quite a few critics, but his maxim that 'a society can only hope to be just and healthy if it is blessed with an independent, critical and courageous press' had stood him in good stead in the English media.

– 38 –

A day after I had finished a book of William Howard Russell's, the *Pendennis Castle* nosed its way into Cape Town harbour. It was 1963, early in the morning, when the sky was a mix of milk and pearl, and in the clear, slightly salty air we saw Table Mountain for the first time, standing guard over the city, with a wisp of floating cloud on its summit.

We lifted the children up to see the seals diving and playing in the sea below and later went into a city that I fell in love with for ever.

We walked under giant oaks where squirrels chased each other and in gardens where we saw old men playing chess under the trees. A nurse in uniform, coming off duty, walked down a cobbled street holding hands with a young naval officer, her cape thrown over her shoulders making a splash of navy and red. It's odd how tiny cameos like that stick in your mind.

We drove to see fine old Cape Dutch houses, and vineyards, and a Malay quarter with pink-washed houses in sloping streets. So many strands of history had come together here. The French Huguenots had landed in Cape Town, fleeing the revocation of the Edict of Nantes, just as they had fled to Cork city in Ireland. Dutch, Malay, English, French and Khoi had all been here for centuries. There was an embroidery of cultures wherever you went.

We went to Kirstenbosch Botanical Gardens and saw

strange flowers called proteas, like large glamorised artichokes. Kirstenbosch had a fragrance garden where scented flowers and shrubs were chosen for the blind to savour; and later came the braille trail, where plants were all labelled in braille, for the same reason. Grandfather would have been in seventh heaven here with all the exotic shrubs and trees, and the talk of the old rose cuttings brought out to the Cape by the Dutch as early as 1659 would have enthralled him.

Some of the later cuttings, a nurseryman told us, had come to Cape Town from Persia and China, where the Dutch East India ships had once plied their trade. A great rose industry had thrived in Cape Town in those days: rose cuttings were exported and the rosewater distilled from the petals of the damask rose was sold to buyers in the Middle East for their ladies. I had always thought the Dutch rather unimaginative, but I was wrong. They had made not simply utilitarian vegetable gardens in the Cape but had brought over herbs, lavenders, roses and numbers of plants from Europe and coaxed them to flourish and grow beautifully in African soil. They were great gardeners, these Dutch, and I could imagine the air of expectation and the news crackling on the Cape winds when a Dutch East India ship came into port. I could picture eager botanists flocking to the docks to collect cuttings, and the excited talk in High Dutch and French of mulching and pruning.

What, I thought, wouldn't I give for a painting of it all – the vessels in port, the cluster of farmers, the market gardeners and viticulturists, the burghers stolid in their high hats, their ladies holding onto their bonnets in the strong south-easter winds – waiting for cargo to be unloaded. And over it all Table Mountain, a brooding watcher. If only, I thought, one could channel-hop from one fragment of time to another and see and feel the magic of another age.

'I could live here quite happily,' I told Robin. I felt that I could turn my back like a traitor on Ireland, so bewitched was I by Cape Town. If this was what South Africa was about, it was marvellous. But Robin's job with the oil company was in Johannesburg, so we had to leave the Cape.

Unfortunately Johannesburg was to bring me down to earth with perhaps the biggest bump I had ever encountered.

Johannesburg was a shock. A culture shock. For a long time after we arrived I tried to write but I had total writer's block. It was like a wall of concrete. Everything I wrote during the seventies and eighties seemed stiff and contrived. There was no flow. It was not a good time. I was unhappy because it was not a place where I wanted to be. There was no magic for me here, no sparkle.

Looking back now, I realise there were elements which hung over the place like a stifling cloud. The most tangible was the hatred and the resentment emanating from millions of the black community who were in bondage to crippling laws.

The resentment was gagged but, however silent, it was nevertheless in the pool of South African consciousness, and it seeped insidiously into the psyche. The other powerful element, of course, was fear. The government system seemed to operate on fear. Ministers made speeches warning chillingly of the *swart gevaar*, the Black Threat to the north of us which could sweep down any time and engulf us. If you are told anything often enough and are cut off from mainstream thought at the foot of Africa, you begin to lose your sense of perspective; you begin to believe or half-believe what you hear and become frightened.

The fear was unconscious for the main part, but the propaganda did its work. When we were up in Kenya on holiday after three years in Johannesburg and went into a rainforest to look for the green lourie birds, I came face to face with an old black honey gatherer and screamed my head off. I don't know who was the more surprised, he or I.

Another element which stemmed creativity was the segregation laws. We were cut off from the pulsebeat and colour of Africa in Johannesburg by draconian laws. They did not affect *us* to any great extent as we were white, but there was always that underlying feeling of tight control, of watchfulness. Police could raid your maid's room in the small hours, looking for illicit visitors, such as her husband. They could arrive and search your house if someone reported that you had subversive literature in your bookcase. Telephones were sometimes tapped and people taken in for questioning. After the freedom of Tanganyika I did not want to be in this strange place so full of repression and violence. It was too raw, too brutal and too disturbing, not like anything I had ever known.

I became very depressed. Dar es Salaam seemed remote, normal and peaceful. I longed with desperate homesickness for it and for the walks on the white beaches of Mjimwema with our vervet monkeys on our shoulders, for the crimson sunsets, the coffee sellers with their tall copper jars clinking, and for the sight of the great Arab dhows at anchor. Had we ever really lived like that? And were we going to be in Johannesburg for ever?

I began having vivid dreams. In most of them, strangely, instead of East Africa, which I longed for and missed so much, was the haunting figure of a tall monk in a long black habit. I never saw his face clearly, but it always seemed that there was some deep significance surrounding his appearance in my dreams and some connection with this strange city where we now lived.

We made new friends who, like most of the South Africans we met, were charming, concerned people but who took the racial laws and divides as a matter of course. 'Concerned' seems a paradox, but a lot of them had imbibed segregation propaganda with their mother's milk. Brought up to believe that the Africans were happiest left in their own culture, and without official permission they could not go into African townships to see for themselves what was happening, so how the blacks lived their lives day by day was a mystery. And yet a lot of Europeans felt guilty, but could not analyse their guilt.

Not long after we arrived there was an upsurge in resistance. More people were put under house arrest, and the restrictions and tensions of life intensified. People were being arrested or jailed for speaking out against the state, but we did not know the details or why. Because much of the news was suppressed, the press struggled and fought against censorship with limited success. Dark rumours began to spread but none were substantiated. People were jumpy, and disturbing stories came to us from young conscripts in the South African Defence Force.

At this time Robin had given up on oil and was locally a British vice-consul commercial, which was why I was asked to lunch at one of the Foreign Office houses. It was to be a multiracial women's lunch at a huge house in Houghton.

When we arrived, a couple of Special Branch men in vehicles were parked in the road outside, noting down the registration numbers of the guests' cars as they drove in. It gave me a creepy feeling because, by now, I was sufficiently South African to feel a frisson of alarm when I saw them; after all, I was doing something that was illicit in South Africa – sitting down to table with black women! Special Branch cars always generated a feeling of tension in any case, and Special Branch plain-clothes men, like the KGB, were everywhere. They sometimes went to plays and sat at the back of the theatre checking to see if the script might possibly encourage integration. They had their spies throughout the country – making notes, tapping telephones, intercepting mail and shadowing people.

Inside the house were a number of well-dressed and highly articulate black women, a few consulate wives and a couple of intense women in arty clothes, the sort who are always allied to some cause or other. There were two of them and they leaned forward, almost bent double, to listen intently to every word the black women uttered, as if they, the African women, were from another planet. I suppose in a way they were. When we sat down to lunch I realised why they had been so attentive and was about to be riveted myself. During some small talk with my neighbour – I think we were discussing black nursery schools and I was just about to pass her the vegetables (the fact that it was cauliflower cheese still sticks in my mind) – she suddenly said, 'The streets of this country will be running soon with rivers of blood.' She said this perfectly calmly, as if we were still discussing kindergartens in Soweto, with no particular inflection in her voice. I suppose I had expected the usual safe cross-cultural conversation on the lines of 'How many children do you have? Boys or girls?'

As there didn't seem to be any proper reply that I could think of, I nervously waved the cauliflower under her nose. She waved it away.

'They are arming in Soweto,' she said with a sort of calm satisfaction. 'And then the killing will start. Rivers of blood in every street. It won't be long now at all. AK47s under every bed.' She reached for the salt.

'Do you think that is a very good idea?' I asked, floundering, feeling inept and very Anglo-Saxon. I did not ask why they were arming. The answer to that was as clear as crystal. 'I mean, everyone will suffer. Your children may be killed and mine too. Couldn't there be negotiations?'

She looked at me as if I were mad. 'We have been negotiating since 1910. The time is past.' She turned away from me and began speaking to the woman on her left.

And so life went on in this strange city. The children went to school and we bought a house in a garden full of old jacaranda trees and yellow mimosa. Here on the Gold Reef the air was clear and sunny, even the birds were brilliantly coloured. Glossy starlings were a technicoloured blue, hoopoes pecked near the azure swimming pool and the rainbirds called, a rich wine-pouring-gurgling sound, down by the river.

We lived across the Little Jukskei River, opposite Rivonia, and one afternoon the bank of the river suddenly teemed with policemen and their walkie-talkies, guns strapped to their belts. We saw all this through the plate-glass windows of the house and heard shouting in harsh, guttural voices. We didn't know what had happened until the news that night at eight. There was a property known as Lilliesleaf Farm which lay just across the river from our house in Bryanston. The river was seldom high unless in flood. Friends at the Sleepy Hollow Hotel on the opposite bank had crossed it earlier and walked to tea with us. They were from Dar es Salaam and were full of talk about the men by the river.

What neither they nor we knew was that Lilliesleaf Farm was being used by the African National Congress, and during the months that we had been settling into our new house Nelson Mandela had been living there disguised as a servant, supposedly employed by a man named Goldreich. That afternoon the South African Intelligence and the police uncovered their secret hideaway and moved in to arrest Walter Sisulu, Arthur Goldreich and others. Mandela was not there at the time, but, as he says in his book *Long Walk to Freedom*, that day the South African government raided and captured almost the entire ANC high command of Umkhonto weSizwe, detaining them under the new 90-day Detention Act.

The raid ultimately led to the arrest of Nelson Mandela.

But strangely enough, after that day a very curious feeling started to filter through, nothing specific that you could put your finger on, but as if a curtain was about to go up on a scene which as yet had no script or choreography, but for which the actors were well prepared.

– 39 –

Johannesburg is a city where you come face to face with yourself. It is a tough town with a façade of culture.

It was Mr Van Rensburg who told me this, and that I would never understand the Afrikaners because, he said, the suburb in which we lived was an 'English-speaking ghetto' and completely out of touch with what South Africa was all about.

I met Mr Van Rensburg at a French Consulate party, a real dyed-in-the-wool Afrikaner of the old school. He talked to me because he had got the idea in his head that I was some kind of Irish nationalist. If Grandfather had heard this he would have had a fit, although in truth he and Mr Van Rensburg had a certain amount in common. They both saw things through blinkers and were convinced that only their angle on things was the right one.

Mr Van Rensburg was heavily anti-British. Thousands and thousands of Boer women and children had perished in the concentration camps set up by the English during the Boer War, he said, when the British 'scorched earth' policy destroyed Afrikaner homesteads. He had had relatives among them and the family memory from 1900 was still fresh in his mind.

It was an unusual sort of party in Johannesburg that night because there was such an odd mix of people. This was not typical: usually everything in this strange country was compartmentalised and there was so much mistrust. I had never met an Afrikaner nationalist before, although we had been in South Africa for some time. His home tongue was Afrikaans and he spoke English with a strong accent. I didn't tell him that my current stepmother was a Krige and Ouma Smuts's niece, because he didn't approve of General Smuts either! He said Smuts was too pro-British.

'I can't keep calling you Mr Van Rensburg,' I said. We were both sitting on cushions on the floor, drinking wine.

'My name is Hennie,' he smiled. He was not at all what I expected him to be, not the stereotypical racist monster of apartheid, and it was impossible not to like him. He was gentle, softly spoken, yet absolutely convinced of the rightness of his philosophy. The Bible featured a lot in his conversation and he quoted biblical texts to emphasise that God intended the black man to be born only to hew wood and draw water.

'So you see,' he said, 'there was no real need to educate them. God did not intend them to be educated men.'

When I suggested that the Boers seemed to be interpreting God's will to suit their own policies, he wasn't angry at all. He just wore the patiently courteous expression of someone who sees that the foreigner (me) understood nothing; for himself, he sincerely believed that the Afrikaner nation was chosen by God for the special care of the blacks. He became very emotional about this, and about apartheid. 'God,' he said, 'did not intend black and white people to live together.'

'There you go again,' I said. I was dying to ask him about the 'purity of race' syndrome, because it was known that some of the early settlers had intermarried with the Khoi and many of their descendants had Afrikaner names. I wanted to know what biblical texts he could possibly introduce for this, but I contained myself.

His *ouma* (grandmother), he told me, had left the Cape with her parents and trekked with others by ox-wagon thousands of miles into the interior to escape what they saw as the cruel strictures of British rule. They had suffered terrible hardships on the trek, dragging their ox-wagons to form a *laager* (stockade) at night against leopards and lions and local black tribes.

Then after the Great Trek his family had settled in the Transvaal, he said, and to thank God, who had brought them safely through so much, the Afrikaner Voortrekkers had built a huge edifice near Pretoria called the Voortrekker Monument. It was to commemorate their deliverance into the Promised Land. They were like the Israelites in the desert, and some of the carvings I saw later on the Monument walls looked like scenes from the Old Testament.

As time went on we occasionally met other Afrikaners. I saw that, like Mr Van Rensburg, they were not evil people, but many of them were simply obsessed with Calvinism and their role in Africa, and absolutely convinced of the rightness of all they stood for.

'We are not wayfarers,' Hennie had said that night, 'not like you. You are not committed here, but this is the only country we have, and given by God to us. We will never leave it; never give in to the *swart gevaar*.' I was to remember this in the years to come.

Meanwhile, I was still struggling to adapt to this strange culture. In Ireland people made religious barriers; in England, class barriers. Obviously neither were legally enforced, because they were free countries, but South Africa was not a free country and the barriers here were not only social but enforced by law, which threw everything into a stark focus of black and white. The full significance of apartheid hadn't really percolated through my mind before we came to South Africa, but it was quickly visible as we settled in.

Less dire but nonetheless galling were some extraordinary regulations affecting women which would have made any feminist have a seizure. I nearly saw a drink actually being poured in a hotel bar in Port Elizabeth and had to be hustled away, so that the law that women might not see drinks being physically poured in bars was not infringed! Another peculiar rule meant that I was not allowed to open a bank account without my husband's permission. This strange society was like nothing I had ever encountered.

There were park benches with notices above them that said 'Whites only'. No blacks could sit on these iron and wooden benches. What did they do, I wondered, to enforce this? Did they have squads of municipal workers employed solely to make sure these laws were not contravened? And what about any swarthy Mediterranean types who might come to sun themselves and go almost black on South African beaches? Were they, too, obliged to sit on the grass?

All this was happening in Johannesburg, the town where I was born. It occurred to me that I had come full circle but I had not the faintest idea of when I left it – had I been a year or eighteen months old? What sort of person would I have become if I had grown up in Johannesburg? I wondered. Would I have accepted apartheid as a perfectly normal way of life, unquestioningly? And all these endless racial laws – would I have seen how cruel they were? The law that prevented children staying with their mothers in a white area once they were past a certain age? The law that said black people could not live in a white suburb except as servants or watchmen and, if found loitering in a white area, could be booked for trespassing?

Would I, if I had grown up in South Africa, have found all this quite normal? I like to think not. As it was, even apartheid in the post office upset me: long queues of black people waiting to be served grudgingly by sullen white civil servants and the contemptuous way Africans were treated by the police made my blood boil. But we ourselves at this stage had little to do with people of colour, because in the peculiar life that we lived it was as if we were in glass boxes. We were separated from other races, seeing one another but without any real contact. The glass boxes were soundproof into the bargain, so that the only black people we really knew were our servants and they, wanting to hang on to what little privacy they were allowed, did not open up to their white employers.

This was to change when Nico, a little Sotho boy, came to live with us, illegally, when he was two. But that was still in the future.

– 40 –

One evening in 1984 an African who was an old friend, and whom we had once rescued from the police when he was much younger, came to see us. He had worked in our garden in the early days and was now a carpet fitter and house painter. 'You must go!' he kept repeating. 'Trouble,' he said, 'very serious trouble is coming very soon.' He said that we would be in danger.

Curiously, we had felt not shock but a sensation almost of relief – relief that something was about to break and things hidden might now come fully into the open. We had a constant feeling these days of living on the slopes of a volcano that was slowly becoming active, but with everything still below the surface.

What had made the previous few months more frightening than anything else was that we, the white public, knew very little of what was going on. The black townships were now sealed off except to the army. All we saw on TV were short clips of what was happening in Soweto, the black satellite city. Screaming, toyi-toyiing Africans, most of them teenagers, hurled rocks and stones and tins among the flaming barricades of upturned motorcars and burning motor tyres. These scenes were usually followed by some bright-eyed TV lady announcer in a pretty dress rhapsodising about rugby scores or basketball wins, while a thick pall of smoke hung over a black township a few miles from the TV station as the crow flies.

One evening I was held up while a sinister procession went past. It was dusk, and I think the way it moved so silently made it all the more menacing. Army tanks with gun turrets, line after line of them, rolled in front of my headlights. Standing in the open hatches were soldiers, wearing what looked like black perspex helmets with visors. The vehicles were moving in perfect convoy towards the townships. I stared, mesmerised. It was chilling, and I felt a goose walk over my grave.

The weeks passed. It was summer time and we often drove past tennis courts on hot evenings while there were tennis parties in progress. On one of the worst days, when Alexandra township was ablaze and army helicopters overhead, we drove past a foursome on a floodlit court in Morningside. The women were in whites, in short pleated skirts, and the men in crisp white shorts. Black servants were carrying out trays of drinks in tall glasses. Behind this cameo huge billows of smoke made a dark smudge on the horizon. The smoke was from barricades of burning tyres. Sometimes the tyres had people inside them, being burnt to death. They were victims of other blacks, who saw them as traitors to the liberation cause. Revolutionary forces were growing stronger and the security police doubled their efforts.

But life went on. There was a feeling of living on the surface in an extraordinary, blindfolded, ostrich-head-in-the-sand sort of way. For my own part I, too, was blinkered and did not know what to think, except that I hated apartheid, but I think if I were to be totally honest, I felt that the war and violence was a showdown between black people and the Boers that had started long before we were posted here; that it had its roots a half century before, and that we would hold no coats for either protagonists. But I feared recriminations all the same, which might come against all the black people, many of whom had been dragged into violence against their will. The police and army were strong and would show no mercy if a rebellion such as this got out of hand.

In the meantime, South Africa seemed to be burning. Flames and smoke were portrayed daily on TV now. Buses with smashed windows drove by, and police cars had wire grids across the windscreens to protect them from rocks and hurled stones. Hatred seethed, and the whites were the pariahs of the world. I wished, as I had wished a hundred times in the past months, that fate had never sent us here. We had tried to leave in much earlier days but were always thwarted. A job with Anglo-Iranian Oil had been offered but our mentor there, the Emir Hoveyda, had been made prime minister and severed his links with the oil company overnight. A Gulf Oil job had flickered on the horizon for a time, then vanished. Like it or not, we were still here. I had made some very good friends and felt a little less alien, but I still did not write although I kept a diary. What I wanted to write would have been banned.

We downplayed our uneasiness in our letters home and kept them light. I wrote to Moll every month, dredging up anecdotes about the children or day-to-day happenings in the home, and leaving out any mention of 'unrest', as the official sources coyly put it.

– 41 –

'I've had a witch in the kitchen these last few months,' I told Moll, 'doing the cooking.' I could imagine Moll reading my letter in the Servants' Hall at Annes Grove among her pots of geraniums, with her plump toes stretched to the stove and the Sacred Heart glowing red on the dresser. She would cross herself at the sound of this! Not that it would surprise her, mind you. She was convinced that Africa was full of heathens, and she collected clumps of silver paper which, for some inexplicable reason, helped to send Little Sisters of Mercy to the heathen.

Moll, always deeply suspicious of the goings-on in Africa at the best of times, saw it as peopled with cannibals dancing round steaming pots with luckless missionaries inside them being cooked up. None of the postcards I sent her from Johannesburg showing skyscrapers and neon lights could persuade her otherwise, so my letter would only confirm what she already suspected – that we were in a heathen place and we should only venture out if we were clanking with rosaries and holy medals. Her letters were full of injunctions 'not to let the blacks near the silver or the Irish linen'. I smiled as I thought of her, picturing her face when she opened my letter. She was getting very old now but she wrote religiously and sent me recipes which never turned out like hers.

'Mind you beat the cream well, and use bantams' eggs,' she wrote, or 'you should use fresh salmon for the kedgeree'

– as if we could get fresh salmon in Johannesburg! She sent me recipes for my favourite sponge cake and a rich Irish salad dressing. Her cooking was always delicious, partly I think from the fresh country ingredients, and as I read her letters I could almost taste the Jersey cream and rich brown sugar in my mouth.

I missed her and Ireland. I was tired of the dust and cold of the Transvaal winters. It was as dry as the Valley of Bones. No rain had fallen for months, and my skin felt that if it was stretched any tighter it would crack. I was sick of the 'unrest' and the whole political structure. The children, the house and the garden had become my world. I wrote children's stories for Marnie and Hugh, and made a herb garden filled with African herbs and grasses and hedged it with wild aloes. We acquired a donkey, dogs, guinea pigs and geese.

The witch I described in my letter to Molly was a young Basuto woman called Emmeline from the kingdom of Lesotho, a neighbouring country where horsemen galloped their ponies over stomach-lurching mountain passes, wearing brilliant blankets and high conical hats made of Poli and Moseha grass.

Robin and I had driven down to Lesotho at the beginning of winter to see a remote breeding station where Connemara stallions had been brought from Ireland to cover Basuto mares. We had driven high into the mountains to the centre, passing thick snow in drifts near 'God Help Me' Pass, where the land dropped steeply down to moonscape scenes. We had drunk whiskey against the chill and talked for hours to the Irishman who headed the project, watching mares race on the mountain slopes, their tails streaming in the snow-flecked wind. Lesotho's harsh, dramatic landscape had its own charm. Dinosaurs had once prowled there and left fossilised footprints. Thatched villages were tucked in the folds of high mountain ranges. It was aptly called the Kingdom in the Sky, one of the few countries in the world with all its land more than three thousand feet above sea level.

A few weeks after we got home, Emmeline had turned up on our doorstep in Johannesburg, complete in a Basuto conical hat and brilliant blanket, looking for work. There were always Basuto people looking for work because Lesotho is such a poor country. She had chosen a good time to apply; we were fresh from our trip to Maseru, her home town, enamoured of it and fascinated by anything to do with it, so we employed her. She was all blankets, and bustle and smiles.

For a while there was nothing to regret. Her references were good. They said she loved cooking. And so she did, but not, it turned out, always as described. The first intimation that there was more on Emmeline's mind than stew and rice pudding was something slimy and evil-smelling simmering on the stove in the kitchen. It turned out to be dried snakeskin and some part of a lizard's anatomy. Clutching her stomach, Emmeline said it was for pain and that she had got the ingredients from the Mai Mai market in Johannesburg. My heart sank, because Mai Mai had recently been in the news. It was a sinister place where it was rumoured that human parts were sold for spells and medicines, under the counter. Recently police had reported that some very young black children had disappeared and been found dead and mutilated. Strange dried-up pieces of anatomy had surfaced in Mai Mai. People were stabbed there. It was talked of as a bad place, yet Emmeline had shopped there and come away unscathed.

'God knows what she may cook up next,' I said to Robin after we had spoken to her sharply, but she seemed repentant and after that contented herself with cooking up leaves and tree bark to make, she said, a potion against lightning. She always asked politely if she could and, thankfully, then used her own saucepans. She knew an amazing amount about medicines made from plants and trees because there had been no chemist shops in the mountains and in the remote village where she had lived as a child. The old people, she said, did their own healing. She knew the right plants to give a cow so that it did not abort, and what brew to use to dose a horse with colic, which was fascinating, if useless, to me. I taped some of the things she told me about pinwheel aloes and mountain legends, together with the names of the famous Lesotho hats, the Mokorotlo, the Illhoro and the Mohamyeoe, whose designs were inspired by the amazing Lesotho mountain peaks.

And so life gradually settled down again, with Emmeline cooking nothing more exotic than macaroni cheese or shepherd's pie. Sometimes she begged the odd old jam pot with a screw lid for some liquids, which she stored under her bed, and now and again her friends slipped into the yard, bringing money for one of her potions, but she was becoming far more citified, abandoning her conical hat for a smart red beret and her blanket for a jersey, and seemingly putting her mountain village ways behind her.

And then one hot summer's night it started all over again. It began with stomach-heaving smells percolating down the passage, and Emmeline stirring away at a concoction on the stove. She was crouched over the pot like a witch, with bands of crocheted knitting wool wound around her wrists and ankles. Someone, she said, had hexed her, so she was cooking up a storm. After that her incantations and witchcraft became more and more menacing. Her spells while she kept to stewing roots and bark had been tolerable, but now things were reaching a climax.

Next she accused Florrie, who did the ironing, of sending a tokoloshe to torment her. The tokoloshe was under her bed and would not let her sleep, she declared, and had lodged a ball of horsehair in her throat so that she could not swallow. Accusations and denials raged in the yard over the presence of the tokoloshe. The noise was terrible and no one did any work. Emmeline was apoplectic, losing sleep and weight, convinced that she was bewitched. Her face was that strange grey colour that I remembered from Ali when he was ill, and she was undoubtedly in the same boat. The tokoloshe, who according to Emmeline was lodged under her bed, was a dwarf spirit with thick facial hair, the familiar of a witch, who sent him out by night to bring sickness to people, kill cattle and cause havoc.

Poor innocent Florrie, the ironing 'girl' with her amiable moon face and propensity for chewing gum and wearing layers of sagging jumpers, denied all accusations, but Emmeline would have none of it. Like the Spanish Inquisition, she was determined to force confession through pain. She came at Florrie in the yard, knocking the bottom off an empty bottle and pointing the jagged edges towards Florrie's terrified face. But before she could do any damage, the gardener gripped her wrist till she dropped the bottle, and Emmeline, still shrieking, was told by Robin to collect the money due to her and leave. Banshees were one thing, I thought wearily – I could still hear Emmeline screaming in the yard – and the odd fairy and Foxy Woman, but murderous shards of broken glass and black magic another.

I read what I could find about tokoloshes, but the descriptions varied. In one book he seemed a jolly troll of small stature, visible only to children; in another he was a sinister creature who crept under beds and was controlled by a witch. Various substances could exorcise him, I read, and maybe that was what Emmeline had brewed on our stove!

After she had gone, stamping down the drive in her blanket, with her hat over her eyes and an acolyte trailing behind carrying her suitcase, the gardener showed me a packet of blue powder which he said was *amalingo* (magic) tokoloshe salt to be sprinkled on doorsteps to keep the little man out.

'Is better that person went away,' he said, throwing Emmeline's pots into the dustbin. 'She make too much trouble.'

But I noticed that he did not throw out the tokoloshe salt.

– 42 –

A few days after Emmeline had vanished down the drive, Eunice, a Zulu lady, very large and full-bosomed, appeared at our kitchen door. She had heard the whole story of Emmeline's departure through the grapevine. I liked what I had heard of the Zulus and I liked the look of Eunice. 'No tokoloshes in your bag?' I asked cautiously.

'Aikona, ma'am – no!' and her plump body shook like a jelly with laughter. She had a face which lit up like a Christmas tree when she smiled. Eunice was what Ned would have described as a 'fine mansion of a woman' – large and stately, with a wonderful laugh.

She wanted to start work immediately once we offered her the job. Whipping an apron out of her capacious bag and dispatching a cadaverous-looking companion lurking near the gate to go and fetch her blankets, she rolled up her sleeves. She could iron, which was just as well, as Florrie, unnerved by events, was never seen again. And Eunice *could* cook, producing delicious crisp roast potatoes by partially boiling them and then dropping them into very hot oil. She made garlicky, herby lamb dishes, banana bread and strange sugary things called koeksisters that looked like plaited doughnuts and tasted like heaven. Now there were no more evil-smelling brews stewing on our stove and the air was fresh and sweet in the kitchen. She was a relief after Emmeline, who had upset everyone in the end.

The gardener, in consultation with Eunice, was all for summoning a black exorcist from Soweto to drive the spirits, he said, from Emmeline's room, but I had had enough of witchcraft and told him to sprinkle the tokoloshe salt if he was worried.

Eunice's passion in life, apart from her church, was embroidering. She embroidered vast acres of calico bedspreads which had strange prehistoric creatures creeping across them in scarlet and poison-green silks, and when she sewed, stitching in the sun, I could sometimes hear her singing a Zulu lullaby about a guinea fowl.

'Ndokwe, Ndokwe!' she sang. She taught it to Marnie, who adored her, and she made Hugh a little beaded talking-stick. 'When the talking-stick is in your hands,' she told him, 'only you have the right to speak.'

On Sundays she donned a biblical white robe that reached to the ground. Across the back a blue cotton cross was stitched into place. The whole effect was magnificent, and as she went off down the road, a great billowing statuesque figure, she looked like a biblical matriarch. Her home was in the Valley of a Thousand Hills in Natal, where her people lived in huts shaped like a plaited straw beehive up winding paths. It was green and lush, like parts of Kenya. In the Zulu language, and in Swahili, strangely, exactly the same words were used for snake, wood and fat, for example, so sometimes we could pick up the sense of what was being said when Eunice's Zulu friends spoke amongst themselves. Not that many people came to see Eunice – her family lived so far from the Transvaal that she had few visitors. She rested on her day off, went to church on Sundays and occasionally caught the bus to the shops to buy fresh sewing materials. Usually she wrapped herself up like a parcel in a large brown shawl when she went out because she'd had a weak chest since childhood.

One afternoon I saw her leaving the yard, in a great hurry

this time and without her shawl, wearing blue slippers and a flowered dress. It was a hot, drowsy afternoon and there was a rumble of thunder. The stillness hinted at the usual build-up before a Highveld storm. I watched her sailing majestically down the drive, a small wind making her dress bell out like a spinnaker, and thought how well she fitted into our family and how in some ways she reminded me of Moll. She had left two freshly baked loaves cooling on a rack in the kitchen, filling the room with a sweet warm smell; and as I stood revelling in the peace and the sunlight, Ireland at that moment seemed very far away. Deep inside me, and stirring for the first time, was a reluctant feeling that it might after all be possible to be happy here.

Nothing stirred. The dogs were asleep at the back door and for a time there was no sound except doves calling, that beautiful liquid call which, like the rain and dust, is part of Africa.

As I stood, I heard the squeak of a bicycle and an African man came up the drive pedalling very fast, almost bent in two. The dogs woke up and set up a frenzied barking at his approach. He was dressed in a torn shirt and khaki shorts, and worn veldskoens with flapping soles. He was not someone I knew. Hushing the dogs, I went down the steps to see what he wanted, but he was so much out of breath that at first I could not make out what he was trying to say.

'They got Eunice, ma'am. They took Eunice.'

'Who took Eunice?'

'The police, ma'am. They took her.'

'But she only left here minutes ago,' I said, bewildered. 'She has only just gone.' Surely nothing could have happened in such a short time.

The wind had dropped and the sound of thunder was closer. Sweat was pouring down the man's face and he was clearly agitated. 'They took Eunice,' he repeated. 'So she want her passbook, ma'am. Eunice left her *dompas* in her room,

that's why the police they threw her in the gumba gumba.'
His voice was urgent.

'The gumba gumba?'

'The police van, Mama.'

Then I remembered. So far were white people removed from these laws that it had gone out of my mind. Every black person had to carry a passbook at all times or risk being taken to jail in the wire-windowed police trucks that cruised the white suburbs. The police were usually out in force on Thursdays, the servants' day off, and today was Thursday.

'Who are you?' I asked.

He took off his cap. 'I am Lukey, ma'am, Eunice's young brother.' African relations were confusing to me. Cousins and second cousins and even more distant cousins were referred to as 'my brother' or 'my sister'. Uncles and aunts were reasonably simple to sort out in the scheme of family, but the circle of 'cousin brothers' could run into twenty or thirty. I stood staring at Lukey, not sure what to do.

'Where is her *dompas* – her passbook?' I asked, holding the collar of one of the bigger dogs.

'In the room, ma'am, in Eunice's room. In the suitcase under the bed. She give me the key.' He proffered it. A coloured beaded disc that I had given Eunice a few days before hung from it. I made a decision, beckoned to Lukey, and the two of us went up the steps, unlocking the door to Eunice's room. The bed and the chairs were draped in embroidered calico with a pile of stitched cushion covers laid out on a stool. She must have been on her way to get more silks. A surplice she was embroidering lay half-sewn on a stool, the needle still in it.

Lukey scrabbled under the bed, which was raised on bricks to keep any menacing tokoloshes at bay. Eunice, in spite of the white robes and the blue Christian cross, had great respect for tokoloshes although she denied it. For some reason, not clear, tokoloshes couldn't get you if you were in a high bed, and so the legs of Eunice's bed were propped on four large bricks from a nearby builder's yard. Still half under it, and muffled by yards of bedspread, Lukey, emerging sideways like a crab, produced the passbook with a flourish and handed it to me.

'We'll take it to her in the car,' I said. 'It will be quicker and you can show me where to go.' The dogs hurled themselves against the gate, trying to nip Lukey as he lifted his bicycle into the kitchen yard. I opened the passenger door of the car for him and we went down the drive, passing a tame hoopoe, its beak stuck more than an inch in the grass, and past the sky-blue plumbago bushes. As we reached the road another African stood waiting for us and held up his hand for a lift. This was an old man who sometimes visited Eunice on Sunday afternoons. He was one of the elders of her church, bulky and bearded, with the apt name of Elijah. I stopped and he climbed into the back seat, holding onto his stick and puffing slightly.

'Thank you, ma'am. Ma'am knows they took Eunice?'

'The news has travelled fast,' I said. 'Which way, Lukey?'

'The holding station in Randburg, ma'am.' We gathered speed. The precinct wasn't far, only a couple of miles from home. It was a grey and dismal-looking building made more forbidding because the sun had gone in, the sky was overcast and it was beginning to rain. The South African flag, blue, orange and white, hung limply on a flagpole outside and the door was open.

No one appeared in the outer office when I went in, and although I tapped on a counter bell no one came, but I noticed a narrow passage and, going down it a few yards, to my great relief I saw Eunice, visible through a barred gate, in an open courtyard. She was standing with a dozen others, herded like patient sheep with no shelter. The rain was beginning to fall quite heavily now and she was getting wet, but her face lit up when she saw me and she put her hand through the bars for her passbook. I made a sign of encouragement and went back down the passage to find someone in authority. It was eerily silent. There was no sign of anyone. Lukey and Elijah had elected to stay outside near the car. Nothing would induce either of them to come into the police station with me. They had brought the news of her plight and fetched me. Now it was up to me.

I had left Eunice clutching her passbook with raindrops beading her hair and I had money in my purse if there was a fine that she had to pay on the spot, but there was no one in sight to ask. Standing, uncertain of what to do, I had a curious feeling as if this strange building was part of a meaningless dream. The silent prisoners huddled in the courtyard seemed unreal – pure Chekhov – the rain drumming on concrete, the faint smell of disinfectant, and myself alone in a deserted passage. Everything had happened so suddenly, breaking into the peaceful afternoon. Lukey and his bicycle, Eunice snatched mysteriously away. Perhaps it *was* a dream, one of those dreams when you look for something you can never find.

On either side of the passage were offices with their doors open, the desks scattered with papers, but no sign of life. I began to walk slowly back when a very young blond police constable came up the passage towards me looking surprised. He seemed unsure of his authority and spoke very bad English with a thick accent. He was clearly astonished to find a woman wandering around the police station, and he indicated with courtesy a notice on the door to the passage which said in Afrikaans '*Verbode*' and in English 'No entry'.

'I didn't see it. I'm sorry,' I said, and I had not seen it. The door open to the passage had hidden it from view. 'I have brought my maid's passbook.'

'I beg yours?'

'My maid's passbook,' I repeated earnestly. 'She was arrested. She was not carrying it. She's here' – I pointed back down the tiled passage – 'in the yard. I have just given it to her.'

But he had lost me. I spoke too quickly for him and English was not his home language. He looked bewildered. 'Your maid, Mevrou?' And then, more boldly, 'You should not have gone in the passage, Mevrou. The Commandant will not like that.'

'But I couldn't *find* anybody,' I said. 'Is there a commandant here?' He nodded, relieved of responsibility, and stood back to let me pass, lifting the flap of the counter and beckoning me through a door and down another corridor. I followed him as he led the way, our shoes clicking on the tiles, up a flight of stairs and onto a landing which faced a heavy door.

The constable knocked, waited a few moments, and then ushered me into the office of a huge man who was smoking a cigarette and flicking ash onto the floor. He was a powerful man with the build of a rugby fullback. He did not move from his chair but he eyed me chillingly, head half-bent over a pile of documents. A rapid conversation in Afrikaans took place between the two men. The constable was deferential, the commandant irritated.

I watched him, thinking this was no Hennie Van Rensburg, no well-meaning 'Ons Volk Ons Land' man full of quasi-religious dogma. This was a type I hadn't met before, a granite-faced monolith in a blue-grey uniform with his pips up, who would give no one quarter. For a moment he said nothing and then, his eyes narrowing, 'Ja, lady?'

'My Zulu maid, Eunice Dlamini …'

'Ja, lady?' He seemed exasperated, impatient, bored with the trivia of women and their servants.

'She forgot her passbook. She was only a few hundred yards from our gate when the police caught her.' Damn you, I thought, don't try to intimidate me! 'I have brought her pass so that she can be released.'

He tapped his teeth with a ballpoint pen, his eyes

expressionless, until the young constable, hovering deferentially, placed a piece of paper down on the desk in front of him and he read from it aloud. 'This Bantu, Eunice Dlamini. She is in your employ?' He sounded accusing.

I nodded.

'This Bantu, lady,' his voice was guttural, measured and ponderous like a judge, 'this Bantu has been charged with not being in possession of a passbook, and as such she cannot be discharged.' He was staring at me, daring me to argue.

'But why? It seems a perfectly reasonable request to me,' I said.

He looked down, continuing to read. 'She was in a white area without a passbook, lady, and this cannot be permitted. This Bantu must now appear in the magistrate's court in Alexandra tomorrow morning in terms of the influx control regulations under the Urban Areas Act.' He stopped reading and cleared his throat.

'But this isn't anything to do with influx control,' I said. I was not even sure what influx control was. 'I mean, she isn't here illegally, she works for us. She just forgot her passbook and I brought it.' But I had made a tactical error. I could see that this man would never bend a rule. It was written as it was written. It was carved in stone, and I had dared to argue with him. Laws to him were set in concrete, and he reiterated them like an automaton, one felt, and with satisfaction. The public were his serfs, the blacks pawns in a meaningless chess game. He knew the rules and I did not.

He despised me, I could see it in his face. He went on reading, glancing up from time to time to fix me with a steely eye. 'Any person who fails, without reasonable cause, to produce a passbook on demand to an authorised official under Act 25 of 1945 is guilty, lady.' He glared up at me and repeated, 'Is guilty, lady, of an offence against the state.'

'But there *was* reasonable cause,' I said patiently. 'She forgot it but then I brought it.'

His forehead had an angry red weal from a too-tight cap band just below his slightly crinkley hair. His long fingers were stained with nicotine and he was beginning to tap them. He was losing patience, but then so was I. He said, as to a cretin, 'I don't think you understand me, lady.'

'I understand well enough.' I could feel anger boiling up. 'You must discharge her, you can't leave her there. It's raining. She has her pass. There are no grounds.' Our eyes locked. The thunder, hovering in the background for the past hour, had now come closer and the rain was pelting, drumming, coming down in a solid curtain of water. Eunice and the others in the open courtyard would be soaked.

I had a wild urge to lean over his desk, grasp him by his blue gabardine lapels and shake him. I fought back the urge, which was just as well, and banged on his desktop instead. 'You *must* get those so-called offenders out of the rain,' I said. 'Holding them there is illegal. It must be.'

He was all attention now, looking me full in the face. Now it was I who was in the wrong. 'Be very careful, lady, be very careful.' His voice was smooth, silky.

But out of control I stormed on, making matters worse, saying inflammatory things about a police state and about tinpot officials who abused power. I had a temper that was not easily controlled, and when I eventually left, shaking with rage, complete with a fine he had given me for obstructing a policeman in the course of his duty, I turned back at the top of the stairs and saw him through the open door, reaching for a cigarette with nicotined fingers and watching me leave, without a flicker of expression on his face. He was not prepared to let Eunice go, and because I had shouted at him it might now go badly for her in the courtyard. I had made things worse. I loathed him and everything he stood for, and the system, which treated people like animals.

Driving home in the wind and rain of the Highveld storm to get poor Eunice her blanket and a coat, I felt a sense of frustration and utter smouldering rage. As a family we had always tried to put right what we saw as wrong, but here, although I could see injustice, I was helpless.

Elijah and Lukey, sensing my anger, were clucking away in the back of the car like two old hens, but I knew in my heart of hearts that they had never expected me to emerge with Eunice. They knew the ropes and how things went, and I did not, but I saw clearly for the first time how diabolic this system was, and how *inhuman*.

I drove back later with Eunice's blanket and with more money to take with her to court, and this time the young constable barred my way. He took the clothes and the money from me, promising to see that she got them, and said in a low voice that he was sorry. Sorry for me or for Eunice was not clear.

It is a singularly helpless feeling to be up against a force far stronger than the individual, but more particularly to know that the force is wrong and to be powerless in the face of it. Now that I had come up against the system, I could not believe that it was not possible to do something. I drove to see a judge who was a friend, and poured out my anger. He listened carefully, his head on one side, and then asked me whether I was prepared to lead a crusade against the state – which he said people did but which could, he said, end with my being confined under house arrest and labelled as a troublemaker. It would, he pointed out, impinge on my family and affect Robin and the children, who needed me. Draconian as the laws were, they were still the laws of the country.

'You must obey the laws of the country in which you live.'

As I listened, I had to face the fact that I was not brave enough to try to fight the system but could only bide my time and wait. Meanwhile, I tore up the fine the Commandant had given me. The judge said it was of no consequence and was only given to frighten me, and in fact I did not ever have to pay it.

The next afternoon Eunice, bubbling with bronchitis and with swollen ankles, came home. They had allowed her and the other pass offenders out of the rain and into the cells quite soon after I had left, but in the early cold hours of the morning the black warders had sluiced the cells with jets of icy water and Jeyes Fluid, and Eunice had had to stand there until dawn in the cell, packed in with a dozen others, with the water seeping through her slippers.

I complained to the local magistrate, and there was an inquiry and a reprimand for the warders, but Eunice was not well for some time. She had always had a weak chest, which we knew, and the episode in the cells had brought on her asthma. We nursed her, and when she recovered she told us that she was anxious to go home for good and get work nearer her children. She gave me a huge tablecloth embroidered with purple chameleons and cried a little when she left.

'*Hamba kahle!*' (Go well!) she called in Zulu out of her cousin's battered old car, piled high with mattresses and luggage, that took her and her trunks of embroideries back to the Valley of a Thousand Hills.

– 43 –

When I first met Maggie Seakamela I had no idea that the young African woman in the straw hat with red ribbons hanging down her back would become an integral part of our lives, or that one day, far into the future, I would strike a blow against apartheid because of a child of hers, as yet unborn.

On an afternoon just before Easter I had set off to interview two maids. Eunice had gone back to Natal and we needed some help in the house. It was late summer and the countryside was a swaying mass of delicate wild cosmos flowers like butterflies, pink, burgundy and white. They came at Easter time, like a promise, lining the dusty roads with colour.

I was to meet the two girls at a farmhouse but, when I drove in, one of them was no longer available and the other, who was waiting to see me, was Maggie. She was twenty-two and the very antithesis of Eunice. She looked so young and inexperienced that when I saw her I was sure she would not do at all. I wanted someone more like Eunice, someone older and motherly, not a young girl, and particularly not a young girl without references – and she had none.

'If we took you on,' I said hesitantly, 'when would you be able to start?' I spoke without any enthusiasm, almost inviting a snag.

'Now,' she said. 'I can come now.'

'But your clothes? Your luggage?' I said, taken aback.

'They are here.' She pointed to a suitcase at her feet.

'And wages, Maggie. We haven't even discussed wages.'

'Whatever the madam wants to pay me.'

It was becoming difficult to say no in the face of such enthusiasm, but still I was uncertain. 'I really wanted to employ a Zulu person,' I said, because I knew she wasn't a Zulu. 'What tribe do you belong to?'

'Northern Sotho,' she said, 'from near Pietersburg.' She looked me straight in the eye, smiling, strong-willed and eager, and the die was cast. She told me many years later that she had made up her mind straight away that she wanted to work for us, but neither of us could have known on that afternoon that her family and ours would become close in the way they did.

And so it was, almost against my will, that Maggie came into our lives and, with her, all her problems, which were legion.

To begin with, there was her common-law husband Robert, who came to live on our property, slipping into the yard at night after work. Later came the birth of her son Duff, whom she sent off to her mother in the Northern Transvaal once he could toddle. There was an unwritten law at that time that allowed blacks to keep their babies in white areas for only a limited time. After that, they went off to the *Gogo* (grandmother) who, when too old to work, had charge of them in remote places far from the cities. And so little Duff learnt to crawl and walk in our garden and then left us.

Next there was the abrupt departure of Robert. He was thrown out bag and baggage by Maggie soon after the birth of their second son, Nico. Robert had provided her with nothing, Maggie said, washing her hands of him. She had cooked for him, ironed his shirts for work every day, laundered his muddy football clothes and given him two strong sons, but in return, she said, she had not seen a penny of his wages. Come to that, neither had we, and most of his food came out of our kitchen! It appeared that Robert gambled away every cent of his earnings on games of chance, and there was another woman waiting for him in the wings who was more accommodating than Maggie.

Robert's departure nevertheless caused us some uneasiness, because we now seemed to be the only buffer for Maggie and her children in a country on the brink of war. Not only that, but the doctor who delivered Nico had talked of eclampsia before his birth, and was adamant that this should be Maggie's last pregnancy if she valued her life. Her blood pressure, he said, was dangerously high. Could she have a stroke if she went on working? we wondered. And what of her children? There was no state social security to speak of, no safety net, no grant for the unemployed.

While we were mulling over all this, down from an African village hundreds of miles away came Maggie's mother, like a small black Queen Victoria, indomitable, and with the unmistakable intention of making a long visit. She was tiny, and seemed far too old to have a 27-year-old daughter.

She was as wrinkled as creased tissue paper, with twinkling, wise eyes. She still had a tooth or two, but her pate was very short of hair, which gave her the look of an endearing tortoise. Her name was Serena Seakamela, and she was of the old school. She had reared more white toddlers than she could count, wiped their noses, carried them on her back in a blanket, and spooned porridge into their mouths while their mothers were off playing tennis or golf or bridge.

She wore a crocheted cap like a Victorian grandmamma and took a little snuff for her health out of a small tin lozenge box. She sat in the sun, watching over and admonishing Nico, who crawled about her feet putting everything he could find into his mouth. I called her 'Tortie' and she called me 'my darling', smiling at me benevolently as I went in and out of the garden.

'Now my darling,' she was to say to me eighteen months later when she was ill and down in Johannesburg for treatment, 'now my darling, if anything happens to me you must promise ...' She opened her snuff tin.

'You must promise to keep my child with you.' She looked at me twinkling and wheedling, so I said laughing, and only half serious, 'But I can't promise, Tortie. Maggie might not want to stay!'

'She *must* stay,' Tortie said fiercely, more like Queen Victoria than ever and brooking no argument. 'She must stay. Because I worry for her. She is my only child.'

'But what's all this talk about something happening to you?' I asked. 'It's rubbish, you will live for years yet.' I smiled at her as she took a pinch of snuff, putting a little up each nostril like a Georgian dandy and lifting her wrinkled old face to the sun.

A week after that Tortie had a CAT scan and was kept in hospital for observation. We visited her and found her sitting up in bed in a towelling dressing gown, her little brown pate shining like a new pin, eating grilled fish and beetroot. She had under her thumb a young doctor called Garth whom she also addressed as 'my darling', and when things went badly for her, she explained, as if it were perfectly natural, she simply sent for him and he appeared like a genie out of a bottle. She had worked for his mother when he was a child, carried him on her back and spooned porridge into him, and he had never forgotten her. She summoned him to meet us, a nice tousle-haired young intern who said it was amazing for him to meet up with Serena again. But then Tortie had some magic about her. She was just one of those people!

When she was discharged with a clean bill of health and some medicines, she came to us for a while in very good heart, smiling away, taking her snuff and wearing a new crocheted cap she had made in the hospital. Bad as apartheid was in those days, the teaching hospitals were marvellous, and with Garth at her beck and call Tortie said she had never felt better. A grateful employer had left her money years ago to build a little house in her village and she was anxious to be off and back to it and to little Duff, who was with an octogenarian cousin. And so, a month later, she packed her traps, gave us a present of an enormous wooden spoon she had whittled herself, and departed, taking Nico with her.

But sadly, Tortie was not cured. She was a diabetic and there were complications. She was to die six or seven months later and then Nico, who had nowhere to go, was to come back to us.

He was not really supposed to be in the white suburb, but no one knew he was there except us. In any case he was a very quiet child, and if perhaps he cried or screamed occasionally his mother must have quickly silenced him. Not because of us, but because if there was any continual noise the neighbours might complain and call the police. Maggie said it had been done in a nearby suburb.

There was talk for a while of sending Nico to a distant relative in Soweto, but the townships were no place for a baby without his mother. There were riots and killings every day, the burning of schools was rife and so was the burning alive of people thought to be disloyal to the cause. There were shoot-outs, tear gas, and soldiers everywhere. With Tortie dead and little Duff with an ancient and only available relation, we tucked Nico away with his mother at the end of our long drive and held thumbs. But no flinty-eyed policeman came anywhere near us. They had their hands full as the 'unrest' grew in the black townships of Soweto and Alexandra.

And so Nico stayed and grew a little taller and played with his toys in the yard. We were getting fonder and fonder of his mother, who had become an indispensable member of our household.

The first time I saw Nico properly, and not just as Maggie's baby, was one evening when he was just over two and a half.

He had been down the drive with his mother to collect the evening newspaper, and he was walking slowly back, not holding his mother's hand but walking by himself, solemn and independent. He was wearing an enormous straw hat of hers with a brim that hid his face so he looked like a walking mushroom. Under the hat were two small milk-chocolate legs, and as he came close he grinned up at me and handed me the newspaper, which had been rolled up and secured with a rubber band.

I saw him then, not as any baby, but as Nico, a small person in his own right.

As he grew up, things fell into place. He had a black mother, Maggie; a white mother, me; and he had Robin to teach him how to throw and catch a ball.

And then it was time, it seemed almost overnight, for him to go to school. He was four. He needed pre-primary and more friends, so off he went to the Rudolf Steiner Waldorf School just across the road. It was a private school for children of any colour or race, where the government had no jurisdiction. He was blissfully happy. And then it seemed that in no time at all he was six and it was time for primary school.

But the Rudolf Steiner Primary School fees had escalated. We didn't really have enough money to meet them. We had reached the end of the road financially. Nico couldn't go back to the farm, Soweto was in an uproar, so there was only one thing to do – send him to a state school, which only took white children.

I took counsel with Robin and Maggie, and one morning in 1991, with my heart pounding but knowing we had to find a solution, I drove to the local government school which had hundreds of white children and no black ones, and I put Nico's name down for admission. I almost expected to be tapped on the shoulder and lectured but, oddly enough, no one asked me any questions. A few people looked at me with surprise and a vague interest, as if I belonged to some strange political group, but they were perfectly polite and smiling. I held my breath as I filled in the application forms and handed them in. No one said anything at all. It was almost too good to be true. Looking at the worst scenarios, I imagined that perhaps they intended to discuss it amongst themselves later and see what line should be taken, and whether to write us a polite letter spelling out government policy; or again, there was a chance they might say there was no vacancy and there must have been some misunderstanding. But there was no sign that anyone condemned anything that I had done. The bursar took the form, smiled at me when I said he was a black child, and I left and drove home.

All that week I waited for repercussions but none came. There were friends Nico had made at nursery school who were going on to primary school. Some of them had been to his birthday parties and he to theirs, and they came to play and talked of the new school.

As the time for the academic year to begin drew nearer, I went back to the primary school, this time with Nico holding my hand tightly; and we met Mrs Clarke, a wonderful woman, who did his school readiness tests and said that Nico was well up to standard.

'Is he accepted?' I asked.

'I think so.'

Maggie and I went shopping for his school uniform. As for Nico, he was so excited he could hardly eat. The uniform was hung where he could see it, on a knob at the end of his bed. It was all like an answer to prayer. We photographed him in his new uniform with his cap on, with his cap off, and carrying the school case. I had bought him a lunch box and a juice bottle and coloured crayons because no letter of rejection had come at all.

And then the telephone rang.

It rang when we were least expecting it, and when we were at our most euphoric.

The voice at the other end said, clearing his throat, that Nico couldn't come to the school. He *didn't* say that it was because Nico was black, it was not as bald as that. What he said was that it was necessary for Nico's parents to produce a paid-up rates account showing that they owned property in the area. A perfectly reasonable request except, as everyone knew, no black people were allowed to rent or buy land in a white area.

'You know that is not possible,' I said. 'You *know* that!'

'I know it,' the voice said. It was sympathetic. 'But it is the law.' He cleared his throat. 'It's not my decision. It's a government school and it *is* the law.'

'We have bought his uniform,' I said, a catch in my voice. 'He is so excited. He has had the school readiness test. He passed it and after that we *promised* him. You can't *do* that to a child, refuse him now. He is only six. You can't *do* that!'

The voice at the other end of the telephone did not sound inexorable. It sounded sad and uncertain. 'It's the law,' said the voice again. There was a pause and then, 'I'll get back to you,' and there was a click as he replaced the receiver.

The next call from the school was extraordinary. To this day I do not understand the significance of what I was asked.

This time the voice said, 'Does Nico sleep under your roof?'

Sometimes he did, but he almost always slept with his mother.

'Yes,' I said boldly.

'And meals. Does the child take meals with you?'

I had a feeling of being gently nudged by the voice, so I said 'Yes,' because in some way my answer seemed to be crucial. And it seemed to have been the right one, because the next day Nico was formally accepted into the school.

And so it came about that on the first day of term

something happened that had never happened before in the annals of the school – a small black local child, Nico, was allotted a desk where he sat next to a little white girl. Amazingly the earth continued to revolve on its axis as he drew and coloured in, drank his fruit juice and ate his biscuits like everyone else. The kindness he received at that previously white school was heartening, to say the least. Teachers, children and their families took him to their hearts and he was in a fair way to have his head turned, except that Maggie, more than I, kept his feet on the ground.

This acceptance of Nico showed that many white families hated apartheid and were more than ready for change. Change was coming, whether the diehards wanted it or not, even as the township troubles grew.

Of course many, many black children came into that school after 1994, but Nico was the first, and we watched him with pride as he captained a cricket team and a soccer team and learnt how to swim, work a computer and fly a kite. He was class captain too, and it was a great day for us when we heard the headmaster say that he was one of their star pupils, on merit and merit alone.

– 44 –

While South Africa became a less and less pleasant place to live, I dreamt of Kenya with great nostalgia, particularly of Nanyuki and sacred Mount Kenya, where Mungu (God) had created Gikuyu and Mumbi, the African Adam and Eve. I wanted very much to go back to Nanyuki, to drink from the ice-cold streams off the snowline of Mount Kenya and stand on the line of the equator which had run through the old Silverbeck Hotel just outside Nanyuki village. Nanyuki had some magic quality of its own, a little town under the mountain, almost the last outpost (because Isiolo wasn't really a town) before the Northern Frontier District where the roads, like rock-strewn river beds, led to Ethiopia.

I had not heard news of my father for some months. In his last letter he had seemed to be in better health than he had been for years. His medication had been changed and he had begun to walk with a stick and get about a little more. Lisa had been looking after him as tirelessly as she always had.

Then, quite suddenly, although everyone implored him not to think of such a thing, he announced his intention of offering himself to a neurosurgeon as a guinea pig for a new and complicated operation. It was a little-known procedure for Parkinson's which might or might not succeed. In a way it was a brave thing to do, because if it was a success it could be a trail-blazer for other sufferers. On the other hand, if it failed, he would merely, as one pointed out, be the subject of an interesting paper at some Neuro conference.

Everyone close to him tried to dissuade him but he was as obstinate as a mule. Once set on course, nothing would deflect him from the idea. I knew from past run-ins with Grandfather in the old days that my father was impossible to sway when the bit was between his teeth. Nothing said, threatened or advised would persuade him to change his mind, and he admitted himself to hospital, to a cacophony of fury and dismay from his family.

Amazingly the operation appeared to improve his quality of life, but as time went on his condition became worse than before. He had indeed been a guinea pig but, as the surgeon pointed out, it was my father who had insisted on it.

After that he began to go downhill. Sometimes it was impossible to hear what he said. He grew stiff, his muscles contracted and his face often set in a rigid mask which was characteristic of the disease. We had seen little of each other, he and I, over the years, and I knew his faults, but I was fond of him. One could say of him that he never gave up, and he hated inactivity. I think he decided on the operation as a new challenge when he was bored.

The monk still haunted my dreams from time to time, although he seemed to recede further and further away nowadays or, in my dream, stand with his back turned so that I never saw his face.

At this time I suddenly received a letter from my mother. Her missives had always struck me as extraordinary in that she wrote to me as to a daughter with whom she had had a very close relationship since babyhood. I found this very irritating. So it was with no particular feeling of interest that I found a letter from her in the postbox.

She wrote that a Colonel Stallard had died in Johannesburg.

Who on earth, or hopefully now in heaven, I wondered, was Colonel Stallard?

The letter went on to say that I should contact a certain lawyer in Johannesburg who would tell me about the funeral arrangements. My mother added that she felt I ought to make a real effort to attend.

'After all,' the letter concluded in a somewhat peremptory fashion, 'Hope Willith, and the farm, is part of your past.'

I put the letter down with a feeling of irritation. Colonel Stallard, whoever he was, was of no consequence to me, and if she had only just heard of his death the funeral would have been over long ago. The postmark on the envelope was over ten days old.

I tore up the letter, threw the pieces into the fire and put the whole thing out of my head. But it came back at odd moments during the day.

Who was Colonel Stallard and why should Hope Willith have any bearing on me? Still the thought nagged at me and then, extraordinarily, when I was reading the newspaper that evening, a paragraph came into my line of vision. It said, in fairly large type, that Colonel Stallard had died. It gave a summary of his life and not inconsiderable achievements. He had commanded a South African regiment, been a Member of Parliament, left over a million in his will, and had lived on an estate south of Johannesburg called Hope Willith. It gave the time of a memorial service for him, scheduled for three days ahead, and mentioned the name of the lawyer in my mother's letter.

Why *was* Hope Willith anything to do with me? It seemed there was more to this Colonel Stallard than I knew myself, and this nagged at me like a recurring toothache.

If there were unknown fragments of your life, however small, then it meant that whole areas of it were out of focus. After all, your life was very personally yours, and unique to you. In my life, areas were definitely out of focus. I sat with the newspaper on my lap and stared into space. Uneasily I remembered my mother's earlier letters about Norman and how I had got in touch with him in the end. How many other unknown things would she spring on me after years of silence?

These intermittent letters of hers were like scraps of paper in a paper chase and could lead down a trail which might bring something I did not know into focus. Did I *want* to know? Did I *really* want to know what it was? I looked at the paragraph in the paper again. It said that a memorial service would be held in a private chapel on the farm Hope Willith. There was even a telephone number for people who needed directions to get there or who wanted to send flowers. On impulse I picked up the telephone and dialled. For some strange reason my heart started to bump but – anticlimax – the phone just rang and rang. Just as I was about to put it down, a man's voice said, 'Hope Willith.'

He must have thought I was a reporter, because when I asked him how to get to Hope Willith he asked me unexpected questions. He hadn't 'caught' my name, he said, and then, 'What's your connection with the Colonel, or is it with Hope Willith, perhaps?'

'No connection that I knew of till recently,' I said, explaining the circumstances and giving my name.

My story sounded not only lame but peculiar, so I was amazed when he said, with considerable warmth in his voice, 'We heard you were back in the country.' He actually sounded quite pleased. 'We wondered if you would be coming to see us.'

'Coming to see you? How do you know who I am?' How did he even know I existed? I thought.

'But you said who you were, and that you had heard of the Colonel's death through your mother,' he said, reasonably enough. In this totally strange country where we knew only a handful of people, this was a bombshell. How could there be even the smallest niche reserved in anyone's memory for me when I so patently was a stranger?

Who *was* this man?

'There are two people who know of you and whom you might be interested to meet,' he said, when the silence had gone on for a moment or two. 'It's been a long time. It was a long time ago. My mother, who loved you dearly when you were a baby, is, sadly, dead. We will expect you at the memorial service.'

And so it was that on a golden winter's afternoon I went to find Hope Willith. All of us went: Marnie and Hugh, Robin and I.

It was one of those magic days that the Transvaal produces on the cusp of autumn and winter. Crisp, clear blue skies and with bars of sunshine slanting through the trees. Golden mimosa hung in clouds of yellow. South Africa has the most wonderful autumnal grasses which turn a tawny pinky gold in the early autumn. They seem to glow, particularly in the sunlight of late afternoon. This afternoon they fringed the road in billows of colour.

We drove down a farm road and parked with other cars near an old farmhouse with a corrugated-iron roof and an old colonial veranda, and we walked with a group of people along a grass path towards a chapel and down through a wood, the silence of the woodland broken only by the full-bodied gentle cooing of doves calling in the trees above us, and the footfalls of people walking on crisp, fallen leaves.

In the chapel a group of monks from a community nearby were already seated in old chairs, some broken and rotted through. One actually collapsed when a plump man sat on it. Dust motes danced in the still air and I could still hear the doves.

I heard a woman in a black hat in front of us say that she thought the chapel had been an old cowshed for a time, which was why the walls were thick and rough and covered with an uneven whitewash. Its total simplicity gave it, for some reason, a feeling of being close to God. With my low Church of Ireland upbringing I felt very comfortable with it.

The service was simple, and the monk who read the address spoke very affectionately of the Colonel and his interest in their Order. After the blessing we stood outside near some graves. The one which was Colonel Stallard's was marked with a tombstone, and someone had laid a bunch of fresh flowers on it. The woman in the large black hat was tottering just ahead of us on high black patent shoes. She walked flanked by two monks. I heard her say, half in English mixed with some Afrikaans, 'He was buried here, the Colonel, because he always said that was how it would be. His old coachman is buried at his feet and his chauffeur at his head. He never drove himself in his car, you see, and if there were horses in heaven his old black coachman would have to manage them, he said, but if there were cars the chauffeur would drive them.' She lapsed into Afrikaans.

Presumably, I thought, the coachman and chauffeur had died some years before. They wouldn't have committed some sort of African suttee on his demise.

She seemed to be a great authority on the Colonel and had a carrying voice because I heard her say to a woman who had joined the group, 'He never really liked women, you know. Never married, so I don't know who will get the Hope Willith diaries or his library now. He had wonderful books. Did you ever go into his house?'

I didn't hear an answer, because at that moment I was suffused with the most extraordinary emotion. Coming towards me was a very old but upright fair-skinned monk with a fine face and the clearest of clear blue eyes. His thick white hair was blowing in the breeze which had just sprung up. He was wearing a long black cassock and he seemed exactly like the monk I had seen so often in my dreams. This time he was not part of a dream, but flesh and blood.

The afternoon, the chapel, the wood and the farm suddenly

became so unreal that for a few seconds I wasn't sure whether I was awake or dreaming. Time rushed backwards and forwards and to and fro so that I felt dizzy. The feeling of *déjà vu* was overpowering. Was the whole scene a dream? The woman in the black hat with her flat Afrikaans accent, was she real? The man on the telephone who had said, 'We heard you were back!' How did I know them?

When the monk spoke, I expected, as you do with *déjà vu*, that something profound would be said; that the whole afternoon was leading up to a climax and that some mystery would now be explained.

Nothing happened. The present came back into focus and the wood stopped spinning.

Taking me by the arm and guiding Robin with a hand on his shoulder, the old monk said, 'There is a very good tea in the farmhouse. Shall we go there? I think, but I am not sure, that you are Diana?' His hair blew in the wind and formed an aureole around his head, exactly as I had seen it in my dream.

'It's very strange,' I said, feeling shaken as we walked along, the children running ahead to pick up pine-cones, 'this has knocked me quite a bit. I feel almost in shock, but when I saw you I had the oddest premonition. Not only about you but that I had been here before.' I didn't like to mention that I had dreamt about him!

'But you *have* been here before,' he said, 'as a baby after your parents separated.' And seeing my enquiring look, 'Your mother was not granted custody of you, but I think she felt entitled to it. You see … she made some attempts to take you … so your father brought you here. It was safe. This is a peaceful spot. Tucked away. A lady, a Mrs Ritchie, who was a wonderful woman, looked after you. Later she nursed the Colonel. I seem to remember you were very attached to her and she to you. Then of course,' he negotiated a flight of steps to a wooden veranda, 'then of course you went to Ireland.'

'Who was she? Is she dead? And the Colonel?'

'A wonderful man. He lived to be a hundred. You probably saw him often when you were a baby. He liked children. And he liked the monks. We are from the Community of the Resurrection and we sometimes took services here when the Colonel was alive.'

We queued next to a trestle table for cups of tea and I stole another look at him. So there was significance in the dream after all; the only improbability lay in dreaming about someone and then meeting him.

We walked along the veranda into an old colonial high-ceilinged house with a tin roof and I was suddenly hit by another wave of *déjà vu*. It was like switching on a light in my mind. It was not because I had been told, but because I actually *knew* now that I had been here before.

I must have learnt to walk in this quiet place with the hundreds of doves cooing in the tall green trees near the little chapel in the wood. This is where I had begun my journeyings to Ireland, Annes Grove, Kenya and Dar es Salaam.

I had come full circle.

And so the afternoon had indeed led to a climax, and one that was very important to me. I realised, perhaps for the first time, that South Africa was an integral part of my life, warts and all, good and bad.

There was a significance after all, I discovered later, and as the significance became clear I saw it as not at all earth-shaking but in its way a kind of healing – an unbundling of unadmitted anger towards my mother, which had set up unconscious tensions in my mind.

When I looked back on that strange afternoon, I realised that it was to change my perceptions for ever. Hope Willith, and the monk that I had met there, became a watershed in my life. There was so much I had not known about my parents and more especially about my mother. The monk, who *had* known her and had felt sad for her, made me see, in a gentle way, that things had gone badly for her in those early days. I knew now that, as a young girl of twenty-two, she had lost a baby son through illness and had run to a man older than my father for support and understanding. Disasters, he explained, can sometimes bring a family closer, or cause unbridgeable rifts. The death of the child, in my parents' case, was the beginning of the end.

Not that my mother was an angel. She was, he said, a person from whom one could not expect too much because, like my father, it was impossible for her to give, or to be, what other people demanded.

I saw the monk several times after that service at Hope Willith. He had been a successful lawyer and had given it up to join a religious order. His kindly wisdom healed a wound I never knew I had.

'She wanted *custody* of you, you see. Perhaps you did not know that.'

'I didn't even know I'd had a full brother,' I told Robin later. 'No one told me.' There seemed to be a good many things I knew nothing about. Things swept under the carpet at Annes Grove.

Oddly enough, after these talks, it was as if a large boulder blocking off a part of my mind had been pushed aside, and now I had access to old forgotten feelings I had not even known were there. I had not even known that the boulder was there! I had to examine and work through the feelings beneath it, which was not always comfortable and took a great deal of courage, but the time was right for me to do so and I managed. Gradually I shed old guilts and began to accept that my grandparents' attitudes had not always been the right ones but had reflected their own experiences. Both their mothers had run away from impossible husbands and so perhaps they, too, had their own boulders in place.

As for me, I no longer wanted to carry baggage from the past now that it was opened and sorted. What was it that Mr Van Rensburg had said? 'Johannesburg is a place where you come face to face with yourself.' How right he was.

– 45 –

Meanwhile, we were punch-drunk in South Africa. The world had imposed sanctions upon us. Bombs were going off, and the troops were in the townships. Bits of the morning newspaper were blanked out, hinting at stories they were not allowed to print; things the government said we had no right, or need, to know.

People talked about extraordinary situations as if they were run-of-the-mill and normal, instead of horrific. 'I wouldn't go into the big shopping malls!' they told each other. 'If they set off a bomb there, the blast will funnel all the smashed glass windows down the sidewalks. Cut you to bits.'

I scuttled nervously to Sandton City, the largest of the shopping malls, to buy Robin a birthday present. It was almost deserted. People rushed past like startled rabbits. None of the ritzy Sandton matrons were stopping to gossip in the glossy shops these days and the coffee shops were almost empty, cakes on display grew stale and dry.

Outside, buses with smashed windows whizzed past, the drivers peering like knights in visors through their wire windscreen protectors. They were brave to drive; half the time they couldn't see where they were going, but if the wire wasn't up, a rock could shatter the windscreen in their faces.

Robin's brother, who was an ear, nose and throat specialist, gave serious advice in case we ourselves had to run the gamut of rocks coming at us through windscreens.

'Don't,' he advised, 'crouch *down* in the driving seat. You'll get a rock on your head that way, and head wounds are serious. Stretch upwards, so that the damage won't be so bad.'

'Only a hole in your chest!' I thought. I had visions of myself, my neck stretched like a giraffe's, speeding like Jehu through a bunch of rock-hurlers.

To get away from Johannesburg for a few days, we went up to the Northern Transvaal to try to see the Rain Queen. Driving edgily past a small knot of students, rocks in hand, outside the University of the North, I stretched my neck as high as it would go, and asked St Jude – the Saint of Lost Causes – to look out for us. In the event, no one threw any. The police had scattered students earlier that day, after a car had been bombarded and a driver badly cut around the face.

The Rain Queen lived in the Devils Kloof area. When we arrived, driving through thick mud, it was pouring with rain. It seemed a good omen for the visit, after the dusty dryness of Johannesburg. But although we walked through the sacred grove of ancient cycads and saw her palace on the hill, we were told that 'Her Majesty was not granting any audiences that day.'

I was disappointed and so was Robin. We had both read Professor Krige's book about the Rain Queen and her Lovedu tribe, and we knew that this Modjadji was the fifth of the Rain Queens. All of them had been called Modjadji, meaning the Ruler of the Day, and all had had the power, according to legend, to call up or withhold the rain at will through the sacred gomana drums and ancient rain beads stolen and brought from far to the north.

Rider Haggard on his visit so Africa in 1875 had based his famous book *She* on the first Modjadji, who, not surprisingly, had captured his imagination. There was enough history, I thought, surrounding these mysterious black queens to entrance any writer or researcher – that is, if you could stomach some of the more sinister rituals.

For example the skins of all the previous Rain Queens and the skull of the first Modjadji were kept in the sacred rain pots. Then there was the dark history of incest starting with the son of the great chief Monomatapu, who had once held sway over most of Zimbabwe. Monomatapu had been the first Rain Queen's grandfather. There was another ritual too, which decreed that when the reigning queen reached a certain age she had to end her own life, usually through poison. Never being seen as old or infirm gave rise to the story that the Rain Queens never aged, but it seemed a grim price to pay. Hardly anyone ever saw her, which added to her mystique. The Zulus, we were told, held the Queen in absolute awe, called her Mabelemane, and believed implicitly she had four breasts and that she could bring drought through incantations to those who did not placate her. True or untrue – she was treated by tribes of the south and well to the north of her as a dark and delphic power, and her tribe grew rich on the cattle offered by supplicants.

'This one's Grandmother was half white,' one of the locals told us, 'a Boer girl kidnapped in a Voortrekker raid by the Lovedu a hundred years ago. Brought white blood into the kraal.' But that was another story in a string of half-told tales. We were told in turn that her ancestors were Arab traders, that she was the descendant of a Great White Queen who had ruled Zimbabwe, and that she was – and this we believed – a remnant of the dark mysterious magic rites that had once been part of the heartbeat of Africa.

Back in Johannesburg it was a crazy scenario and getting worse. Army tanks were on the highways and more and more helicopters overhead, and in the last days of P. W. Botha's presidency there was a feeling of being on a powerful boat heading at speed for the rocks with a mad pilot at the helm.

The telephone rang late one night. It was a friend in England. Waking, and reaching for the telephone, Robin heard her say that there was going to be a bloody revolution in

South Africa. She had heard it on the news. 'Take the minimum. Pack a case. Just get on the first plane you can and come to us.'

Nadine Gordimer, I think, had written a book about white people fleeing a revolution in Africa and being sheltered by kindly blacks. Would we have to flee? And what would we manageably take? Valuable things that were re-saleable? Irreplaceable things of sentimental value? I lay awake and made mental lists. And what about our animals? Maggie would look after everything as best she could, but would she be safe? And Nico? Was our friend in England overreacting? Or could we not see the wood for the trees?

And then suddenly everything started happening at breathtaking speed, like a video on fast forward: De Klerk was to release Mandela after he had spent twenty-seven years in prison as a dangerous enemy of the state. We switched on our television – we had been allowed television decades after the rest of the world – and saw a tall, charismatic figure with a gentle face, smiling and waving as he walked free. He looked an unlikely terrorist. This was a turning point for many people who had to begin to question what they'd always believed, to revise their firmly held opinions.

After that, tensions began easing in many quarters. Then came the general elections when for the first time blacks voted alongside whites. They voted the African National Congress into power with Nelson Mandela as the first black President of South Africa. The day he stood, hand on heart, in Pretoria, being sworn in, with the new South African flag fluttering in a gentle breeze, people all over the country had tears of joy streaming down their faces.

The bell was tolling for white supremacy after more than three hundred years. Black South Africans went mad with joy and thousands of – though not all – white South Africans rejoiced with them, feeling a weight lifted from their hearts. The iron grip the Nationalists had had on the country was loosened. The stories of brutal torture by the secret police of black people, no matter how they had been suppressed, had somehow filtered through. Tales of people being taken away for interrogation at night and never seen again had chilled the blood.

But how would men like Hennie Van Rensburg cope with these changes? I wondered. Would they adjust to the new order? Would they say it was the will of God? Would they recant or would it destroy them? It was impossible to tell. It was said that Afrikaners would trek again as they had in the past – to Mozambique or Zambia or South America. But no one knew for certain.

Meanwhile, we had lived through a miracle. There had been no bloody revolution. In retrospect, South Africa could so easily have been another Kosovo, another Rwanda or East Timor, but it had not happened.

'Blood all round you,' Mrs Barry had said that night at Annes Grove. Hopefully there would be an end to it now.

Ireland was changing too. I went back, flying over the green of it after a long time away. It was becoming commercial, industrial. More factories were being built, and huge housing estates. One day I supposed there would be palings around the holy wells, the druid stones, and the fairy raths. People would perhaps queue at kiosks that sold tickets to see them. The stories John Joe once told, holding the listener in the palm of his hand, would be long forgotten or thought quaint and outlandish.

But Annes Grove was still the same when I saw it, the house solid and welcoming, still like an old lady with a hat pulled down over her eyes. Some of the old copper beeches were still standing. A few rhododendrons were out and the key beds in the walled garden were still in place.

I wandered down to the killeen and stood looking around, touching the cromlech with hands that were old now, tracing patterns of lichen as I had done as a child.

Next to his parents' and his brother's graves stood my father's headstone. His ashes, sent from Africa, were scattered here in the place that he had loved. The prodigal son was home at last.

And then it was time for Robin and me to leave. To fly back to the warmth and the space and the pulsing life that was *our* Africa. Where we had met and married and had our children. To what was now our home.

www.summersdale.com